Becoming *Frum*

Jewish Cultures of the World

Edited by Matti Bunzl, *University of Illinois, Urbana-Champaign,*
and Jeffrey Shandler, *Rutgers University*

Published in association with the Allen and Joan Bildner Center
for the Study of Jewish Life, *Rutgers University*

Advisory Board

Yoram Bilu, *Hebrew University*

Jonathan Boyarin, *University of North Carolina*

Virginia R. Dominguez, *University of Illinois, Urbana-Champaign*

Susannah Heschel, *Dartmouth College*

Barbara Kirshenblatt-Gimblett, *New York University*

Jack Kugelmass, *University of Florida*

Riv-Ellen Prell, *University of Minnesota*

Aron Rodrigue, *Stanford University*

Mark Slobin, *Wesleyan University*

Yael Zerubavel, *Rutgers University*

Becoming *Frum*

How Newcomers Learn the Language and Culture of Orthodox Judaism

SARAH BUNIN BENOR

RUTGERS UNIVERSITY PRESS

NEW BRUNSWICK, NEW JERSEY, AND LONDON

LIBRARY OF CONGRESS CATALOGING-IN-PUBLICATION DATA

Benor, Sarah, 1975–
    Becoming *frum* : how newcomers learn the language and culture of Orthodox
Judaism / Sarah Bunin Benor.
        p. cm.—(Jewish cultures of the world)
    Includes bibliographical references and index.
    ISBN 978–0–8135–5390–0 (hardcover : alk. paper)—ISBN 978–0–8135–5389–4
(pbk. : alk. paper)—ISBN 978–0–8135–5391–7 (e-book)
        1. Jewish way of life. 2. Jews—Return to Orthodox Judaism. 3. Orthodox Judaism—
Social aspects. 4. Hebrew language—Social aspects. 5. Yiddish language—Social
aspects. 6. Sociolinguistics. I. Title.

    BM723.B427 2012
    296.8'32—dc23   2012000002

A British Cataloging-in-Publication record for this book is available
from the British Library.

Visit our website: http://rutgerspress.rutgers.edu

Manufactured in the United States of America

This book is dedicated to my parents, Roberta and David Benor.
Thank you for giving me life, love, education, Judaism,
and everything else.

CONTENTS

FIGURES

TABLES

PREFACE

This book is intended for multiple audiences: scholars, students, and anyone else who is interested in language, identity, or Jews. While the primary fields that have influenced my research are sociolinguistics, anthropology, and Jewish studies, I have also written this book with other academic fields in mind, including sociology, religious studies, folklore, cultural studies, and American studies. I have tried to keep the writing accessible not only for scholars but also for educated adults, using technical terms only when necessary and adding explanations that most academic work would omit.

While many distinctive Jewish words and phrases are used throughout this book (translated at first use), the three most important are *frum*, *FFB*, and *BT*. The Yiddish word in the title, *frum*, means religious. Many Orthodox Jews use this label to describe themselves in contrast to those who are not Orthodox. Those who grew up in Orthodox families are known as "frum from birth," often abbreviated "FFB." And Jews who were born into a non-Orthodox family and chose to become frum are known by the Hebrew label *ba'alei teshuva* (literally "those who return/repent," masculine singular *ba'al teshuva*, feminine singular *ba'alas/ba'alat teshuva*), sometimes shortened to "BTs." Other Hebrew, Yiddish, and academic terms are defined at first use, as well as on the book's website, becomingfrum.weebly.com. This site also includes audio and video samples of Orthodox language (especially useful for chapter 4), discussion questions for university courses and book clubs, and an interactive blog, in which readers are encouraged to participate.

ACKNOWLEDGMENTS

This book has been over a decade in the making, and many people deserve my thanks. The first and most important acknowledgment goes to the frum Jews who enabled me to conduct my research. Thank you so much for the time you spent as my consultants and for your commitment to *hachnasas orchim* (hospitality). Special thanks to those who went above and beyond in answering my questions and making me feel welcome: the people I refer to as Rabbi Fischer, Andrew, Moyshe, Shelley, Levi, and Shira (all names are pseudonyms, in keeping with academic norms of confidentiality).

Many conversations with friends and colleagues helped me work through ideas. I thank Netta Abugov, Dalit Assouline, Netta Avineri, Shani Bechhofer, Mara Benjamin, Marcy Brink-Danan, Mary Bucholtz, Elaine Chun, Eve Clark, Aryeh Cohen, Steven M. Cohen, Patricia Duff, Penny Eckert, Arnie Eisen, Reuven Firestone, Sharon Gillerman, Hershl Glasser, Chaya Halberstam, Benjamin Hary, Joshua Holo, Samuel Heilman, Jill Jacobs, Lanita Jacobs-Huey, Joseph Kanofsky, Deborah Kaufman, Ari Kelman, Shaul Kelner, Evan Kent, Mark Kligman, Shawn Landres, Chaya R. Nove, Bruce Phillips, Robert Podesva, John Rickford, Mary Rose, Michele Rosenthal, Jennifer Roth Gordon, Adam Rubin, Roberta Sands, Joshua Shanes, Sam Weiss, Walt Wolfram, Malcah Yaeger-Dror, Tali Zelkowicz, Amy Zwas, my Stanford linguistics classmates, my fellow alumni of the Wexner Graduate Fellowship, my colleagues and students at Hebrew Union College and the University of Southern California, and members of the Jewish Languages Mailing List. Special thanks to Ayala Fader and Jeffrey Shandler for going above and beyond in their help on this book.

I appreciate the feedback I received from audiences at talks I gave at HUC, USC, Emory, UCLA, the University of California–Santa Barbara, the University of South Carolina, and several academic conferences, including New Ways of Analyzing Variation, the American Anthropological Association, the Linguistic Society of America, and the Association for Jewish Studies. My graduate education and research was funded by the Wexner Foundation, the National Foundation for Jewish Culture, the Memorial Foundation for Jewish Culture, the Goodan Family Fellowship, the Dorot Fellowship in Israel, and a number of smaller grants. Since then, Hebrew Union College–Jewish Institute of Religion has been extremely generous with maternity leaves, sabbaticals, and extra funding. Thank you for making this work possible.

I would like to thank the staff of Frumster.com for allowing me to turn their online matchmaking service into a wellspring of data. Thank you to Suki and Ding Productions, Abie Rotenberg, and Rabbi Moshe Shur for permission to print song excerpts. I am grateful to all the people who worked on ideas for the cover image, including Levi Tenenbaum, Y'rachmiel Zweig, Chaviva Galatz, Yonah Bookstein, Barb Heller, and especially Bill Aron, Josh Morris, Lev Metz, and Sara Metz. Thanks to Shanghai Garden Diamond for the discounted kosher sushi.

It has been a pleasure to work with Rutgers University Press. The series editors, Matti Bunzl and Jeffrey Shandler, have been very supportive and helpful. The editors and anonymous reviewers improved the book with their extensive comments on previous drafts. Eric Schramm offered not only his meticulous editing skills but also his impressive knowledge of linguistics and Jewish studies. Marlie Wasserman, Allyson Fields, and Marilyn Campbell all deserve hearty thanks for their suggestions and attentive responses.

Finally, I want to thank my family for their love and assistance. My grandmother, Estelle Schultz, my siblings, Miriam Benor and Aaron Benor, and my siblings-in-law have taken a great interest in my work and offered helpful suggestions. My parents, Roberta and David Benor, and in-laws, Ruthie and Alan Bunin, have helped in various ways, including giving feedback on papers, presentations, and chapters. My three daughters, Aliza, Dalia, and Ariella, have contributed their cuteness and enthusiasm. And my incredible partner in life, love, and ideas, Mark Bunin Benor, has regularly served as a sounding board for my academic work—and as an inspiration for everything I do.

TRANSCRIPTION CONVENTIONS

In English writing, Hebrew and Yiddish words can be transcribed in many different ways. Some journals and publishers use the Library of Congress system for Hebrew and the YIVO system for Yiddish. The problem is that in the writing of American Jews, words often come from both Hebrew and Yiddish. If I were to choose one of these systems for all Jewish words, the reader would find the results awkward and hard to read ("Five Books of Moses" and "Jewish law" would be either *ḥumash* and *halakha* or *khumesh* and *halokhe*). I could follow the conventions of linguistic writing and use the International Phonetic Alphabet (xʊməʃ/xumaʃ and haləxa/hʌlʌxʌ), but that would scare away everybody without linguistics training. Within the Orthodox Jewish community in America, some spellings have become relatively standardized, although variation still abounds. For example, the throaty [x] sound is generally written "ch" (*chumash* and *halacha*). In this book I use spellings that are commonly used in materials written by Orthodox Jews, sometimes having relied on Google rankings to decide among multiple options. In instances in which I analyze pronunciation, I use alternative spellings. Whole Yiddish sentences are transliterated using the YIVO system.

Becoming *Frum*

1

Introduction

Orthodox Jews and Language Socialization

The lights come up. In the middle of the stage stands a young man wearing a black hat, full beard, and black suit with no tie. He holds the microphone close and begins chanting a slow Hasidic niggun, a wordless melody, in a minor key. All of a sudden the rhythm section starts up and the singer switches to an upbeat style. The young men and women in the audience sing along, dancing energetically and pumping their arms to the beat. The music is unmistakably reggae, complete with faux Jamaican accent, interspersed with Hebrew words like *Hashem* (God), *golus* (exile), and *Moshiach* (Messiah).

The unique blend of hip-hop and Hasidic style that launched Matisyahu's career is unlikely among those who were raised Orthodox. But it is just the kind of hybrid self-presentation we might expect from *ba'alei teshuva*, also known as BTs. Matisyahu and other BTs exist in a cultural borderland between their non-Orthodox upbringing and the *frum* (religious) communities they have joined. These two worlds differ greatly in dress, food, language, and other important aspects of everyday life. This book describes how BTs navigate this borderland. How do they learn the many cultural norms of their new communities? Which do they choose to make their own? Do they give up burritos and pad thai in favor of gefilte fish and noodle kugel? To what extent do they incorporate Yiddishisms into English sentences and mention God frequently in their informal conversations? Why do some, like Matisyahu, maintain aspects of their pre-Orthodox identities, while others wish to pass as FFB (frum from birth)?

This is a book about becoming, in-between-ness, identity, and community. Based on ethnographic and sociolinguistic fieldwork in an Orthodox community with many BTs, I show how individuals deal with transitions in identity through the creative use of language and other cultural practices. I demonstrate how they and others see themselves, to varying extents, as part of both worlds.

I describe the self-consciousness they experience throughout their transition and how their interactions with community veterans and other novices help to socialize them. And I show how the case of BTs relates to the broader phenomenon of adult language socialization: how newcomers learn new ways of speaking that position them as members of a new community.

The idea for this book came about when I was researching language at a Chabad center in California. A few of the BTs who frequented the center found out that I knew Yiddish and asked me to teach an informal Yiddish class. After the first session, one student said to another, "We're going to sound so FFB!" It was then that I realized how important language is for BTs as they integrate into Orthodox life. While speaking Yiddish is important among Hasidim, I knew from previous observations that a distinctive English, with influences from Yiddish and Hebrew, is the language of choice in non-Hasidic Orthodox communities around the country, including the one I ultimately studied in Philadelphia.

I began floating the research idea among some Orthodox friends. One said, "You mean you want to study how Ivy League–educated people can speak like they're new immigrants?" Another friend smiled and told me a joke about BTs overextending linguistic rules: "What do BTs drink? Ginger Kale!" (Orthodox Jews pronounce El/Ale, one of the names of God, as Kel/Kale in conversation, but only a newcomer would apply this rule to an English word.) It became clear to me that studying the language of ba'alei teshuva would yield fascinating data, rich in ideology and humor. It also became clear that the study should not focus only on language, as the Hebrew and Yiddish words people use are intimately connected with the ways they dress, the foods they eat, and their relationship with God and their communities.

I read up on Orthodox Jews and linguistic anthropology, complementing my graduate education in sociolinguistics. The more I read, and the more I spoke to colleagues in Jewish studies, linguistics, and anthropology, the more I realized that this study could have something to contribute to those fields. While there was a good deal of research on ba'alei teshuva, no study had analyzed their language. And while many linguists and anthropologists had researched how children learn language and how adults learn a second language, especially in the burgeoning field of language socialization, there were few studies of how adults learn new ways of speaking their native language. I knew I had found a niche, but it was not until I had completed my fieldwork and analyzed the data that I realized what my contributions to those fields would be.

Orthodox Jews

My research has led to three main findings about Orthodox Jews: (1) being Orthodox involves not only a system of belief and religious observance but also a set of cultural practices; (2) through subtle linguistic cues, Orthodox Jews indicate their locations along various social axes, including the *Modern Orthodox to Black Hat continuum*; and (3) ba'alei teshuva, through their *hyperaccommodation* and *deliberate distinctiveness*, complicate the culture and social axes of Orthodoxy. The sections that follow introduce these findings and offer the background necessary for subsequent chapters.

Belief and Spirituality, but also Community and Culture

A central finding of this book is that religion cannot be separated from social life and practice; religiosity and religious transformation involve an interplay between the spiritual and the cultural, between the individual and the communal.[1] Orthodox Jews are expected to conform not only to *halacha* (Jewish religious law, literally "way" or "path"), but also to cultural practices—although there is less communal censure for cultural nonconformity. We see this interplay in the languages that enrich the English of American Jews, especially Orthodox Jews: the holy languages of the Torah, rabbinic commentaries, and prayers (Hebrew and Aramaic); the Eastern European Jewish language spoken by the ancestors of many, but not all, community members (Yiddish); and the national language of the country to which Jews have diasporic allegiance and transnational ties (Israeli Hebrew). All BTs in the current study use words from textual Hebrew and Aramaic, and most also use features from Yiddish and Israeli Hebrew. But there is more ambivalence about Yiddish and Israeli Hebrew, as they are not considered central to religiosity. These findings are in line with anthropologist Ayala Fader's study of a Hasidic community in Brooklyn.[2] There, however, Yiddish is much more prevalent as a spoken language, especially among men, and Israeli Hebrew plays a minimal role. Even so, both her study and my own point to the interplay between religion and culture in Orthodox life, manifesting in reverence for both Hebrew and Yiddish.

There is some debate within frum circles about the relationship between religion and culture. Some rabbis involved in helping newcomers transition to Orthodoxy preach that individual spiritual transformation and halachic observance are central, and "walking the walk" and "talking the talk" are peripheral. BT training programs support this assertion, as their curricula focus on Tanach (Jewish Bible), Talmud (compilation of rabbinic commentaries), and Shabbos observance, rather than cooking, dance, or Yiddish.[3] Even so, the current study indicates that culture is also an important part of being—and becoming—frum. Many BTs take on cultural practices with great enthusiasm, sometimes even going beyond the norms of FFBs, a phenomenon I refer to as *hyperaccommodation*.[4] Other BTs, especially in their early stages of Orthodox identification, avoid elements of frum culture that they see as peripheral to halacha and continue to participate in aspects of secular culture that are not common among FFBs.

This *selective accommodation* and *deliberate distinctiveness* serve to diversify frum communities. In addition, when BTs do not fully accommodate, they effectively critique the cultural conventions of Orthodox life. When halachically observant BTs use contemporary slang or add blue trim to their black velvet kipah, they send the message—intentionally or not—that they consider religious mandates to be more important than cultural conformity.

Another finding of this study is that religious and cultural practice may take precedence over full acceptance of the underlying system of belief. Although some Orthodox outreach programs do offer proofs of God's existence, and many BTs become Orthodox only after being convinced of the truth of the Torah, newcomers may take on religious laws and cultural practices before they fully accept the theology.[5] For example, a new BT who has not internalized the concept of divine providence might still answer a frum friend's "How are you?" with "*baruch Hashem*" (blessed be God), conforming to the communal norm. This phenomenon, which has also been reported in several situations of religious and social transformation, is reminiscent of a biblical story. At Mount Sinai, the Children of Israel responded to the revelation of the laws, "All that the Lord spoke *we will do and we will hear/understand*" (*na'aseh v'nishma*).[6] The order of the two actions suggests that knowledge and spiritual transformation can be secondary to religious behavior, a trope common among BTs.

Na'aseh v'nishma also points to the importance of community in religious observance. The nation responds to the giving of the law together in the first-person plural: *we* will do and *we* will hear, rather than each individual answering in the singular. The centrality of the community persists in contemporary Judaism: certain prayers can only be recited when a quorum of ten is present, and because traditionally observant Jews cannot drive on Shabbos, they tend to cluster residentially within walking distance of a synagogue. As I found in my research, community is central to frum life, and the tight-knit, supportive social networks are a major draw for many BTs. As such networks tend to do, they also create pressure to conform to communal norms, not only in religious observance but also in cultural practice.[7] Some BTs embrace that communal conformity, and, as the case of Matisyahu suggests, others creatively tap into the cultural repertoires of Orthodox and American life to highlight their in-between status.

Ideology and Practice

The linguistic and cultural practices common in Orthodox communities are not arbitrary; they are influenced by a number of ideologies, beliefs, and worldviews.[8] These include belief in an omnipotent, omniscient God (*Hashem*); an expectation that the Messiah (*Moshiach*) will come; a complex system of laws (*halacha*) and customs (*minhagim*); reverence for great rabbis past and present and confidence that their knowledge of Torah endows them with special insight in other spheres (*daas torah*); high value attached to the study of biblical and rabbinic texts ("learning"); maintenance of distinct gender roles; connection to the recent Eastern European Jewish past; sense of Jewish peoplehood and descent from the biblical Children of Israel; connection to the contemporary state of Israel; and a sense of distinctiveness from non-Orthodox Jews and non-Jews.

As previous literature has shown, these ideologies, though not exclusive to Orthodox Jews, are central to Orthodox life.[9] They are relevant to the current analysis because they influence cultural practices, like dress, food, and language. For example, Orthodox Jews frequently discuss Bible stories, give their children biblical names like Rochel (Rachel) and Shmuel (Samuel), sing Hebrew songs, and use Hebrew words within their English—practices connected to the ideology of descent from the biblical Children of Israel, the value of study, and the attachment to contemporary Israel. Many Orthodox Jews prefer Eastern European foods, minor musical modes, and Ashkenazi (Central/Eastern European) pronunciation of Hebrew words, all of which are influenced by a connection to Eastern Europe. The differences in women's and men's dress, activities, and language are dictated by a complex set of ideologies surrounding the relationship between gender, modesty, and piety.[10] Many practices are also affected by Orthodox Jews' complex and stringent system of laws and customs, such as the length of women's sleeves and the avoidance of gossip and profanity. The belief in an omnipotent, omniscient God encourages the use of common interjections like *baruch Hashem* and *im yirtse Hashem* (God willing). An expectation that the messianic age is imminent leads to the formulaic *dvar torah* (sermon) ending: "May we be zoche (merit) to witness the coming of the Moshiach speedily in our days." And reverence for rabbinic leaders influences the home-based custom of prominently displaying portraits of elderly, bearded rabbis and the *yeshiva*-based practice of addressing esteemed rabbis in the third person. While previous literature on Orthodox Jews discusses many of these cultural practices, especially Yiddish and conservative dress, this book highlights the centrality of culture in differentiating Orthodox Jews, not only from non-Orthodox Jews but also from each other.

Demographics of Orthodox Jews in America

To understand the analysis in this book, readers should be familiar with the demographics of Orthodoxy. In 2001, studies estimated the U.S. Orthodox population between 530,000 and 700,000, which is about 10 to 13 percent of the U.S. Jewish population.[11] Because of high birth rates, these numbers are poised to jump in the coming decades. Currently, at least 39 percent of the Orthodox population is under age eighteen, compared to 20 percent of the overall Jewish population.[12] The U.S. Orthodox population is heavily concentrated in the

Northeast, especially the greater New York area, but there are also Orthodox communities in most major U.S. cities and some smaller towns, as well as in several cities in Canada, Europe, Latin America, and elsewhere. While Orthodox communities today have high retention rates, there are also defectors, as recent research has pointed out.[13]

Within Orthodox communities, a number of social, cultural, and religious distinctions are salient. These oppositions and axes, which emerge from community discourse and cultural practice, are important for understanding the socialization of BTs. As BTs transition from non-Orthodox to frum, they also necessarily position themselves along several social axes (with varying levels of intentionality). As they do so, they contribute nuance to this social landscape. Not only do they add a new axis (BT–FFB), but, through unusual cultural blends, they also complicate some of the other axes.

ORTHODOX AND NON-ORTHODOX JEWS. Although I use the term "Orthodox" in this book, I note that this term seems to be less common among insiders than *frum*.[14] Many of the frum people that I encountered in my research say that they prefer not to make distinctions like "Orthodox" versus "non-Orthodox." Several talked about *klal yisroel*—a unified Jewish people—or commented, "Jews are Jews!" And many have close ties and regular interaction with non-Orthodox Jews, especially with prospective BTs who take classes in Orthodox outreach centers and visit them in their homes. Even so, there is a strong ideology of distinctiveness from non-Orthodox Jews and their forms of Judaism.[15] For example, I heard several FFBs and, especially, BTs contrasting their communities, synagogues, and forms of observance to those of "secular" Jews or "Reform and Conservative" Judaism, often with a disparaging tone.

A song by the popular Orthodox children's singer Uncle Moishy illustrates these conflicting attitudes:

> My name is Dedi,
> *V'ani medaber Ivrit* [and I speak (Israeli) Hebrew].
> *Un* [and] Shimmy knows Yiddish too.
> Whenever Dovid speaks,
> He prefers to stick to English [British accent].
> Yet everyone can get along with you.

> You're my brother, my sister, my friend—Together we're *Am Yisroel* [the People of Israel].
> We share one Torah, one nation, one dream—We are all the children of *Hashem* [God]. . . .

> Yitzi wears a different *kipah* [skullcap].
> His father's hat is tall and round.

Baseball caps are Yossi's favorite.
Yet both can walk hand in hand.

Ahuva wears a different uniform.
Her school has a Spanish name.
Sometimes we seem so very different.
But really we are very much the same. . . .

You know, when I grew up,
Our family lived in the most interesting building.
Shloymi loved to roller skate,
And Dovid loved to read . . .
Mr. Golding ran a restaurant . . .
Mr. Goldbaum taught us all about the Torah.
And with so many people . . . we called the building
Chaverim kol Yisroel [all Israel/Jews (are) friends][16]

To many of the children and parents who listen to this song, it is an accurate representation of the diversity they encounter in their daily lives. But Jews who did not grow up Orthodox recognize that the song portrays diversity only within the frum world, despite its claim to represent all Jews in the phrase *kol Yisroel*. Shloymi, Shimmy, and the other names mentioned are used almost solely by Orthodox Jews. Not one of the children eats cheeseburgers or watches Saturday-morning cartoons, actions prohibited by halacha but common among secular Jews. Yitzi wears a different kipah, but the song does not say, "Jeremy goes out bareheaded," and certainly not "Jennifer wears a kipah" (some religiously observant non-Orthodox women wear skullcaps). This song highlights the unity of frum Jews despite linguistic, ethnic, and religious diversity, but it also offers evidence of the implicit understanding that this unity does not necessarily extend to non-Orthodox Jews.

The ideology of distinction and separation from non-Orthodox Jews and non-Jews plays a role in the origins and maintenance of many Orthodox cultural practices. For example, although the use of Hebrew and Yiddish words and grammatical constructions may be related to Orthodox Jews' ties to the holy texts, Israel, and Eastern Europe, they are also influenced by the desire to maintain communal boundaries and distinguish from non-Orthodox Jews and non-Jews.

TRAJECTORIES OF OBSERVANCE. A distinction that is central to this book is whether or not people grew up as Orthodox Jews. Two categories refer to those who did not: ba'alei teshuva and *gerim* (converts). A *ba'al teshuva* (singular) refers to a Jew who transitioned from not halachically observant to halachically observant. The original meaning was simply someone who repents for having violated Jewish law (*teshuva* means return or repentance). Some still use it this way, but today the term generally refers to a frum Jew (born to a Jewish mother) who was not raised frum. In Israel, BTs are often referred to as *chozrim b'teshuva* (returnees to repentance). A *ger* (singular of *gerim*) is someone who was not born Jewish (not born to a Jewish mother) but who converted to Judaism through a process of study and socialization, *mikveh* (ritual immersion), and, for men, *milah* or *tipat dam*, actual or symbolic circumcision.

While most of the Orthodox Jews in this study were FFBs or BTs, a few were gerim. This included one who grew up as a practicing Catholic, one who grew up with no religion and non-Jewish parents, and a few who grew up with a Jewish father and non-Jewish mother. Even though some of the gerim had always considered themselves Jews, they were still required to go through an official conversion process, in keeping with halacha. Some of the gerim I met during my fieldwork were open about their non-Jewish past, but some mentioned it for the first time in an interview and requested confidentiality because their communities assumed they were born Jews.

Compared to BTs, many gerim have different experiences in their path to Orthodox Judaism and their socialization into frum communities, especially if they were active participants in another religious group. Those differences would be fruitful material for future research. On the other hand, some BTs had even less childhood Jewish education and socialization than some of the gerim. And some of the gerim had a stronger connection to their half-Jewish ancestry than some of the BTs. Because of these overlaps and the small numbers of converts in the study, I include gerim under the label BT, except where an individual's non-Jewish past is relevant.

In Orthodox communities, both gerim and BTs are contrasted with the Orthodox label FFB. In some ways, "frum from birth" is a misnomer. Orthodox children are not born with the moral system and knowledge to be pious and halachically observant; they too are socialized to the religious and cultural norms of their community.[17] For this reason, some scholars prefer the term "raised Orthodox" over FFB.[18] In this study, I use FFB, acknowledging its irony, because it was the term I heard most often in my fieldwork.

Another category of Jews who have shifted in observance is formerly Orthodox Jews, also known as *chozrim b'she'ela* (returnees to "question" [the opposite of another meaning of "teshuva," response]), *yotzi'im* (those who leave), and Jews who are "at risk" or "off the *derech* [path]."[19] Recent studies in Israel and the United States show that the socialization process formerly Orthodox Jews go through is similar to that of BTs, but with less communal infrastructure.[20] "Defection involves unlearning lifelong roles and the community's idiomatic ways of speaking, thinking, and acting and learning new, unfamiliar ones."[21] As with BTs, this transition results in unusual cultural combinations. For example, one study describes a group of formerly Orthodox Jews and questioners sitting around smoking marijuana, disobeying the laws of *negia* (touching members of the opposite sex), and debating secular philosophy. Some of them are still dressed in frum styles, while others are wearing tank tops or combat boots. Some are using curse words, some are using Orthodox speech styles, and some mix the two.[22] The language and culture of formerly Orthodox Jews clearly has parallels to the current study and would be a fruitful topic for future research.

MODERN ORTHODOX AND BLACK HAT. A major axis of distinction is a continuum between "Modern Orthodox" Jews at one end and "Black Hat" Jews at the other, based on observance, insularity, gender ideology, and, especially, cultural practices.[23] The label "Black Hat" is comparable to *Haredi* (those who tremble [before God]), a term common in Israel and in academic research, as well as Ultra-Orthodox, used in the popular press and among outside observers. The social category "Black Hat" is based on the headgear that distinguishes men closer to the right end of this continuum from those who cover their heads with only a kipah. Although "Black Hat" symbolically excludes women, I did hear Orthodox women use it to refer to entire communities. In this book I use mostly "Black Hat" because, more than Haredi or Ultra-Orthodox, I heard it in the communities of my fieldwork.

Many Orthodox Jews make shifts in observance and identification along the Modern Orthodox to Black Hat continuum. Some Black Hat Jews become more Modern, but more frequently Modern Orthodox Jews take on stringencies and cultural practices associated with Black Hat communities, as recent research shows.[24] As we might expect, language plays a role in this transformation. Sociologist Samuel Heilman writes that a Haredi (Black Hat) Ashkenazi Hebrew accent "and the worldview it represents are often imitated by young Orthodox who grew up with the American or modern Israeli pronunciation but wish to display that they have been 'transformed' following an extended stay in a Haredi yeshiva."[25] Clearly, trajectories of observance and identification are salient within Orthodox communities, and language and other cultural practices play a central role in how these trajectories are performed and perceived.

In chapter 5, I explore how the Modern Orthodox to Black Hat continuum is constructed in the community, including how individuals use linguistic cues to locate themselves and others along the continuum—and how BTs complicate the picture. For the time being, readers should know that the main community in which I conducted research for this book, for which I use the pseudonym "Milldale," is located between the middle and the Black Hat pole of that continuum, according to community discourse and symbolic practices.

HASIDIC AND NON-HASIDIC. Among those toward the Black Hat pole, another social, cultural, and religious dimension is the distinction between Hasidic and non-Hasidic Jews. This difference stems back to eighteenth- and nineteenth-century Eastern Europe, when Hasidism, a mystical, leader-centered approach to Judaism, spread rapidly through Jewish communities. Opponents of Hasidism, known as *Misnagdim* (opponents), emphasized traditional Jewish study over ecstatic prayer and revitalized the institution of the *yeshiva* (academy of advanced traditional Jewish learning for men). Despite their differences, Hasidim and Misnagdim were united in their opposition to the *Haskalah*, or Jewish Enlightenment—trends toward modernization, secularization, assimilation, and religious reform that had begun in Western Europe and were making their way eastward. Hasidim and Misnagdim gradually became more similar, and they even banded together politically.[26]

In the contemporary United States, these two groups continue to influence each other culturally and religiously, although they remain mostly distinct in their religious and educational institutions. The actual and spiritual descendants of Misnagdim are now generally known as "Yeshivish," as the yeshiva still holds great importance, or "Litvish" ([Yid.] Lithuanian Jewish), as their ancestors were mostly from Lithuania and surrounding areas. Hasidic Jews sometimes refer to themselves as *Chassidish* ([Heb./Yid.] Hasidic) or *heimish* ([Yid.] homey).[27] The community highlighted in this book is not Hasidic, although a few community members follow some Hasidic practices or have ties to Hasidim. Even so, Milldale residents tend not to refer to themselves as Misnagdim, Litvish, or Yeshivish, but rather with more general terms like "frum," "Torah Jews," and "Torah-true Jews."

GENDER. Gender is a central dimension in frum communities, where there are very different expectations for males and females, especially surrounding religious observance and family roles.[28] Men are expected to pray three times a day and set regular times for intensive study of rabbinic texts. Women are not required to participate in these activities and are often discouraged from doing so. One reason for this difference is that women are expected to be the primary caregivers for children. As one Orthodox rabbi teaches, "A woman should sacrifice her study of Torah for the raising of children."[29] Even so, Orthodox women often juggle childcare with work outside the home, sometimes as the sole breadwinner in families where men study full time.[30] In Milldale, such full-time study is rare: most of the men, and many of the women, pursue careers in diverse fields.

A number of studies have looked at Orthodox conceptions of gender, including how formerly secular women reconcile them with feminist orientations.[31] As the current study shows, gender differences play an important role in the socialization of male and female BTs. They can no longer sit together in synagogue and at many public events. They must conform to stricter gender norms in dress and hairstyle. Women are expected to fulfill the *mitzvos* (commandments) of *neros* (lighting the Shabbos candles), *challah* (separating bread dough in keeping with the biblical commandment in Numbers), and *niddah* (laws regarding menstruation that include refraining from sexual relations during part of the menstrual cycle). Men are expected to acquire the skills of *davening* (praying) and learning (Talmud study). Both men and women must adjust their understanding and performance of gender as they integrate into Orthodox life. This necessary adjustment contributes to BTs' experience of infantilization, feeling like children in comparison to the adults around them who are veterans of the local gender systems. In addition, BTs' presence in Orthodox communities complicates, to some extent, local conceptualizations of gender difference (see chapters 6 and 8).

ANCESTRY. A social dimension that applies to Orthodox and non-Orthodox Jews is ancestry, especially the distinction between *Ashkenazi* and *Sephardi/Mizrachi* Jews. These Hebrew labels stem from biblical and rabbinic literature and refer to ancestral locations: *Ashkenaz* refers to Central and Eastern Europe, and *Sepharad* to Spain and Portugal. Jews are considered Ashkenazi if their ancestors stem from Germany, Poland, Hungary, and surrounding countries, and they are considered Sephardi if their ancestors were expelled from Spain and/or Portugal in the late fifteenth century (most of whom settled in Western Europe, North Africa, or the Balkans). *Mizrachi* (Oriental or Eastern) is a more general term for Jews who are not Ashkenazi, including Sephardim and the long-established communities in Syria, Iran, Iraq, Yemen, and elsewhere. Jews from longstanding communities in Greece, Italy, India, and Ethiopia are either not included in this classification or are subsumed under Mizrachi.[32]

According to survey data, the majority of American Jews (60 percent)—and a large majority of Orthodox American Jews (79 percent)—self-identify as Ashkenazi.[33] In various parts of the country, especially the New York and Los Angeles areas, there are sizeable communities of Jews from Iran, Syria, North Africa, and elsewhere, but many Jews of Sephardi and Mizrachi descent have assimilated into Ashkenazi-dominated communities. In Milldale, the vast majority of Orthodox Jews I met seemed to be Ashkenazi; only a handful identify as Sephardi or Mizrachi through their surnames, divergent religious practices, and/or talking about their ancestry. Apparently, most of the Ashkenazim in Milldale descend from Eastern European immigrants who spoke Yiddish.

GEOGRAPHY. Community size and location are also important dimensions of Orthodox demography. The New York area is home to hundreds of thousands

ｊews, as well as hundreds of synagogues, schools, yeshivas, kosher mar-
ｊudaic bookstores, and other Orthodox institutions. New York serves as
ａtional and international frum hub, as many Orthodox Jews in other cit-
ｅs maintain connections with people and institutions there and visit regularly.
People in and out of New York talk about the frum communities in New York
being more insular and homogenous than others. When an Orthodox Jew in
New York has unconventional speech, dress, or other cultural practices, people
might assume he or she is from "out of town," a phrase used to refer to communities outside of the New York area.[34]

This study is situated primarily in Philadelphia, Pennsylvania, a large city
on the east coast of the United States about two hours by car or train from New
York. The Philadelphia area is home to a few medium-sized Orthodox communities. Many of the Philadelphians I met in this study maintained ties with and
paid regular visits to family and friends in larger communities in nearby cities,
including Brooklyn, New York; Monsey, New York; Lakewood, New Jersey; and
Baltimore, Maryland. Several had moved to Philadelphia after growing up in
these and other cities around the United States.

Some also maintained ties with Jews in other parts of the world, either
because they had grown up there, traveled or lived there, or met them while
studying in Israel. Transnational ties like these are common: as a number of
studies point out, Orthodox Jews travel, study, migrate, marry, do business,
and conduct religious outreach across international borders.[35] American Ashkenazi Jews are not only part of this transnational scene; they represent the
hegemonic wing of it. Because of the institutional spread of Chabad Lubavitch,
Aish HaTorah, and other Orthodox outreach organizations, American Orthodoxy has influenced communities around the world. In my own travels, I have
met American Orthodox outreach professionals in Mexico City, Madrid, London, Paris, and Jerusalem. While they spoke the local languages to varying
extents, they all also used Orthodox American English. These emissaries are
not only spreading Orthodox forms of belief and observance; they are also
introducing American Ashkenazi Orthodox language and culture to Jewish
communities around the world.

While other dimensions are also salient, such as age, life stage, and specific schools and yeshivas where individuals studied, the distinctions discussed
above—and presented in table 1.1—are most important to the current analysis,
because they are connected to expected and observed differences in language,
dress, and other cultural practices. Orthodox Jews and others familiar with
their communities tend to view these differences in a *recursive* way; that is,
they believe that two groups exhibit a linguistic or other cultural difference,
and then they expect a similar difference in other social distinctions.[36] They
expect the groups on the right side of table 1.1 to be more distinct, and—for

TABLE 1.1

Social, cultural, and religious distinctions

Dimension	Categories seen as less distinct	Categories seen as more distinct
Orthodox identity	Non-Orthodox	Orthodox*
Orthodox continuum	Modern Orthodox	Black Hat*
Ancestry	Sephardi/Mizrachi	Ashkenazi*
Hasidic orientation	non-Hasidic*	Hasidic
Geography	not in New York area*	in New York area
Gender	female*	male*
Religious background	BT*	FFB*

*group represented in the current study

some practices—more closely associated with Eastern Europe. When it comes to language, Black Hat Jews are expected to have more Yiddish influence in their English speech than Modern Orthodox Jews, Ashkenazi more than Sephardi and Mizrachi Jews, Hasidim more than non-Hasidim, those in the New York area more than those in other communities, men more than women, and FFBs more than BTs. Within the Hebrew of their prayers and blessings and the Hebrew words they use in their English speech, the groups on the right of table 1.1 are expected to use more Ashkenazi Hebrew pronunciation, as opposed to Israeli Hebrew.

These expectations are confirmed by my observations, but, as I explain later in the book, some of the oppositions act more like continua than hard-and-fast distinctions. This social structure is relevant to the language socialization of BTs, because they necessarily position themselves (intentionally or not) along these axes through their language and other cultural practices.

Ba'alei Teshuva

This book takes place several decades into the "teshuva movement," the modern-day transition of thousands of non-Orthodox Jews into Orthodox Jews.[37] Several studies, conducted from the perspectives of sociology, anthropology, religious studies, and feminist studies, deal with BTs in various stages of their integration into Orthodox communities around the world.[38] A major focus of this research is why these modern, secular-leaning Jews are attracted to nonliberal religion.[39] Common motivations include filling a spiritual or moral void, attraction to the tight-knit, family-oriented communities they encounter when they visit, rejection of the vacuous values they find in American society, finding appeal in the strict structure and discipline of halacha, and being convinced of the truth of traditional Judaism through lectures or conversations with frum Jews. Some BTs find Orthodox Judaism after dabbling in other religions; some are seeking solace after a personal tragedy. Some are brought by a friend or relative, and others walk into an Orthodox institution on their own out of curiosity. Many BTs have their first encounter with Orthodoxy during a visit to Israel, sometimes after meeting a charismatic outreach professional at a tourist site.

These studies have also looked at the process BTs go through when they become Orthodox. They tell stories of mostly young single men and women studying in BT yeshivas (men) or seminaries (women), moving to Orthodox neighborhoods, taking on new forms of observance, especially Shabbos and *kashrus* (dietary laws, also known as keeping kosher), and adopting new worldviews. Some of these studies explore how BTs negotiate their changed relations with their non-Orthodox family, often a source of tension and concern on both sides. Some studies look at how BTs see themselves and are seen in relation to the FFB majority. And some look at the institutions in Jerusalem and cities around the world that help BTs make the transition to Orthodoxy, including Aish HaTorah, Ohr Somayach, Chabad, and B'nai Akiva (the independent outreach center in this study, for which I use the pseudonym "Ner Tamid," is not affiliated with any of these institutions), as well as various synagogues, outreach centers, and *kollels* (institutions of full-time advanced study).[40] The people who work and volunteer for these organizations are crucial in the socialization of BTs. These groups are supplemented by a small industry of websites, recorded lectures, pamphlets, and books.[41] These resources describe individuals' religious journeys, deal with women's issues, provide practical guides to observance and integration, and offer translations and interpretations of holy texts.

Distinctive Orthodox language makes an appearance in all these studies. Whether the interview quotes are in English, Spanish, Portuguese, or Dutch, they are peppered with Hebrew and Yiddish words. Some of the books and articles even append lengthy glossaries. A few mention the linguistic and cultural changes BTs go through. For example, in Argentina, BTs of Syrian descent take on Ashkenazi forms of Orthodox observance and incorporate Yiddishisms into their Spanish, due to the influence of Black Hat Orthodoxy from the United States and Israel.[42] Similarly, Sephardi BTs in Paris use Ashkenazi linguistic and cultural practices: "A Tunisian who had become a fervent Chabadnik could be seen eating his aunt's couscous while wearing his black *rebbe* hat and singing imitation Hasidic songs. . . . Some affect Ashkenazi pronunciations during prayers."[43] Even Israeli BTs in some Ashkenazi Orthodox communities in Israel encounter Yiddish-influenced Hebrew.[44]

Despite brief mentions of language and culture, these studies do not offer systematic treatment of them. This book addresses this gap by asking three questions: What linguistic and cultural practices do BTs encounter in Orthodox communities? To what extent do they adopt them? And how do they learn them? In conjunction with the impressive body of research on BTs from the last thirty years, this book enhances our understanding of the complex process of cultural change and language socialization that individuals go through as they become frum.

Diversity among BTs

As previous literature shows, it is important to examine each Orthodox community in its local context.[45] The unique history of each country's Jewish population—especially with respect to immigration patterns and institutional landscape—leads to sociopolitical, religious, cultural, and linguistic differences. For example, BTs both in Argentina and in South Africa see their religious intensification as a response to the lawlessness or immorality of the society around them.[46] In contrast, the legacy of the Holocaust is a driving factor for many Dutch BTs, whose parents or grandparents are survivors. Religious seeking plays a role in some of these communities, such as Brazil and the United States, but less so in others, such as the Netherlands.[47] Brazilian BTs encounter a more porous Orthodox community, in which individuals might attend all three São Paolo synagogues rather than identifying with just Chabad or Modern Orthodoxy as in some other countries.[48] And studying abroad in Israel is not as common among Dutch BTs as among BTs in South Africa, the United States, and elsewhere.[49] In addition, the experiences of BTs in Modern Orthodox communities differ significantly from those in Yeshivish or Hasidic communities.[50] While this diversity should not be overlooked, I believe, based on my brief visits to other Orthodox communities and conversations with many BTs, that many of the current study's findings apply to BTs around the world. All BTs encounter new linguistic and cultural practices and learn to adopt or avoid them through similar processes of socialization, even as local dynamics differ.

In addition to intercommunal differences, I also found that, in any given community, individual BTs have diverse experiences, varying according to personality, life stage, and gender. Some non-Orthodox Jews get very excited about Orthodoxy early in their exposure to it, and they take on religious and cultural practices as quickly as they can. These people might become fully observant and move to an Orthodox community within a year or two. On the other hand, I met a number of interested prospective BTs who had been attending classes and events at the Ner Tamid outreach center for years but had not started to observe halacha. I also met a few BTs who had been observing some of the laws for five or more years but had still not attended yeshiva/seminary or moved to an Orthodox community.

People become Orthodox at various ages and life stages. Some are married, and they take on the laws and customs with or without their spouses (BTs in the latter category often have marital problems—as a cause or a result of the transition). Young BTs often find themselves in sticky situations with their parents.[51] Some are parents themselves, and they have to deal with their children's reactions to their newfound religiosity. Some are parents of BTs, and they become frum in part because of their children's urging. Single BTs, especially those over age thirty, are expected to begin the matchmaking process soon after becoming Orthodox. Several BTs at Ner Tamid moved to an Orthodox community as soon as they married another BT. All this points not only to BTs' diverse experiences related to age and life stage but also to the importance of interpersonal relationships in the socialization process.

Gender is a very important factor in the diverse experiences of BTs, as men and women begin to participate in different roles as they gain increasing access to Orthodox activities. Gender differences are present to some extent at the Ner Tamid outreach center where non-Orthodox Jews often get their first taste of frum culture, but they become much more pronounced when BTs shift their participation to a residential Orthodox community like Milldale. At a Shabbos meal, it is common to find female guests serving and clearing plates while men chat and sing. Men are expected to attend synagogue religiously, and women may attend for part of the service or not at all. While women do attend classes and lectures and sometimes participate in one-on-one study sessions, men are more likely to make daily or weekly study a priority. These differences in activities have an impact on language: men tend to get more practice in the language of prayer and text study, and women tend to get more practice in the language of informal socialization and child rearing. In short, although this book points out trends and posits some common phenomena, readers should remember that every BT has a different experience.

Stages in BT Trajectories

Despite the diversity, in my research in Philadelphia I noticed a common trajectory: most BTs spend at least some time peripherally involved with Orthodox life, most move to an Orthodox community, and some study in a yeshiva or seminary (often before moving to an Orthodox community). I found these stages, which I call Peripheral, Community, and Yeshiva/Seminary, to be important in the cultural socialization of BTs. Although these labels do not seem to be used in Orthodox communities, people do discuss the important transitions that happen when BTs move to an Orthodox community and/or spend time at a yeshiva or seminary. In the paragraphs that follow, I discuss this progression of integration based on my research at Ner Tamid, an outreach center in downtown Philadelphia, and in Milldale, a neighborhood within driving distance that has an established Orthodox community. Ner Tamid and Milldale are closely connected, as a number of the teachers at Ner Tamid live in Milldale and often invite students to their homes.

INTERESTED PROSPECTIVE BTS. The director of Ner Tamid Jewish Study Center sees his institution as "the first step in the learning process." Through educational, religious, and social programming, Ner Tamid provides traditional Jewish experiences to non-Orthodox Jews in the hope that they "will go on to higher learning" in a yeshiva or seminary, the director says. After prospective BTs attend some events at Ner Tamid, the rabbis who teach there invite them to spend Shabbos and holidays with them and their families in Milldale. Throughout these early exposures, the non-Orthodox Jews are what I call Interested Prospective BTs. When they begin to observe the laws and customs of Orthodox Judaism in their everyday lives, they enter the category of Peripheral BTs.

PERIPHERAL BTS. Peripheral BTs are marginally affiliated with Orthodoxy and have diverse levels of observance. Some keep strictly kosher; others eat in non-kosher restaurants. Some observe all the laws of Shabbos; others observe strictly when spending Shabbos in Milldale but are more lax in their own homes. Some BT men wear a kipah all the time, some do so only in private and at Orthodox events, and others borrow from the basket of kipahs at the entrance to Ner Tamid. What Peripheral BTs have in common is that they have all increased their observance of Jewish laws and customs and currently identify as Orthodox Jews. As sociologist Lynn Davidman found in her research among women in a beginners' prayer service at a Modern Orthodox synagogue, some Peripheral BTs stay in this "experimental" stage for some time.[52]

COMMUNITY BTS. Eventually, most BTs decide to move to an Orthodox community, becoming what I refer to as Community BTs.[53] Making the major commitment to live among Orthodox Jews is considered an important step in the BT "journey," as it generally also involves increased peer pressure to attend synagogue and observe halacha. For their annual banquet, Ner Tamid chooses one or two people to honor as students or alumni of the year. These are often people who have moved to Milldale or other Orthodox communities. One year the banquet program reported what synagogue the alumni of the year attend and praised their religiosity (in language geared toward a diverse audience): "They observe the Sabbath, keep kosher and love being Jewish." Thus these former students were rewarded for taking the step of becoming Community BTs.

YESHIVA/SEMINARY BTS. Several of the BTs in Milldale followed the path out-
lined above—Ner Tamid or a similar outreach center and then a move to Milldale. But a number of BTs took an additional step before or after moving to
Milldale: spending time in a residential program geared toward BTs. These
usually younger BTs live and study for months, a year, or longer in a yeshiva
or seminary far from their home, sometimes interrupting or ending a career.
They study traditional texts of Judaism (mostly Talmud for men, mostly Bible for
women), and they learn the intricate laws and customs of traditional Judaism
in a formal setting.

As Davidman argues, residential programs for BTs tend to encourage rapid
transformations because of their "physical, social, and ideological encapsulation."[54] This is also the case for other situations of adult socialization, including
professional training programs, addiction rehabilitation programs, and religious enclaves.[55] In addition to being relatively insulated from outside influences, yeshivas and seminaries foster a culture of peer pressure: participants
tend to share their zeal about Orthodoxy and often convince their classmates to
extend their stay and take on halachic observance, as well as cultural practices
involving dress and language.[56]

When BTs leave a residential program and return or move to an Orthodox community, they are assumed to be more knowledgeable and to have
solidified their observance. One rabbi talks about Yeshiva BTs as "mainstream
ba'alei teshuva": "They've now fit in. They speak the language, they know how
to learn, they've gone to yeshiva. They have it. They know what's going on."
Attending yeshiva/seminary is not a necessary step in the path to Orthodoxy;
I met several longtime Community BTs who never felt they could take time off
work but are still well integrated religiously, socially, and culturally. Even so,
the residential program for BTs is seen as a useful and important institution
of socialization.

The yeshiva/seminary is so important in the BT socialization process that
some studies use it as the primary research site.[57] Building on this work, my
study includes BTs in all four stages: Prospective, Peripheral, Community, and
Yeshiva/Seminary. As I explain in chapter 7, I found that when people move to
an Orthodox community and when they spend time in a yeshiva or seminary,
they experience a significant increase in access to distinctive linguistic and cultural practices, as well as increased opportunity—and pressure—to adopt them.

How BTs Are Changing Frum Communities

As BTs progress through these stages, they contribute to frum communities in
several ways. Of course, they grow the ranks of Orthodoxy with their presence
and their progeny, and they offer their professional and other skills to animate
organizations and informal social networks. But they also have a significant

impact on Orthodox life through their hyperaccommodation and their deliberate distinctiveness.

Previous research has documented a "Haredization" or "slide to the right"
in Orthodox communities since the 1960s: Jews toward the Modern Orthodox
pole of the continuum have taken on halachic stringencies and cultural practices associated with the Black Hat pole.[58] In addition to various historical and
sociological factors for this shift, I suggest that BTs' hyperaccommodation could
play a role. When FFBs observe new BTs in their community saying "baruch
Hashem" frequently, growing a long beard, or wearing both a wig and a hat (a
stringent interpretation of the requirement for married women to cover their
hair), they may feel pressure to follow suit (see chapter 8).

At the same time, BTs have also brought elements of secular culture to
FFBs. The explosion in English-language Orthodox publishing has been spurred
in part by a perceived need among BTs and prospective BTs for books that
translate and explain traditional Hebrew and Aramaic texts.[59] Although English books may be disproportionately represented on BTs' bookshelves, they are
also becoming more popular among FFBs. Similarly, international cuisine and
health-conscious cooking are gaining traction in frum kitchens. Kosher Chinese, falafel, and pizza restaurants, which have long been staples of Orthodox
neighborhoods, have recently been joined by Thai, Mexican, and sushi establishments. While this change may be partly a result of cosmopolitan Modern
Orthodox Jews keeping more strictly kosher, it is probably also influenced by
BTs bringing their culinary preferences to their new communities.

We also see the cultural influence of BTs in the linguistic realm. Although
the frequent use of "baruch Hashem" is a stereotype of BTs, some FFBs told me
that they emulate this practice because they admire BTs' zeal. Sometimes BTs'
linguistic innovations influence the speech of FFBs. For example, the Yiddish-
origin word *daven* now means not only the act of saying prayers, as it did in Yiddish, but also "supplication," a change that may be spurred by BTs' using it on
analogy with English "pray" (see chapter 7). In short, through both their hyperaccommodation and their deliberate distinctiveness, BTs are changing not only
themselves but also the communities they have joined.

Jewish Renewal and Religious Seeking

While this book focuses on Orthodox communities, religious intensification is
also a broader Jewish phenomenon. The last few decades have seen a growing
polarization and "shrinking middle" of American Jews.[60] At one end of the continuum, we see a growing number of Jews with little interest in religious observance and little connection to other Jews and to organized Jewish communities.
At the other end, we see a growing number of religiously engaged Jews, both in
non-Orthodox and Orthodox communities. The committed end is represented

by an explosion in Jewish educational initiatives—not only Jewish day schools for children but also new venues for adult Jewish learning, such as the Melton adult education network, Limmud conferences, and thousands of classes in synagogues and Jewish community centers.[61] Adults of all ages have embraced religious practices that they did not grow up observing and have become active in synagogues, independent *minyanim* (lay-led prayer groups), and other spiritual communities with Conservative, Reform, Reconstructionist, Renewal, and other non-Orthodox affiliations. It is common to find Jews who grew up in the suburbs rejecting the Jewish lifestyles they found "passive" or "devoid of spirituality" and moving to urban centers to participate in young, vibrant, progressive Jewish communities.[62]

This renewed interest in Jewish observance and education is part of a broader American trend of spiritual seeking. In an expanding "spiritual marketplace," Jews, Christians, and others are increasingly likely to try out religious practices they did not grow up with. Often at times of life transitions, many see themselves as taking a spiritual journey to find personal meaning and connect to something larger than themselves.[63] This spiritual seeking tends to involve a communal component: many seekers try out religious practices based on friends' recommendations, and they find social stimulation and support in the religious communities they encounter. In contrast to some other religions, Jews' spiritual seeking may also involve an ethnic component: a sense of connection to other Jews and a yearning to (re)discover the religion and culture of one's ancestors.

The findings of this book are similar to the processes of socialization that allow converts and newly religious Jews to integrate into non-Orthodox Jewish communities. Jews are attracted to non-Orthodox religious life for some of the same reasons that BTs become adherents of Orthodoxy.[64] Many non-Orthodox Jews also take on life-changing religious proscriptions, regular prayer, frequent hosting of guests for Shabbat and holiday meals, and new practices like wearing a kipah and *tallit* (prayer shawl) (non-Orthodox Jews tend to use Sephardi/Israeli-influenced pronunciations like *Shabbat* and *tallit*, in contrast to *Shabbos* and *tallis*, more common among Orthodox Jews). In some cases, their transformation is very similar to that of a BT, differing only with respect to gender separation and certain halachic stringencies. But most non-Orthodox religious intensifiers do not commit fully to halacha, and many take on cultural practices not found in Orthodox circles, such as accompanying the Sh'ma prayer with deep breathing and placing an orange on the seder plate.[65]

Like BTs, Jews without much religious education often feel uncomfortable in non-Orthodox services, infantilized by their poor knowledge of Hebrew and liturgical practices. Like Orthodox outreach centers, many non-Orthodox synagogues offer classes and religious mentorship. For example, a non-Orthodox congregation in Los Angeles offers a thirty-seven-session introduction to Judaism class. Organizers acknowledge that Jews who have been away from religious life for many years (or their whole lives) may feel less skilled than their peers, as sessions like this indicate: "Theology and Tefillah: Am I the Only One Who Has No Idea When to Bow?"

Language is also important in the process of becoming more involved in non-Orthodox religious life. Many congregations offer Hebrew classes and instruction on chanting Torah or leading services. One Reform rabbi in California heard me speak about American Jewish language at a conference and was inspired to offer a class at her synagogue called "Mentch, Bentch, and Kvetch: Demystifying Jewish Lingo." She explained to me in an e-mail: "It's not a Yiddish class in that I don't speak Yiddish. It's really about talking Jewish! It occurred to me after your talk that with so many Jews-by-choice and Jews who grew up outside of the shtetls of Brooklyn and Pico-Robertson [a densely Jewish neighborhood in Los Angeles] that it can be hard to learn our 'secret codes.'" This institutional recognition of the distinctive language practices of religiously engaged Jews is unusual but, as this book shows, potentially useful for the integration of newcomers.

Whether or not Jews have become more observant, they often make decisions about how they will present themselves as Jews. Will they use Yiddish words when they *kvetch* (complain) and *kvell* (express pride/joy)? Will they congratulate a friend using the Ashkenazi *mázel tov* or the Israeli *mazál tov*? Will they indicate their Sephardi roots by throwing in Ladino phrases and avoiding Yiddishisms? As I have written elsewhere, Jews throughout history and around the world have used Hebrew words and other linguistic features not only to distinguish themselves from their non-Jewish neighbors but also to indicate their identities as certain types of Jews.[66] American Jews are no exception to this phenomenon.[67] By focusing on language, this book sheds new light on the choices individuals make—conscious or unconscious—as they position themselves within a diverse Jewish landscape.[68]

Language Socialization, Adult Transitions

Many of the findings in this book are relevant not only to newly Orthodox Jews but also to other instances of individuals transitioning to new roles and new communities. This includes major life changes that most people never experience, such as religious conversions, regional migrations, and transitions to new sexual orientations and gender identities. But it also includes smaller, more common transitions, such as picking up a hobby (becoming a wine connoisseur, Pilates pro, or bluegrass fan), starting a new line of work (becoming a cosmetologist, attorney, or midwife), or entering a new life phase (becoming a college student, parent, or retiree). While these transitions differ in many ways from becoming frum, they also involve cultural adjustments: individuals make subtle and not-so-subtle changes in their physical appearance, their activities, and their speech.

In my research on BTs, I found four major principles that may also apply in other situations. (1) Language, in conjunction with physical appearance and other cultural practices, plays a crucial role in adult transitions. (2) Individuals transition with the help of ongoing interaction with others in the roles/identities they aspire to, as well as with other aspirants. (3) Adults in transition may feel self-conscious about their liminal state between their old and new identities, and they may indicate this through hybrid or marked cultural practices. (4) Transitioning individuals take diverse approaches to the identities they aspire to: some may be zealous and others ambivalent, or they may be both zealous and ambivalent in different situations or in progression. This is not intended as a comprehensive theory of adult socialization, but rather as a set of principles that emerge from a study of newly Orthodox Jews and may be tested in other cases of adults transitioning to new roles, identities, and communities.

Becoming Frum joins a growing body of literature on how people learn language and other cultural knowledge through their interactions with others, the research paradigm known as "language socialization."[69] Linguistic anthropologists Bambi Schieffelin and Elinor Ochs formulated its two main concerns: "socialization through the use of language and socialization to use language."[70] Children and other novices learn the language of their community through interactions with their caregivers, peers, and others, and by learning the language, they are socialized to be competent members of their community. Investigating language socialization using longitudinal ethnographic methods combined with interactional analysis can tell us a lot about a community's norms, values, and culture.

While most research in this tradition has focused on children, recent work has also studied adults in language classrooms and professional training programs (nothing yet on Pilates or wine connoisseurship).[71] In language classrooms, the primary competency students are expected to learn is speaking, reading, and writing the language. In professional training programs, such as law school and cosmetology school, students are socialized not only to the core competencies—practicing law and cosmetology—but also to the language practices surrounding these competencies: speaking like experts on law and beauty through the use of certain words and speech acts.[72]

The current study adds to our understanding of adult language socialization by incorporating classroom-based research with data from other settings: concerts, cooking sessions, holiday meals, and the synagogue lobby. While the classroom offers a convenient research site and, certainly, an important locus of socialization, adults transitioning to new communities spend much of their time outside the classroom, even when they are full-time students. Observing individuals in multiple settings can yield a more complete and nuanced picture of the socialization process.[73]

Language and Identity, Second Dialect Acquisition

While language socialization research has focused on how people learn to speak in certain ways, the field of sociolinguistics has demonstrated quantitative correlations between social categories and language use.[74] For example, African Americans are more likely than European Americans to omit the verb "to be" ("He going home" versus "He's going home"), and working-class New Yorkers are more likely than middle-class New Yorkers to drop the "r" sound when it comes after a vowel ("fouth floah" versus "fourth floor").[75] The correlations between social groups and linguistic features are usually not categorical: not all African Americans omit "to be," and those who do also use standard verb structure in certain situations or with certain audiences.[76] Similarly, Orthodox Jews are more likely than non-Orthodox Jews and non-Jews to use certain Hebrew and Yiddish words, Yiddish-influenced grammatical constructions such as "staying *by* them" (rather than "staying at their house") and "I *live* here *already* eight years" (rather than "I have lived here eight years"), and sing-song intonation contours. And they tend to use more or fewer of these features depending on audience and situation.

We also know that people change their language when they transition to new communities. Several studies have found that people who move to other regions or countries where their native language is spoken differently pick up some elements of their new local dialect. Research has looked at children and adults moving from one dialect region to another in Brazil and Scandinavia, for example, and from one part of the English-speaking world to another, including Canadians in England, Americans in Australia, and Brits in the United States.[77] All these studies have found that, although younger children tend to approximate the new dialect more closely, adults also make some changes in their grammar, pronunciation, and especially lexicon (word choice).

As research has found, "situations of sociolinguistic reinvention" are not limited to international and regional migration.[78] Phillip Carter presents the case of Maria, a Mexican American girl who attended a predominantly white suburban elementary school and spoke English like her classmates. At age twelve she moved to an ethnically diverse middle school nearby, and within a year or so she had restyled herself, sporting urban, hip-hop clothing and features of Latino English, including different ways of pronouncing short [a], as in words like "man" and "candle." Carter explains, "In vitiating her suburban persona, a persona that likely would have been culturally unintelligible, undesirable, or infelicitous in her new school for a dark-skinned, immigrant, Latina, Maria rendered herself legible—and unassailable from peer critique—within the already pre-determined limits of her new environment."[79]

The linguistic changes made by these migrants (across the globe or across the neighborhood), as well as the style-shifting we all do, imply that we have some control over how we speak. Language use is an "act of identity" through which we align ourselves with some people and distinguish ourselves from others, with varying levels of consciousness.[80] In combination with our physical appearance, associations, activities, and other cultural practices, we use language to indicate to others which groups we wish to belong to. In other words, language use not only reflects social categories; it also helps to constitute them.[81]

The research on second dialect acquisition also points to the fact that humans do not have total control over their language. Very few of the migrants in these studies completely took on the new local dialect.[82] Research suggests that the "critical period" for learning native-like accents in a second language is between ages six and fourteen, although this is debated, and individual examples of adult immigrants with barely detectable accents do exist.[83] But, as one study found, even children who migrate when they are young, and sound mostly local, might not have total command over the complicated phonological rules surrounding how vowels change when they precede certain consonants.[84] In Orthodox communities, BTs are much less likely to pick up distinctive phonology (the sounds of speech) than lexical and grammatical features. There are various explanations for this, including the frequency and salience of these features, but a major factor is the same cognitive constraints that limit full acquisition in other instances of second dialect and second language acquisition.

The fact that individuals change their language—and the cognitive constraints on this control—makes more sense when we view language as a form of cultural capital.[85] Sometimes this manifests economically, as when people who can more closely approximate the standard language get higher-paying jobs. But often the "capital" is more social in nature: people are less or more accepted as members of a social group when they speak in certain ways. Just as Maria can raise her standing within Latino cliques in her middle school by changing her vowels, so too can BTs raise their standing within frum communities by using Hebrew words and sing-song intonation. The reverse holds as well: immigrants who cannot learn to speak their new language natively will always be seen as immigrants. In the same vein, many BTs indicate their non-native frum status when they speak, even if they wish to pass as FFB.

Language has much in common with other cultural practices; one might write a similar book about how newcomers learn the dress, food, or dance of Orthodox Judaism. But focusing on language offers a unique and important window into the socialization of newly Orthodox Jews—and adult transitions more generally. First, compared to other cultural domains, language is ubiquitous. A woman makes decisions about dress every time she buys clothing and gets dressed in the morning. She plans her Shabbos menu when she goes grocery shopping on Wednesday, and then on Thursday night or Friday she decides how sweet to make her kugel and how thick her chicken soup. In contrast, she makes decisions about language every time she opens her mouth (or chooses to remain silent). Whether or not she is conscious of her language variation, every word, grammatical structure, and pronunciation send signals to others about her identity, including where she positions herself along various social axes in the Orthodox world.

Another unique feature of language is how complicated it is. The cognitive burden of learning a new language, dialect, or even set of words far outweighs the cognitive burden of learning a new brisket recipe or circle dance. One must learn the forms and meanings of words and figure out when and with whom it is appropriate to use them. One must learn the intricate rules of pronunciation and grammatical structures. One must learn how to modulate the voice appropriately for different types of utterances and when to throw in an "um" or a "like." And one must learn the ideologies that connect linguistic features to social stances or activities and those stances and activities to identities.[86] Once this information has entered the mind (if it does), one must access and apply it quickly in any interaction. Learning other cultural practices, like cooking or dance, is certainly not simple: one must learn not only the embodied actions but also the ideologies that connect them to social structures. Even so, language learning is especially complicated, loaded as it is with cognitive constraints.

Finally, unlike other cultural practices, language is an essential component of adult socialization. Novices do not acquire competencies and their related cultural practices merely by observing others and imitating them. They learn through their interactions with experts and other novices, and these interactions generally involve language (spoken, written, or signed). Experts may explain their actions directly or offer advice, and novices may ask questions or otherwise initiate discussion. Aside from these interactions of socialization, novices must learn to speak about their new activities, roles, and communities with insiders and outsiders. While a study of adult socialization might omit analysis of dress and eating habits, ignoring language would overlook a crucial component of how adults transition to new identities.

Socialization: Legitimate Peripheral Participation

Like previous research on adult socialization, I found that BTs' linguistic and cultural learning is a social process akin to apprenticeship, which scholars have labeled "legitimate peripheral participation."[87] Novice Orthodox Jews begin participating in their new communities only peripherally, and, as they gradually w roles and responsibilities, they are able to try out the Hebrew words, ammatical constructions, and other practices they observe. They are ₁ the acquisition process through interactions of socialization with veteran community members, as well as other newcomers at various stages of integration. The overt practices of socialization initiated by others include translation of Hebrew and Yiddish words, explicit language instruction, and correction of language errors and other cultural breaches. In addition, BTs initiate practices of socialization, including questioning, repetition, and self-teaching. These interactions, as part of a broader process of legitimate peripheral participation, enable newcomers to learn not only Orthodox language but also other cultural practices and, of course, the religious rituals and proscriptions that are central to traditional Judaism.

The socialization process BTs go through is in many ways similar to that of pre-professional trainees and people acquiring new hobbies and other roles.[88] But, as I explain in chapter 9, there are important differences. While law students, for example, are socialized to behave and speak like lawyers in a community of adults, some of the "experts" who help to socialize BTs are children, a situation that leads to greater feelings of infantilization,

Self-Consciousness: Infantilization, Inauthenticity, In-Betweenness

Compared to children learning their mother tongue and native culture, adults transitioning to new identities may experience heightened self-consciousness. They likely recognize that more experienced community members can participate in linguistic and other cultural practices with much less effort and thought. In my research among BTs I found that this self-consciousness can manifest in feelings of infantilization, inauthenticity, and, especially, in-betweenness.

Unlike many other religious converts, newly Orthodox Jews tend not to refer to themselves as "born-again."[89] Even so, they sometimes feel that their religious transformation has rendered them like children. Their interactions with more experienced BTs and native-born community members often highlight their religious and cultural incompetence, even though the veterans tend to treat them with respect. New BTs may feel infantilized simply by noticing that an Orthodox child has full ownership over a cultural repertoire while they are just trying to make sense of it. This feeling may be crystallized on the rare occasion when an adult or child publicly corrects a mistake they made.[90]

Another manifestation of self-consciousness is inauthenticity: adults in transition may not feel full ownership over certain linguistic and cultural practices. When BTs try out new Hebrew words and Yiddish grammatical structures, they sometimes feel phony—like they are wearing a costume. They may have a similar reaction to their new wardrobe, head coverings, and, to a lesser extent, dinner recipes. Because these cultural practices are different from what they are used to, and because they associate them with people they want to emulate in some ways, they may feel that they do not have full authority to use them—with certain audiences or at all. Some BTs avoid practices that feel inauthentic to them, and others use them despite their discomfort and eventually grow to feel ownership over them. A common way that BTs deal with their feelings of inauthenticity is to mark new linguistic features as foreign to them. For example, they might joke about their own use of a Yiddish grammatical structure, or they might attribute a new Hebrew word to someone else. Although this phenomenon seems to be an important difference between child and adult language socialization, I have not found discussion of it in other research.

The third manifestation of self-consciousness in adult language socialization, in-betweenness, has been discussed in many other contexts. Anthropologist Victor Turner analyzes rites of passage as a period of transition between two states of being. During transitions, neophytes—or people being initiated into a new state—are neither in their previous state nor in their future state. They experience this phase as a state of limbo, or "liminality," from the Latin word for threshold.[91] Cultural theorist Gloria Anzaldúa discusses the permanent and painful state of in-betweenness, or "borderlands," imposed by colonialism. When a colonial power takes over a country and imposes cultural norms, the colonized people are necessarily changed. They never fully return to their precolonial culture, and they never fully take on the culture of the colonizers.[92]

As I found in my research, BTs are in a state of in-betweenness, a cultural borderland, even as they make this transition voluntarily. When they take on Orthodoxy, they necessarily give up elements of their former self. And, within the social structures of their new communities, they will never be considered FFBs.[93] As in postcolonial societies, BTs indicate their in-between status through hybrid linguistic and cultural practices—sometimes consciously and sometimes unconsciously. They may use a slew of Hebrew and Yiddish phrases in combination with some slang expressions that mark their secular past (e.g., "Just keepin' it real, *mamish* [really]"). Or they may keep modern art on their walls along with new additions of Jewish images. Even when BTs attempt to pass as FFB, their in-between status may become apparent to those in the know, based on the tilt of a hat, the slit of a skirt, or the shape of a vowel.

Diversity in Language Socialization

In my research, I found a great deal of variation in BTs' approach to their transition. Some sever their ties with their non-Orthodox and non-Jewish contacts, and others keep more diverse company. Some wish to pass as FFB, and others intentionally highlight their BT identities. Some take on religious and cultural practices as quickly as they can, even going beyond the norms of FFBs (hyperaccommodation). They might use *mamish* and *baruch Hashem* more than their FFB peers, just as they take an overly stringent approach to halachic observance. Others adapt gradually, making efforts to maintain aspects of their pre-Orthodox selves (deliberate distinctiveness). They might wear modest clothing but keep their nose ring or their goatee. Their music collection might include Orthodox bands like Journeys and Mordechai Ben David alongside Rush and the Rolling Stones. Many BTs participate in both hyperaccommodation and deliberate distinctiveness in different situations or with different audiences. Some BTs do both in a progression over time that I label the *bungee effect*: at first they go overboard in their use of Orthodox practices, and then they bounce back to a more comfortable level. It is clear that there is no single way of being a BT; differences in ideology lead to differences in behavior, including how they speak.

The notion of ideology—and its connection to language—calls for some discussion. In any community, ideology plays a significant role in how language is structured, used, and perceived.[94] As linguistic anthropologists understand it, "language ideology is the mediated link between social structures and forms of talk."[95] For example, individuals may associate curse words with a stance of toughness, and they may associate toughness with masculinity, but these three levels are connected only because of the ideologies that associate curse words with toughness and toughness with masculinity.[96] Even if those ideological connections remain unstated, they fuel our desire to use or avoid certain linguistic features as we align ourselves with some people and distinguish ourselves from others.

When individuals join a new community and encounter new ways of speaking, language ideology is important in their process of acquisition.[97] If newcomers did not recognize a connection between a linguistic feature and an individual or group they wanted to align themselves with, they would likely have no desire to use that feature (although they might acquire it unconsciously). In addition, newcomers' positive or negative views about individual linguistic features influence whether they want to incorporate them into their repertoires. For example, a number of BTs avoid the Yiddish-influenced usage of "by," as in "Are you staying by us?" because of an ideology that "by" represents substandard grammar. And many BTs replace certain English words with their Hebrew equivalents because of an ideology that Hebrew is a holy language. This is not to say that all adult language change is intentional or influenced by ideology. Newcomers sometimes use features they view negatively, and they sometimes acquire features they are not aware of. Even so, ideology necessarily plays a role in adult language socialization. And because newcomers have diverse ideologies, they are also likely to have diverse linguistic practices.

Another factor leading to diversity in adult language socialization is individual cognitive differences. Just as some people have more ease learning a foreign language, some people have more ease learning variations on their native language."[18] Indeed, I found that some of the BTs in my study picked up linguistic features with ease, while others struggled with them. I also found that variation in skill interacted with variation in ideology. The four BTs who scored highest on a test of Orthodox speech perception had diverse views about language. Three of them applied their linguistic perception skill to their linguistic performance to such an extent that they were sometimes mistaken for FFBs. The fourth, who has a master's degree in applied linguistics, noticed distinctive Orthodox features that were not salient to others but avoided some of them for ideological reasons. In short, individual differences in ideology, as well as linguistic skill, are important in how people approach a new identity and its associated ways of speaking.

Organization of the Book

By now it should be clear that language is thoroughly intertwined with other elements of culture, with identity, and with social structure. The analysis throughout this book brings all these together. Even so, some chapters focus more on language than others. In chapter 2, I explain my research methodology, and I discuss how my experiences as a non-Orthodox Jew encountering an Orthodox community compared to those of BTs. I explain the unique issues that arise when a non-Orthodox fieldworker conducts research in an Orthodox community. Chapter 3 introduces Orthodox cultural practices aside from language, including dress, music, and home decoration. I explain how BTs take on many of these cultural practices, often in distinct ways.

The fourth and fifth chapters return to language. Chapter 4 offers background on the languages Orthodox Jews have access to, and then it details some of the Yiddish and Hebrew features that make the English of Orthodox Jews distinct from the English of other Americans. Chapter 5 looks at the relationship between language and the continuum between Modern and Black Hat Orthodoxy. Individuals vary in their pronunciation of Hebrew words and use of Yiddish grammatical influences, as I show using data from an Orthodox matchmaking website, an online survey, and recorded study sessions.

The next three chapters turn the ethnographic spotlight back to BTs. Chapter 6 offers evidence for BTs' diverse approaches. It explores BTs' self-representation, as well as their ideologies about specific linguistic features, including the Hebrew phrase *baruch Hashem* and the Yiddish-influenced "by." While chapter 6 focuses on the "why," chapter 7 turns to the "how": BTs learn language through a progression of increasing access as they interact with community members in more intensive ways. A comparison of classes and videos presented at Ner Tamid and in Milldale illustrates the differential access BTs have before and after they make the leap to living in an Orthodox community.

This chapter also analyzes the interactions of socialization BTs have with FFBs and other BTs, as well as the stages BTs go through as they learn Hebrew and Yiddish words.

No matter how much linguistic skill BTs have, they are bound to make some mistakes or otherwise identify themselves as BTs through their language. Chapter 8 examines the distinguishing practices of newly Orthodox Jews, including hyperaccommodation, deliberate distinctiveness, and the bungee effect. Chapter 9 discusses the infantilization involved in becoming frum and asks whether the "BT borderland" is a temporary or permanent state. Finally, I offer reflections on other situations of adult language socialization, including becoming a doctor, becoming a parent, and the most famous fictional account: Eliza Doolittle in *Pygmalion/My Fair Lady*.

2

"Now You Look Like a Lady"

Adventures in Ethnographic and Sociolinguistic Fieldwork

To find out how BTs learn Orthodox language and culture, I carried out a three-tiered methodology: a year of ethnographic observation and interviews, recordings of community members' speech, and an experiment using recorded speech samples. In this chapter I explain these methods and the issues that arose during my fieldwork, and I compare my experiences as a non-Orthodox researcher to the experiences of BTs.

Ethnographic Methodology

Ethnography is the study of people, their culture, and their social organization through participant-observation and interviews and the subsequent written presentation of selected aspects to an audience. The researcher spends a significant amount of time in the community, getting to know people, observing events, asking questions informally, and conducting interviews. This is what I did during my year of fieldwork at Ner Tamid and in Milldale.

I spent the first six months—October 2001 through March 2002—attending lectures, prayer services, concerts, and social events at the Ner Tamid Center. I audio recorded classes, social interactions before and after class, and one-on-one study sessions. I interviewed the rabbis who teach there and some of the non-Orthodox Jews and BTs who attend their classes. Gradually, I began to spend more of my time in Milldale, where the Ner Tamid rabbis and several former students live. From April to November 2002 I did fieldwork mostly in Milldale, visiting people in their homes, celebrating Shabbos and holidays, and attending classes and services at Shomrei Emunah (also a pseudonym), the largest synagogue in that densely Orthodox neighborhood.

In addition to these centers of my fieldwork, I also visited a few other Ortho-dox synagogues in the Milldale area, the mikveh (ritual bath), and three schools that Milldale Orthodox children attend. I ate several meals at the two kosher restaurants (one pizza and one Chinese food), bought books, gifts, and wine at the two Judaica shops, and shopped at a few of the supermarkets with large kosher sections. I read the bulletin board at the synagogue, community news-letters, and several Orthodox newspapers and magazines. I took a research trip to Israel to experience some of the BT hotspots there. And I made brief vis-its to Orthodox communities in Brooklyn, Monsey, and Mexico City. Overall, I spent about five hundred hours at the field sites, observing and participating in classes, festive meals, prayer services, and social events, and interviewing—formally and informally—members of the communities. In addition, my obser-vations are backed up by my previous research in other Orthodox communities: a Modern Orthodox group of college students, a small Chabad Hasidic commu-nity in Northern California, and brief visits with Orthodox Jews in other Ameri-can cities.

Outsiders Coming In: The BT and the Non-Orthodox Ethnographer

To some extent, my ethnographic observations simulated the three-phase pro-gression that many BTs go through: attending classes and events at an outreach center like Ner Tamid, studying in an intensive BT training program or yeshiva, and becoming part of a tight-knit Orthodox community like the one in Mill-dale. I started by attending a social event at Ner Tamid. Then I attended some classes and prayer services there and began to get to know the rabbis and other students. On my third visit there, one of the regular teachers, Rabbi Hollander, invited me and a few other students to spend Shabbos—from before sunset Fri-day to after sunset Saturday—at his home in the Milldale community. I eventu-ally did spend a Shabbos there, along with a Ner Tamid student in her sixties and a few other guests, and I started to meet people in the neighborhood. I con-tinued to attend classes and other events at Ner Tamid and gradually became more involved, gaining increased access to roles and responsibilities there. The rabbis at Ner Tamid asked me to collect tickets at the door for a lecture and to set up for a concert, roles they often give to relative newcomers (both to make them feel welcome and to fill the center's need for person-hours).[1] After a few months of classes at Ner Tamid, I started attending classes at Milldale's Shomrei Emunah synagogue. I got to know several families in Milldale and accepted their invitations to spend Shabbos and holidays with them. I danced at weddings, comforted mourners, and celebrated at birth festivities.

In the middle of my time in Milldale, I visited *Erets Yisroel*, the land of Israel. I spent a week studying in one of the women's seminaries where three of the BTs in my study had "learned." While in Israel, I also visited other seminaries in Jerusalem, met with a number of rabbis and *rebbetzins* (wives of rabbis), and spent Shabbos with a few BTs at an outreach-oriented youth hostel in Tsfat, a city that draws many religious seekers because of its mystical character and history.

According to my observations and interviews, as well as previous literature, the path that BTs take to Orthodox life is often similar to the progression of my research.[2] And as a non-Orthodox Jew encountering Orthodox communities, I shared a number of experiences with BTs. In some cases I was able to use my experiences as data. For example, when an FFB referred to me with the Orthodox Ashkenazi Hebrew pronunciation of my name, Sora Ben-Or—even though I introduced myself with a more Anglicized pronunciation—I made a note in my Names file. Some BTs in my study started to refer to themselves by their Hebrew names after similar interactions with community veterans. And when an FFB corrected my plural of *shadchan* (matchmaker) from English shadchans to Ashkenazi Hebrew *shadchonim*, I added that to my growing list of instances in which newcomers were corrected by community members.

The first time I attended Shabbos services in Milldale, I realized that some of the same things that made me feel like an outsider also affected other newcomers and even longtime BTs. Because of my Jewish educational background, I was usually able to follow along in the *siddur* (prayer book). But there were occasions, especially on holidays, when I was confused. Was there a special *musaf* (additional service) for *yomtov* (holiday), or was it the same as on Shabbos? I knew I was supposed to keep my feet together during the *Amidah* (standing silent prayer), but that made me feel unsteady, so I moved my toes a few inches apart. And I was one of the few married women wearing a hat rather than a *sheitel* (wig). These things made me feel like I stuck out in the women's section of the synagogue. But I looked around and realized that several of the women around me were BTs, and some had even less background than I did in Hebrew and liturgy. After the rabbi's complicated dvar torah that day, I turned to the recent BT next to me and asked, "Did you understand what he was talking about?" "Hardly at all," she said with an uneasy laugh. I was not the only one feeling like a sore thumb.

Another experience I shared with BTs was being shamed by young children. One day when I was staying overnight with an Orthodox family, I took a shower and left my hat off for my hair to dry. The father was not at home, so I did not need to worry about a man seeing my hair (the reason behind the hair-covering rule). But the five-year-old girl, Rina, asked, "Why aren't you wearing your hat?" Her mom told her, "It's OK." Later, as I was about to leave the house, Rina reminded me not to forget my hat. She asked if she could put it on for me. She did, and she tucked my hair behind my ears and under the hat. "Now you look like a lady," she said with a smile. I felt ashamed, belittled, and grateful. And I realized that this five-year-old, who often interacts with BT guests, would probably help many women to "look like a lady" according to Orthodox standards.

Other ethnographers of Orthodox Jews have had similar experiences of being shamed. Anthropologist Tamar El-Or tells of her second visit to a Hasidic community, when a young girl asked her sister in Yiddish if Tamar was a *pritse* (loose woman, prostitute). The girls' mother explained that the comment referred to her uncovered hair, never seen among married Ultra-Orthodox women. From then on, El-Or always covered her hair when she visited the community.[3]

Through interviews and observations, I learned that BTs also endure comments and shaming from children. When Jacob was starting to become more religious, he used to drive a few hours to spend Shabbos with an Orthodox family. He would arrive in his street clothes and then change into his suit in time for Shabbos. One day he happened to arrive in a suit, and the thirteen-year-old son said, "He's a regular guy." To this FFB boy, regular guys wear suits all the time, not just on Shabbos. Jacob said that this comment had a big impact on him and coaxed him toward his eventual decision to wear suits every day. Similarly, when Leonard was first becoming involved in the Orthodox community, he sometimes wore a kipah and sometimes did not. One day when he was bareheaded, a three-year-old girl asked, "Why aren't you wearing a kipah?" Since that little girl's question, he says, he has always worn his kipah in the community to avoid uncomfortable situations like this.

Another instance of shaming happened in the linguistic realm. Hank is a successful professional in his fifties who has only recently become observant. He has trouble with the [ch] sound in Hebrew and Yiddish words, and his [ch] usually sounds more like [h] or [k]. Zev, an eleven-year-old FFB boy, often makes fun of Hank's pronunciation. One evening, in a very public setting, Hank asked someone, "Can you pass me a *humash* [Pentateuch]?" Zev interjected, "*CHHHUmash*. It's not *humash*; it's *CHHHUmash*." Hank responded with a smile, but based on my own feelings in similar situations, I imagine he felt belittled and annoyed.

These examples show how BTs and I elicited similar reactions from community veterans. I also found that we sometimes made similar hypercorrective mistakes (mistakes that occur when someone tries too hard to speak or act correctly). One sweltering June day, I went to visit a BT woman in her home in a mixed Modern–Black Hat community near Milldale. Although as a pregnant woman I felt ten degrees hotter than most people, I decided out of respect to wear knee-high stockings with my sandals. When she greeted me, I was surprised to see her toes uncovered in her sandals. When I asked about this, she said that she made a conscious decision only to wear socks when she goes to more "*shtark*" (intense [Black Hat]) communities like those she has visited in Milldale and Brooklyn. Interactions like these taught me about the nuances of distinctiveness within the Orthodox community—and allowed me to relax my dress code and feel more comfortable on hot days.

Ayala Fader reports a similar interaction in which she felt uncomfortable wearing only a bathing suit in an all-women's pool in a Hasidic vacation area. Because she was accustomed to dressing modestly when doing ethnographic fieldwork in the community, the Hasidic women had to urge her to remove her bathrobe.[4] Similarly, Samuel Heilman begins his book *Defenders of the Faith* with a description of immersing himself in a mikveh crowded with Haredi Jews. He says he drew irritated looks when he spent too long in the water. And, after he got out, someone even corrected him when he audibly said the blessing for putting on the tzitzis, informing him that he should say it only the first time he puts it on in the morning. Like me, these researchers of Orthodox Jews learned from their hyper-corrective mistakes and were able to better fit into their research communities. Socialization of the researcher parallels socialization of other newcomers.

While my own interactions helped me to understand the experiences that many BTs have, I also kept in mind that our experiences were different in a number of ways. Many Jews in the process of becoming Orthodox are not sure where in the Jewish landscape they will end up and how they will get there, but I expected all along that I would remain a non-Orthodox Jew. My participation in Orthodox communities and cultural practices was a temporary measure, while their use of Orthodox clothing, language, and other practices is part of their long-term integration into the community.

Unlike BTs, I did not completely take on the system of laws required of Orthodox Jews, nor did I come to believe in some of the central tenets of Ortho-doxy. Because of this, I did not feel like a hypocrite when I wore a skirt in Milldale but changed into pants as soon as I got home—or when I stopped at a non-kosher Dunkin' Donuts shop after interviewing someone at the kosher pizza place.[5] New BTs do similar things and, according to their reports, sometimes feel hypocritical. In addition, once they take on full-time observance, they often have trouble negotiating their new practices in the presence of non-Orthodox family and friends. I never had to deal with these issues, which are commonly discussed among BTs. I also never experienced the same intensity of integra-tion as many transitioning BTs do, since I did not move to an Orthodox neigh-borhood or even spend every Shabbos there. Finally, I entered the Orthodox community with a relatively strong knowledge of Jewish texts and of traditional observance and culture, both from my childhood (non-Orthodox) Jewish educa-tion and from my previous research in Orthodox communities. Many BTs begin their journey with little or no Jewish education and have much more to learn in their process of becoming frum.

Lynn Davidman, a non-Orthodox ethnographer who did research among BT women in Lubavitch and Modern Orthodox settings, had a similar approach

to her own fieldwork experiences: "I used myself as an instrument, realizing
that my reactions to the setting were a valuable clue to what the other women
might be experiencing. I also strove, however, to pay attention to what made
their experiences distinct from mine. They, after all, were involved in a process of 'conversion,' while I was there to study this process."[6] No matter how
deeply involved an ethnographer becomes in the community, her experiences
will always be somewhat different from the people she is studying. As ethnographer James Clifford says, "The ability of the fieldworker to inhabit indigenous
minds is always in doubt. Indeed this is a permanent, unresolved problem of
ethnographic method."[7] Even people who research their own communities, like
Heilman studying the Modern Orthodox congregation of which he was an active
member, will experience the field differently from their informants, just by the
nature of their role as ethnographer.[8]

Not Quite Insider, Not Quite Outsider

Since the publication of Bronislaw Malinowski's diaries in 1967, ethnographic
writers have offered reflections on their own backgrounds and experiences.[9]
Information like this is useful, as it gives the reader a sense of how much access
the researchers had and why they focused on some things and not others, both
in their observation and in their analysis. In this section, I discuss how I as a
non-Orthodox Jew was viewed by the frum community and how I negotiated my
self-representation to find a balance between access and honesty.

I grew up attending a Jewish day school and joining my family in *Shabbat*
(Sabbath, Modern Hebrew pronunciation) and holiday celebrations. At the time
of my fieldwork, I was an active member of a Reconstructionist *minyan* (prayer
group), which was part of a Conservative synagogue.[10] Judaism pervades many
aspects of my life, from how I spend my Saturdays to how I celebrate life-cycle
events, from the art on my walls to my collections of music and books, from the
toys I buy for my children to the topics I choose for my academic research.

Throughout my fieldwork, I encountered several Orthodox Jews—BTs and
FFBs—who were not sure what to make of me: a non-Orthodox woman who can
speak like an Orthodox Jew and take part comfortably in prayer and meal rituals. Once I was looking through a Hebrew book about holy places in Israel with a
young girl, and I was reading some of the place names to her in Hebrew. Her FFB
mother was listening, and she said, "I'm very impressed. How do you know so
much?" Similarly, a BT woman was amazed when I mentioned that my husband
and I created a brochure for our wedding to explain the rituals to guests. "You
had a traditional wedding?" she asked. "Well, with modifications," I answered.
If she had asked for details, she might have been surprised to learn that we
had both men's and women's *tishes* (pre-wedding celebrations with singing and
speeches, literally "table"), while Orthodox Jews just have a *chossen*'s (groom's)

tish. And she might have been shocked to hear that the seven circles, which the bride traditionally walks around the groom, were divided equally between my groom and me, a new egalitarian tradition that this BT had criticized moments before. I was grateful that she did not ask for details.

Although some BTs were not sure how to categorize me, they assumed that I would become more religiously observant throughout my study. Early on in my fieldwork, one woman was reading the part of the consent form that said, "There are no apparent risks," and she joked to her friend, "Risk—the only risk is that she'll become religious." Another BT mentioned a well-known teacher who has written books about Orthodoxy and told me, with a smile, that he "got into it doing what you're doing"—research on the community. Most of the other ethnographers who have researched Orthodox Jews report similar expectations that they would become Orthodox, just as an anthropologist studying a fundamentalist Christian community was considered a "lost soul on the brink of salvation," not merely a researcher gathering data for a book.[11]

About halfway through my fieldwork, a community member embarrassed me publicly because I was not becoming observant. This shaming may not have been intentional, because it happened on Purim, the festive holiday when there is a tradition for Jewish men to get drunk. At a Purim *seudah* (festive meal), in front of at least twenty other people, a man who was very helpful throughout my study said something like this:

> If Sarah really wants to learn about the community, she must do it all herself—be *shomer Shabbos* [keep the Sabbath], *shomer kashrus* [keep kosher], follow the laws of family purity. . . . You're a *bas yisroel* [Jewish woman], like your *bubby* [grandma] and her bubby and her bubby, and your *zeidy* [grandpa] and his zeidy and his zeidy. An outsider can't understand. . . . My blessing to her is that she should become frum. I know it's hard . . . but I think she should become frum. When she's done she can decide whether or not to continue doing these things.[12]

Despite my embarrassment, I responded with the post-blessing Hebrew word of agreement, "Amen." He was probably right that I would understand frum Jews better had I taken on all the laws. But I did not feel that extra bit of ethnographic depth was worth temporarily renouncing the religious life to which I was so committed.

My "amen" was the only appropriate response, both to the Purim blessing and to people's predictions throughout my fieldwork that I would become Orthodox. I would have alienated many people if I had revealed too much about my own religious observance and how comfortable I am with it. When people asked about my Jewish affiliations, I told them that I am Conservative, not wanting to get into details about Reconstructionism. I did not contradict the Purim blessing by explaining how I observe Shabbos and other commandments, just in nontraditional ways. And although I felt close to several community members, I did not invite any of them to my home or to my baby's *Simchat Bat* (birth celebration for a daughter), where they would have encountered unorthodox egalitarian rituals, in which tradition has "a vote but not a veto" (Mordecai Kaplan's phrase commonly used in Reconstructionist circles).[13] Even though I imagine they would have been respectful and understanding, I was uncomfortable sharing how my Judaism differed from theirs.

Like other non-Orthodox ethnographers of Orthodoxy, I avoided conflicts by maintaining separate Jewish lives. On the *Shabbatot* I spent at home, I lit candles after sunset, talked on the phone, drove to synagogue, and occasionally played violin in my congregation's accompanying ensemble, wearing a tallis (prayer shawl traditionally worn by men). I avoided doing any kind of "work" related to my research. On the *Shabbosim* I spent in Milldale, I arrived with my hair covered a half-hour before their early candle lighting, walked up to a mile to synagogue—even when I was very pregnant—and said the prayers quietly along with the others in the women's section. And, ironically, I spent the entire Shabbos "working," that is, observing and remembering details, to be written down only after *havdala* (end-of-Shabbos ceremony, literally "separation").

Just as I tried to avoid bringing my liberal Judaism into my fieldwork, I rarely brought the Orthodox traditions I was learning about into my own Jewish life (except for a delicious *challah* recipe). However, on the Shabbatot I spent in my own community, I sometimes found it hard to shed the role of ethnographer. After the Purim *shpil* (play) at my Reconstructionist minyan, I rushed home to my computer to add to my fieldnotes a song I heard there: "We don't need to daven from behind a *shtender* [lectern, a traditional venue for leading prayers], but we must alternate by gender!" The differences that I had noticed between Orthodoxy and liberal egalitarian Judaism were made explicit in this parody, in which one of the leaders of the minyan made fun of the minyan's focus on nonhierarchical prayer and gender equality by contrasting it to the traditional Jewish worship I observed every time I went to Shomrei Emunah or other Orthodox synagogues.[14]

By reading about these details of my Jewish observance, the reader should understand that I was both insider and outsider with respect to my fieldwork community. Like them, I am Jewish and Jewishly committed, but I have a different way of expressing my Jewishness. Although I chose not to share many details of my own religious observance with my Orthodox friends, every time I visited an Orthodox community I made decisions about self-representation—in dress, language, and self-reports—that would affect how people viewed me. A challenge throughout my year of fieldwork was trying to remain honest in my self-representation without offending people or losing access to their institutions, homes, and lives.

Balancing Access with Honesty

Near the beginning of my fieldwork at Ner Tamid, I wore a long skirt and a modest long-sleeve shirt, in accordance with the Orthodox laws of female modesty. A man who had recently started to become observant asked if I was Orthodox, and I said, "I'm Conservative." He said, "You don't look Conservative. Did you dress that way just to come here?" I realized then that wearing long skirts and high necklines was not just a matter of being respectful—it also had practical and ethical implications. Throughout my fieldwork, I often tweaked my self-representation in an effort to navigate the boundary between access and honesty. I could have gone to Brooklyn and spent thousands of dollars on a full Orthodox wardrobe (including a sheitel, several modest tailored suits for Shabbos and special occasions, and some housecoats and snoods for casual lounging). But I decided to wear my own long skirts and hats—and not just for financial reasons. Like some newly Orthodox Jews, I did not want people to think I was an imposter, pretending to be a strictly Orthodox Jew. I also did not want to make people feel uncomfortable by wearing short sleeves or going to synagogue with no head covering. So I compromised and dressed like some Modern Orthodox women I know, choosing not to sew up the slit in one of my long skirts and not to tuck most of my hair under my hat, even after the five-year-old girl shamed me into doing so on that one occasion. These details of appearance allowed me to distinguish myself from many of the community members and still remain respectful.

Another area in which I maintained distinctiveness was my language. I did use many elements of Orthodox Jewish English, pronouncing most Hebrew words according to the Ashkenazi norms common in the community. But when I used liturgical Hebrew aloud, such as reading a Bible quote in class or saying the blessing over the candles, I generally used the Americanized Modern Hebrew pronunciation that I grew up with. An example is the Hebrew sentence visitors recite when leaving a house of mourning, which Milldale Orthodox Jews tend to pronounce in the Ashkenazi way: "*hamókom yenáchem eschém . . .*" (May God comfort you). When visiting Mrs. Feig after the loss of her mother, I used Modern Hebrew pronunciation: "*hamakóm yenachém etchém . . .*" This was partly because I felt uncomfortable using the Ashkenazi pronunciation for fear of mistakes, but also because I felt it was appropriate to indicate through my language that I do not identify as Black Hat Orthodox.

My attempts at modest but non-imposter self-representation were sometimes misinterpreted. For example, the first time I met one Milldale woman in her home, I was wearing a skirt but no hat. And when she saw me a few months later at the synagogue, I was wearing a hat, as I always did there. She assumed I had become "observant" in the time that had elapsed. In situations like this, I tried to respond in an ambiguous way. Similarly, one day I asked

Michelle, a BT I had become close to, for the e-mail address of a rabbi who runs a seminary in Israel so I could arrange a visit. She gave me the information and asked if the purpose of my trip was to do research or to advance my own Jewish learning. Research, I replied, "but it'll have the secondary effect of adding to my learning." It was true: I learned a good deal from attending classes in Israel, as in Philadelphia, but it was not the same response I would have given to non-Orthodox friends.

I gave similarly ambiguous answers to community members who asked if my fieldwork was affecting my observance. I told them that I have been observing Shabbos and certain *mitzvos* (commandments) more, which was true in a nontraditional sense. And I made sure to mention that I have enjoyed baking my own challah, using a delicious doughy recipe I got from a rebbetzin in Milldale. This was one of many compromises in my self-presentation that enabled me to remain mostly honest while maintaining access to the community. I often felt like a tightrope walker, trying not to lose my balance on the fine line between access and honesty.

In keeping with contemporary American standards for research using human subjects, my motives in the community were never covert. Any time I met new people, I told them that I was doing research about how ba'alei teshuva integrate into Orthodox communities. Usually, I did not initially mention that my focus was language, so as not to make them self-conscious about their speech. If they asked for details, I added that I was interested in how BTs learn the culture of the Orthodox community, especially the language styles. By the end of the year, many community members had participated in the speech perception experiment, and almost everyone knew that my research focus was language.

Gathering Speech Samples

The ethnographic methodology described above allowed me to spend hundreds of hours observing how people spoke to family, friends, acquaintances, strangers, and an insider/outsider researcher (me). On most days, my fieldnotes include in-depth sections about language, including BTs' mistakes, brief exchanges between BTs and FFBs, BTs' use of Hebrew words with one interlocutor and the English equivalents with another, and use of English and Hebrew plurals on Hebrew nouns.

In addition to observation, I gathered over ninety hours of speech on digital mini-disc or audio cassette. This speech came from dozens of classes and lectures at Ner Tamid, in Milldale, and elsewhere, several one-on-one study sessions, several hours of informal social interactions, and many interviews I conducted. I was present during all the recorded interactions, except for a few of the study sessions, and I always obtained signed consent forms from all present. I collected samples of recorded speech for sixty-nine BTs and FFBs, about an equal number of males and females.

The purpose of taking notes on language use and analyzing recorded speech was to clarify which Orthodox Jews use which linguistic features and in which contexts. I expected variation according to the length of time people have been Orthodox, as well as gender, age, and other factors. Based on the recorded and observed speech of 101 speakers (24 BT women, 28 BT men, 27 FFB women, and 22 FFB men), I compiled a large Excel spreadsheet, where I noted which speakers used which linguistic features, with some data on audience and context. I noted individuals' uses of over four hundred Hebrew and Yiddish words, and I noted when people used English words that generally tend to be in Hebrew or Yiddish (such as "synagogue" or "Passover" rather than *shul* or *Pesach*). And I noted the use of dozens of phonological, grammatical, and other features of Orthodox Jewish English.

Interviews

In addition to observation and speech samples, I conducted interviews with one hundred Orthodox Jews, sixty of which were recorded. Most interviews were individual, but some were in pairs and a few were in small groups, including group interviews with eight BT women and four BT men currently in seminary/yeshiva. The interviews were conducted in the interviewee's home or office or in a semi-public place like Ner Tamid. Family members, colleagues, and others sometimes walked by and interacted with us. Interviews ranged in length from ten to ninety minutes. The breakdown of people interviewed is presented in table 2.1. The FFB category includes a few children and teenagers, but all the BTs were adults.

TABLE 2.1

Number of interviewees by gender and exposure to Orthodoxy

Years of active involvement with Orthodox institutions	Female	Male
0–2 years (BT)	11	8
3–5 years (BT)	8	5
6+ years (BT)	15	13
Entire life (FFB)	25	15
Total	59	41

The interviews had a few goals: to help me understand the process of becoming frum, as well as individual BTs' and FFBs' views about Orthodox language and culture, and to gather additional samples of speech. The interviews were guided by my questions but were open-ended; some felt more like "hanging out." Most interviews with BTs included questions about how they became interested in Orthodoxy, what they have changed since becoming frum, and how Orthodox and non-Orthodox Jews speak differently. Most interviews with FFBs included questions about how they see their role in helping BTs integrate into the community, whether and how they can tell who is a BT, and whether and how BTs change their language.

Often after the first question, whether it was about their childhood or their first interest in Orthodoxy, BTs would launch into a long narrative describing their "journey" to religiosity. As a published collection of BT narratives demonstrates, this has become a common speech act, rehearsed and edited over and over during social gatherings, usually with other BTs.[15] Like other religious conversion stories and gays' and lesbians' coming out stories, the process of co-constructing a personal narrative with peers and more experienced community members plays an important role in BTs' socialization.[16] Although in-depth analysis of BT narratives is beyond the scope of this study, there seem to be some (optional) common features: a journey metaphor, pre-Orthodox life events that prefigured the current state of religiosity, an event or events that led to a desire to explore Orthodoxy, a moment or moments of realization, relationships with Orthodox mentors, and discussion of how the BTs' new observance affected relationships with family and friends.

Like other researchers of BTs, I found that some BTs appreciated the opportunity to tell their stories in such detail.[17] One BT was disappointed when he realized that our second meeting, months after the first, was only to do the speech perception experiment; he was hoping it would be a follow-up interview about where he is in his "journey." One BT requested to be interviewed after he saw me setting up an interview with someone else. Even FFBs seemed to enjoy the interviews. One woman had planned to tidy up during the interview, but, as she pointed out at the end, she found our discussion so interesting that she did no cleaning at all. There were also people who did not agree to be interviewed, or did so reluctantly, as I explain in the "Mixed Reactions" section below.

Speech Perception Experiment: Matched Guise Test

During the interviews I asked BTs and FFBs general questions about Orthodox language, and they sometimes offered opinions on specific linguistic features, like the Yiddish-influenced "by" and Hebrew phrases like *baruch Hashem*. Since I wanted to explore in more depth how people perceive individual linguistic features, I conducted a sociolinguistic experiment called a matched guise test. Based on research by Wallace Lambert and his colleagues, the matched guise test has been used to test stereotypes that listeners have about different languages and dialects.[18] For example, Lambert recorded several English and French Canadians speaking in two guises, French and English. He played excerpts from their speech and asked English-speaking and French-speaking Canadian respondents to rate the speakers on several qualities, including intelligence, sincerity, and ambition. The respondents, not aware that they were hearing the same speaker in both English and French, were essentially evaluating the languages in question rather than the speakers themselves. Overall, Lambert found that both English- and French-speaking Canadian respondents had more positive images of the speakers in their English guises.

I modified this experiment to determine whether people associate certain linguistic features with Orthodoxy and with BTs or FFBs. I enlisted several Orthodox and non-Orthodox "actors" who have no connection to Ner Tamid or Milldale but are familiar with Orthodox Jewish English. I created scripts for the speakers and coached them on how to say their lines in two different guises. The scripts were based on utterances I observed in my fieldwork but were tailored to ensure a controlled experiment. Examples included the following:

[CH] IN HEBREW WORDS

1. Where were you for *kol hamoed*? (lower FFB rating expected due to absence of [ch])
2. Where were you for *chol hamoed?* (referring to the time between the holiest days of a long holiday)

HEBREW PLURALS

1. How many *ba'al teshuvas* do you think there are? (lower FFB rating expected because of the English rather than the Hebrew plural marker)
2. How many *ba'alei teshuva* do you think there are?

[T] RELEASE (T[H] = RELEASED [T], AS IN *ALL RIGHT*[H], WHERE IT IS NORMALLY GLOTTALIZED OR FLAPPED, AS IN *ALL RIGH'*)

1. All right[h]. We're gonna skip the first section, but[h] uh, we'll go back to it[h]. (higher Orthodox rating expected)[19]
2. All right. We're gonna skip the first section, but, uh, we'll go back to it.

The samples were recorded several times on mini-disc, and I selected the best takes for each feature. I copied the samples onto cassette in two quasi-random orders (making sure that the similar sentences were not too close together).

After conducting a pilot version of the experiment for several BTs and FFBs in the New York area, I tweaked it to maximize its usefulness. I conducted this experiment among fifty-seven Orthodox Jews in Philadelphia: twenty-nine BTs and twenty-eight FFBs, ranging in age from ten to sixty-eight. All respondents were native speakers of American English. They received questionnaires with the following directions and the same two questions for each excerpt:

> You will now hear a tape with 45 excerpts of conversation by Jewish speakers. Some of the speakers are ba'alei teshuva, some grew up Ortho-dox, and some are not Orthodox. For each excerpt, please answer questions a and b by circling the number of the best answer.

EXCERPT #1:

a) Do you think the speaker is Orthodox?
   1. Definitely Not. 2. Probably Not. 3. Can't Tell. 4. Probably. 5. Definitely.

b) Do you think the speaker grew up Orthodox?
   1. Definitely Not. 2. Probably Not. 3. Can't Tell. 4. Probably. 5. Definitely.

After the respondents answered these questions for all forty-five excerpts, I discussed their reactions with them. The written responses, as well as the post-test discussions, were very useful in helping me understand attitudes about language, Orthodoxy, and ba'alei teshuva, as well as about specific linguistic features.

Methodological Issues

Loshon Hora

Theoretically, the religious prohibition against *loshon hora* (gossip, literally "evil speech"), talking about others in ways that might be perceived as nega-tive, could have inhibited my fieldwork.[20] People could have been offended by questions like "Can you tell who's BT?" and been reluctant to recount anec-dotes from their experiences with others. In general, this was not a prob-lem. I was surprised that some people, unsolicited, offered names of BTs they thought seemed more or less "BT-like," for example. The rules surrounding loshon hora affected my research only in two minor ways: some people's dis-comfort with the speech perception experiment and my written presentation of personal information.

While most community members I approached seemed happy to partici-pate in the experiment, some felt uncomfortable about it. One BT woman reluc-tantly started to listen to the tape, saying, "I'm just going to say 'Can't tell' for all of them." After she circled "Can't tell" for the first three, I suggested that she stop the test. I asked about her discomfort, and she said, "You can't judge. People who grow up in a close-knit [FFB] family you can tell. You can sense their *yichus* [lineage]. But even if I could tell, I wouldn't tell you what I think." Her concern was not that it is impossible to make a judgment based on a short speech sample (although she did recall having made incorrect assumptions in the past), but that reporting her judgment to me would be loshon hora.

While this reaction was extreme, a few other people—BTs and FFBs, women and men—commented during or after the experiment that they felt uncomfortable making assumptions about people's religiosity and religious background. One recent BT wrote, "I think it is very judgmental to try to [determine whether a speaker is Orthodox]. The only being that can tell is G-d." ("G-d" is a common Jewish way of writing "God" on paper that might be thrown away, based on the prohibition against discarding God's name.) An FFB man, referring to the questions on the matched guise test that ask whether the speaker grew up Orthodox, asked, "Is this testing prejudice?" This comment assumes that judging whether speakers are BT or FFB is making a value judgment. Unlike other matched guise tests, I did not ask respondents to judge whether the speakers are "intelligent," "friendly," or "tall." I asked only whether the speakers are Orthodox and whether they grew up Orthodox. Some people's reluctance to make such judgments stems from their understanding of the rules about loshon hora. But it also hints at the prejudice BTs may face, even in outreach-oriented Orthodox communities.

Since there are stories about Jews throughout the chapters that follow, this whole book could be perceived by some as loshon hora. I have taken a few precautions to avoid this characterization. In line with social science standards and the confidentiality I promised in the consent forms, I use pseudonyms for all individuals and institutions, and I do not report any information that would definitively identify people. Sometimes I use two pseudonyms for the same person. When discussing linguistic "mistakes" and other potential embarrassments, I use even more ambiguous appellations for research participants, like "a BT woman." And I try not to report any anecdotes that might be perceived as involving loshon hora. An example is the time I heard a person joke, "Sometimes I think [so-and-so] is really not Orthodox," based on "things she said." The "things she said" and the informant's reactions to them would have enhanced my discussion of Orthodox ideology, but including them might have revealed the identities of the speaker and the referee to each other and to other community members.

Another feature of my methodology that may help to preserve confidentiality (and steer clear of loshon hora) is the use of data from outside Ner Tamid and Milldale. On my brief research visits to Israel, Monsey, and elsewhere, I observed and interviewed several BTs and FFBs. Therefore, readers familiar with the communities should not assume they know all the "characters" in this book. Precautions like these are ones that any contemporary ethnographer would take to maintain the confidentiality of her consultants. But they may be even more important in a community where loshon hora, or gossip, is considered a sin.

The "Observer's Paradox" and Orthodox Style-Shifting

In the Orthodox community, people change their language significantly depending on who they are speaking to. FFBs grow up using English with Hebrew and Yiddish words with their family and friends, and they use mostly English with outsiders, generally translating any Hebrew and Yiddish words they do use. BTs also learn to shift styles like this (although, as I explain in chapter 8, some of them also use insider speech when talking to outsiders). Based on some people's speech to me, it was clear that I was not always considered an insider. I experienced a serious case of the "observer's paradox" that all sociolinguists encounter to varying extents: the researcher wants to observe speech as if she were not there, but to observe it she has to be there.[21]

One evening at a Ner Tamid class, I heard Marissa, a recent BT, use the Hebrew word *Hashem* (God) several times. When I interviewed her informally after class, she used the word "God" several times. But when an FFB rabbi walked by, she—still talking to me—used *Hashem* instead. Even though she heard me use many Hebrew words, she used the outsider-directed variant when speaking to me. But she apparently considered it more appropriate to use the Hebrew word when a veteran community member was within earshot.

One young FFB man interacts with many non-Orthodox Jews and is accustomed to switching styles. He first introduced himself to me with his English name, Michael, but he later used the name he goes by among community members, Moyshe. Throughout my year of fieldwork, I had many conversations with Moyshe, and he and I both used many Hebrew and Yiddish words, as well as other Orthodox features. Even so, he sometimes used outsider language when talking to me. He once told me that the rabbi was about to lecture, "as he always does between *mincha* and *maariv*, the afternoon and evening services." I said, "I know what mincha and maariv are." Moyshe responded with a smile, "I know, I was just playing with you." However, it did not seem that he intended to tease; I think he was using his outsider voice when speaking to me, perhaps subconsciously.

Many people started using outsider speech to me and then gradually used more Orthodox features when they learned of my Judaic knowledge and linguistic abilities. For example, when FFB Rabbi Nussbaum first met me, he used very few Orthodox features, and he even used the word "Talmud," the rabbinic commentaries he calls "Gemora" when speaking to insiders. In the next conversation we had, he used "with" when he could have used the Yiddish-influenced "by": "Who will you be staying *with*?" (rather than "Who will you be staying *by*?"). But during our interview a few months later, after he got to know me a bit, he used several features of Orthodox speech, including some untranslated Hebrew and Yiddish words (as well as some translated ones and some English words where Hebrew would have been appropriate), and even the Orthodox "by."

I had a similar experience when I was interviewing Mrs. Rifkin, an FFB woman who did not know me well. Near the beginning of her interview, she said "studying" (rather than "learning") and "classes" (rather than "*shiurim*"). But as soon as I asked a question using the word "shiurim," she answered with "shiurim" and began using more Hebrew words. Sometimes the test of my language ability was made explicit, as with the FFB woman who said a Hebrew word and asked if I knew what it meant. When I said I did, she said, "I'm just speaking like I normally would because it seems like you know a lot." These examples show that many community members did speak to me the way they would to an outsider, at least at first.

Other times, I witnessed the opposite trend; people who knew I was focusing on language offered a "performance" of Orthodox language for my benefit.[22] A young BT once greeted me with "*Sholom aleichem*" (peace to you, a traditional Hebrew/Yiddish greeting), rendered in the scratchy voice of an old man. Another wrote in an e-mail to me, near the end of my pregnancy: "Are you ready for a whole new lifestyle? Too bad, you've got 3 weeks to get ready! B'H (I had to throw that in there for you) the birth will be easy, and so will childrearing the next . . . well the rest of your life." "B'H" is short for *b'ezras Hashem* (with God's help), a phrase appended to the statement of a future event. If he had written a similar e-mail to a nonlinguist Orthodox Jew, he may or may not have included "B'H." But he certainly would not have included the parenthetical comment.

Another trend I noticed is that some people changed their speech style as soon as I turned on the tape recorder. One BT used many Hebrew and Yiddish words when talking to me informally or to her friends when I was present. Even in our first phone conversation, before she knew whether I was Orthodox, she used words like *shtark* (intense), *matsliach* (successful), and *kedáy* (worthwhile). But during the interview she used very few loanwords. She could have said *tznius*, *frum*, and *loshon hora*, but she chose instead to say "modesty," "Orthodox," and "gossip." She translated *shiurim* as "classes" and *gashmius* as "materialism," and one time she even corrected herself mid-word: "*ga*- materialism." After the interview, I asked her about this, and she said she was not consciously purging her speech of Hebrew and Yiddish influences. Together we decided that she was using a more formal interview style rather than an outsider style.

Another longtime BT changed her speech drastically when the tape recorder was on. Before and after the interview, she used many Hebrew and Yiddish words and other Orthodox linguistic features. During the interview she used very few Orthodox features and several English words that she normally says in Hebrew or Yiddish. Once she cut herself off from saying "*shul*" and said "synagogue" instead. I later asked her about that, and she said that it was probably because she knows my project is in English. I realized from interactions like these that even a researcher who grew up in the community would still likely encounter the observer's paradox. I mitigated its effects by basing my linguistic analysis not just on interviews but also on everyday interactions and on recorded lectures available in the public domain.

Gender Issues

In ethnographic work on Orthodox Jews, it is almost inevitable that researchers will spend more time with community members of their own gender. Some researchers make this issue explicit and state that they are presenting only the women's side of the story.[23] But some male researchers purport to paint a portrait of an entire Orthodox community even though they had very little access to women's lives. The title of William Helmreich's informative and insightful book, for example, would be more accurate as *The World of the Yeshiva: An Intimate Portrait of Orthodox Men* (rather than *of Orthodox Jewry*).[24] Similarly, Heilman makes several statements about how he assumes women feel (e.g., about not participating in the rebbe's tish) without offering evidence that he observed their reactions or interviewed them extensively.[25] Some researchers give both sides, such as Janet Aviad, who bases her research mostly on surveys and interviews, and Ellen Koskoff, who researches music among Lubavitcher men and women.[26]

In my ethnographic observations and interviews, I believe I achieved a relative gender balance. As table 2.1 above shows, I interviewed fifty-nine women and forty-one men. At Ner Tamid, I spent more time with men, because more men attended classes and events. In Milldale, I spent more time with women, because the norm there is for men to attend synagogue or study sessions while women stay at home with the children. Overall, I spent a good deal of time with both male and female BTs. Among FFBs, I did get to know more women, but I was pleasantly surprised that a few FFB men allowed me to spend time with them. The recorded speech I gathered is skewed toward men, because I recorded many study sessions and classes in which men were the main speakers.

Of course, there were barriers to my observing men's lives, especially the physical barrier called the *mechitzah*, which separates the men from the women in the synagogue and at communal celebrations. I was never able to witness the Torah reading up close, and I never experienced the communion Heilman describes of dancing in an all-men's circle.[27] There was also the figurative mechitzah that prevented me from observing at men's yeshivas. While I observed at a few BT women's seminaries, I was unable to gain access to a comparable yeshiva for men, except to interview people in the office wing. I did visit two men's yeshivas briefly, but when I peered into the large, noisy study halls from the outside, all I could observe was a sea of black and white—both their clothing and the pages of the rabbinic texts. I am sure that these literal and figurative mechitzahs obscured interesting interactions that would have been relevant to my analysis of BT men's acquisition of Orthodox styles.

The ideal scenario for ethnographic research on Orthodox Jews would be for a co-ed team to fan out into the community with common research goals and meet regularly to share findings and construct a joint analysis. While this was not possible in the present study, I did include both men and women in the research in a significant way, unlike most previous studies of Orthodox Jews. This was possible because the Ner Tamid and Milldale communities are not nearly as insular and strictly divided by gender as some of the other Orthodox groups studied, partly due to their emphasis on outreach toward prospective BTs.

Mixed Reactions

In general, reaction to my research was positive. People thought it was an important topic of inquiry, and they were eager to learn what I found. Most of those who attended classes at Ner Tamid and Shomrei Emunah were willing to be recorded during class, and most of those I asked were happy to be interviewed. On the other hand, a few community members were hesitant to be part of the study.

One woman told me right before our interview that she feels uncomfortable whenever I am around, because she thinks of me as spy-like. I offered to cancel the interview and not include her in the study. But she said she wanted to help me, so she signed the consent form and we did an abbreviated interview. Another woman asked to withdraw from the study after a few months, saying she felt weird being a research subject and would rather just be my friend. A few months later, she agreed to be part of the study again.

A third woman signed a consent form the first day I met her and subsequently allowed me to interview her and record her informal interactions on several occasions. Then one day she told me she no longer wanted to be part of the study. She explained that she had talked to an important rabbi in Lakewood, who asked her where I, the researcher, am in my observance. When she told him that I am "in the middle of [my] journey" (that is, not Orthodox yet), the rabbi *paskened* (made a religious ruling) that she should ask not to be interviewed anymore. Sadly, I agreed. The next day, this woman asked me for a ride to the home of a seamstress, whom she had hired to alter her wedding dress. I said, "I don't know if that would be a good idea, because you don't want to be part of my study any more, and I would be observing you." She replied, "It doesn't have anything to do with Judaism. The dress woman isn't even Jewish." Satisfied that she knew my research was not limited to interviews, I agreed to give her a ride. I was pleased to have the opportunity to observe her interacting with non-Jews.

Because some people were uncomfortable with the tape recorder, I chose not to pursue a methodology involving frequent recording of everyday speech (which I had originally planned). One FFB woman allayed her young son and daughter's discomfort with the tape recorder by quoting *Pirkei Avos* (Sayings of the Fathers), a central rabbinic text: "You know what it says in *Pirkei Avos*? It says *ozen shoma'as*, there's always an ear listening. 'Cause Hashem's always listening. You don't have to worry about a microphone, 'cause after 120 years [the length of a full life, based on Moses' lifespan], when a person goes up to *shomayim* [heaven], they hear everything they said their whole lifetime. So you always have to be careful what you say, because you're always being recorded, right?" This approval was suitable for the children, who proceeded to shout glee-fully into the microphone. If only there were a rabbinic injunction to speak "naturally" in the presence of a tape recorder.

Defining Categories

Ethnographic methods tend to find that local social categories can be fluid and even problematic: reality is rarely as orderly as researchers (or their readers) might want it to be. Although "ba'al teshuva" and "BT" are commonly used in Orthodox communities, several people expressed concerns about these terms. Even those who have been Orthodox all their lives are expected to "do teshuva" regularly, repenting for any sins and intensifying their level of observance. One woman who has always been Orthodox was complaining about the ambiguity of the term, and I asked her, "Do you consider yourself a ba'al teshuva?" She responded, "All of us are!"

Even people who dislike the term ba'al teshuva still recognize that some people grew up Orthodox and others did not. But the boundary between these categories is not as solid as I expected. How was I to categorize the woman who grew up Orthodox, shed her observance in high school, and reclaimed it several years later? Although she is a ba'al teshuva according to the original meaning of the word, I categorized her as FFB for this study, because—like other FFBs—she was surrounded by Orthodox language and culture as a child. And the woman who grew up in a non-Orthodox home but attended a Modern Orthodox middle school and high school? I considered her a BT, since she was not exposed to Orthodoxy from infancy and she made a conscious decision to take on strict Orthodox observance. What about the community members who grew up Mod-ern Orthodox and chose to affiliate as non-Modern or Black Hat as adults? I considered them FFBs.

In addition to the issue of ambiguous labels, some people prefer not to box themselves in to a specific category, even if their peers are quick to classify them. This was particularly evident when I asked people to check categories on the questionnaire accompanying the matched guise test, including BT and

FFB. One man who is considered a BT wrote, "Have been observant all my life—but shomer shabbas since age 23. . . . Family always kosher, always went to shul, but not shomer shabbas—right-wing conservative." Despite his aversion to the label BT, I categorized him as such, since he did not grow up in an Orthodox community.

In spite of these issues, my methodologies enabled me to gather the data necessary to answer my research questions. Now I turn to the results, starting with the culture that newcomers encounter when they begin to spend time in the frum world.

3

"He Has *Tzitzis* Hanging Out of His Ponytail"

Orthodox Cultural Practices and How BTs Adapt Them

Erev Shabbos (Sabbath Eve)

One late Friday afternoon, I arrived at the Greenbaums' home on Parker Street, near the middle of a block that had become very familiar to me. During my fieldwork, I spent several Shabboses and holidays with various families on this block, where twenty-five of the twenty-eight families are Orthodox Jews. Since traditionally observant Jews do not drive on Shabbos, they either live within walking distance of a synagogue or regularly spend Shabbos with people who do. This block was about a fifteen-minute walk from Shomrei Emunah, the largest shul in Milldale.

Wearing a long skirt, long sleeves, high collar, and hat, I opened my bag and took out my thank-you gift, a bottle of kosher wine. Mrs. Greenbaum showed me to the basement, where I would be sleeping, and suggested that I dim the lights so that the room would be illuminated enough for walking around but still dark enough for me to sleep. The laws of Shabbos do not permit turning lights on or off. The six Greenbaum daughters who were still living at home—ranging in age from five to twenty—showered and dressed for Shabbos, and Mrs. Greenbaum and I lit the candles. Mrs. Greenbaum changed into her tailored skirt suit and replaced her cloth head covering with a medium-length sheitel.

We then took out some folding chairs and sat on the front lawn to wait for Rabbi Greenbaum to return from shul. "Good Shabbos," we greeted other women walking by, some with baby strollers, as the sky began to darken. Pushing strollers and carrying objects outside the home are normally prohibited on Shabbos, but, like other Orthodox communities, Milldale has an *eruv*, a demarcation made of preexisting structures and wire that makes such activities halachically acceptable by symbolically enclosing the neighborhood.

Two girls in skirts and ponytails, around seven years old, came over from three houses down the road, looking for their friend Chavi Greenbaum. While one girl went into the house to find Chavi, Mrs. Greenbaum asked the other how her mother was doing. She was on bed rest, due to give birth in three weeks, and members of the community were taking shifts watching her children and bringing meals. When Chavi and her friend came out, they saw another friend across the street, who, although also in second grade, was the niece of one of the other girls. Mrs. Greenbaum and I walked them across and chatted with two other neighborhood moms who were wearing long skirts and sheitels and trying to keep track of five young children.

Rabbi Greenbaum, wearing a black suit, black hat, and full gray beard, returned from shul with two other guests, a middle-aged man in a black hat and a young man in a small knit kipah. "Good Shabbos," they greeted me, without handshakes, as physical contact is forbidden between men and women, except between a husband and wife. We went inside the Greenbaum home and sat down at the long table, covered with a white tablecloth and plastic covering and set with china and silverware from a few different sets. The pre-dinner rituals included the parents blessing each of their children by laying their hands on their heads and muttering Hebrew words, as well as Rabbi Greenbaum singing the *kiddush*, the Shabbos blessing over wine in Hebrew, and all family members and guests sipping from tiny silver wine cups. One by one, each of us went to the kitchen sink for the ritual washing of hands, pouring water three times over each hand and saying a blessing. We then returned to the table, where Rabbi Greenbaum said a blessing over the two home-baked challahs, and the meal began.

The first course was a loaf of sweet homemade gefilte fish. Then came the chicken soup. Then the main course: chicken and brisket with side dishes of spinach kugel (like quiche without the cheese and crust), potato kugel, mushroom farfel (egg noodle bits), boiled carrots, and a coleslaw-like salad. Rabbi Greenbaum and the two male guests sang a few Hebrew songs while the women cleared the dishes and brought out dessert. We ate little squares of chocolate cake and vanilla ice cream that was labeled "*pareve*," meaning that it does not include dairy products. (The laws of kashrus dictate that meat and milk products cannot be eaten at the same meal.) Reading along in little booklets, we all *bentshed*—said the Grace after Meals—men in a chant, women in a whisper.

I thanked my hosts for dinner and walked half a mile to the Hollanders' home to join their Shabbos celebration, still in progress. On the way there, I enjoyed looking at the other semi-detached houses on Parker and nearby streets. Many are identical in layout and offer a view of the living room and dining room through their large front windows. I could tell which of the homes belonged to Orthodox families when I saw men in black suits, women in skirts, a large family table, a living room lined with bookshelves of *seforim* (Hebrew/Aramaic holy books), and several children.

As I approached the Hollander home, I could hear singing through the open door. At least thirty people were sitting around or near the large table. The men and boys were singing Hebrew songs loudly, in beautiful harmonies, and banging on the table. The women were mouthing the words to the songs, clapping, or helping to serve little cakes and *cholent*. Cholent (a Yiddish word derived from French "hot" and pronounced "tshuh-lint") is a Shabbos stew typically made with meat, beans, barley, onions, potatoes, and carrots. As with all cooked food consumed on Shabbos, cholent is prepared before sundown on Friday, but because it is generally served with lunch, cholent continues to simmer until midday on Saturday. Every Friday night, the Hollanders have a post-dinner party they call "midnight cholent," where they serve their uniquely spicy cholent along with a selection of beer and schnapps. Rabbi Hollander, a beloved teacher at Ner Tamid, often reminds students of his standing invitation to stop by Friday nights for cholent.

After two or three songs, Rabbi Hollander announced that it was time for another *dvar torah* (literally "word of Torah"). He asked a young man in a black velvet kipah if he wanted to give one. The man agreed and discussed a moral lesson from that week's *parsha*, the section of Torah chanted in shul on Shabbos morning, speaking in English but with many Hebrew and Yiddish words added. Next Rabbi Hollander selected a middle-aged man with a colorful knit kipah. This man talked about how observing Shabbos the past few months had been important to him.

I joined a few of the women in the kitchen and heard a middle-aged woman asking Mrs. Hollander which *hechshers* (symbols on food labels indicating that a product is kosher) she accepts. A younger woman was telling fourteen-year-old Freidala Hollander about the man she recently met through a matchmaker. I thanked my hosts and walked back to the Greenbaums'. I knew I had to get up early to go to shul the next morning.

This Friday evening was typical of my experiences in the Milldale community, and many of the events and images recounted here are typical of Orthodox Jews around the world. Of course, there is a great deal of variation within Orthodoxy, given differences in the practices of Modern Orthodox and Black Hat Jews, Sephardi, Mizrachi, and Ashkenazi Jews, communities big and small and in various places, and other factors. This chapter focuses on the practices I observed in Milldale, a medium-sized Orthodox community near the Black Hat end of the continuum, made up mostly of American-born Ashkenazi Jews.

As many scholars have described, becoming Orthodox entails taking on new beliefs and a complex system of laws that govern most aspects of life, such as which foods can be eaten together, when prayers are recited in the three daily services, which activities are prohibited on Shabbos and holidays, and when during a woman's menstrual cycle husband and wife are permitted to have physical contact.[1] But, as the description above highlights, being frum involves much more than faith and observance. In fact, when I asked one BT what she has changed about herself since becoming Orthodox, she replied enthusiastically, "Everything!" When prospective BTs spend time in an Orthodox community, they encounter distinctive practices in dress, food, language, and activities. Some of these practices have functional purposes, such as the use of plastic table coverings and the prominence of Hebrew and Aramaic holy books. Many are influenced by halacha, such as the laws surrounding modest dress and food restrictions. Other practices may have aesthetic explanations, such as the choices of art and music. But, to some extent, all the cultural practices discussed here serve to construct and reinforce Orthodox identity and community. By describing food, art, names, dating, and other practices, this chapter points to the interplay between halacha and *minhag*, law and custom.

Although some BTs adapt enthusiastically to the cultural standards of their new community, some resist selected changes, at least temporarily, and come up with hybrid cultural practices. As Janet Aviad writes, BTs "may be noticed by the mixture of traditional and modern they display in their dress, manners, style."[2] They distinguish themselves from the non-Orthodox Jews and non-Jews they grew up with, and, within their new communities, they indicate their BT identity (sometimes intentionally, sometimes not) by preserving elements of their previous selves.

Orthodox Practices

Dress

On a Saturday morning in Milldale, standing in the women's section of the shul, I noticed tailored suits of many colors with long skirts and high necklines. Even on this humid summer day, no elbows were showing. I peeked through the lace curtain of the mechitzah and saw a sea of black and white on the men's side—dark suits, white collar shirts, dark ties, black hats, and, among married men, body-length off-white tallises with black stripes (while non-Orthodox Jews begin to wear a prayer shawl at age thirteen, Orthodox Ashkenazi men wait until they are married). These sartorial norms are common not only in Milldale but in other Yeshivish-leaning Orthodox communities as well.

When it is not Shabbos, some men still wear dark suits, and others (especially BTs) are more casual, sporting collar shirts and dark pants. Very few are seen in public wearing jeans, T-shirts, or sweats. Young men who go to yeshiva generally wear white collar shirts and dark pants, even when home on vacation. Pre-yeshiva boys tend to wear plaid or striped collar shirts of various colors.

Starting at age three, all males wear tzitzis, a thin white garment worn under the shirt with four fringe tassels hanging down. Some men tuck the fringes into their pants, others let them show a bit by attaching them to their belt loops, and still others (including many BTs) let them hang down their thighs conspicuously.

On weekdays, women wear long skirts and blouses or dresses, always with long sleeves, sometimes pushed up to just below the elbows. Some women are careful to cover their collarbone; others leave the top few buttons open. At home, it is common to find women wearing robe-like house dresses. Girls tend to wear shirts or sweaters and skirts, sometimes made of denim. It is rare to see sandals (without socks or tights) or bare feet among Orthodox Jews in Milldale.

These sartorial practices stem both from the laws of *tznius* (traditional Jewish modesty) and from the desire to appear conservative—and distinctly Orthodox. In addition, certain details, such as not baring the foot or collarbone, distinguish Jews toward the Black Hat end of the Orthodox continuum.[3]

The laws and norms regarding dress are discussed widely in the community, and leaders make some effort to ensure that even visitors dress modestly. For my first meeting with a rabbi at Ner Tamid, on an unusually hot autumn day, I wore a long skirt and a short-sleeve shirt. After listening to me explain my research and giving his approval, the rabbi suggested that I wear long sleeves when I visit Milldale. From then on, I wore long sleeves on most of my visits to Milldale and other places where I expected to encounter Orthodox Jews, including Ner Tamid. Similarly, when Devora, then an Interested Prospective BT, was going to spend her first Shabbos in Milldale, an Orthodox friend suggested that she wear a skirt. Since then, she has always worn skirts when visiting the Orthodox community. Another example of the expectation that non-Orthodox visitors should dress modestly can be seen in the wedding invitation of two young BTs. Following the traditional text of the English side was an additional line: "Please dress according to Orthodox tradition."

During their early interactions with Orthodox Jews, prospective BTs often continue to dress as they normally do. At Ner Tamid events it is common to see men in T-shirts and women in pants. But people who spend time in Milldale often begin to "try on" Orthodox styles. And BTs who move to Milldale or a yeshiva/seminary community always seem to change their dress to conform to Orthodox norms, at least to some extent.

Esther's first experiences with Orthodoxy were in classes at an outreach center similar to Ner Tamid, and she says she often changed into a skirt before going there, just as I did during my year of fieldwork. But the first time she spent Shabbos with an Orthodox family, she decided she wanted to "dress frum" on a regular basis. Esther's transition was more sudden than most people's. Several women told me that they were at first reluctant to make a major change in their dress. Barbara, a woman in her sixties who became Orthodox during my year of fieldwork, wore pants to Ner Tamid classes for several months. When she spent her first Shabbos in Milldale, she wore modest skirt outfits. A few months later, she saw me at Ner Tamid wearing a skirt and said, "I should wear skirts too." By the end of the year, she was wearing skirts at Ner Tamid and, according to her report, everywhere else too.

For men, wearing and displaying tzitzis are an important part of becoming frum. When Andrew decided to become more observant, he started wearing tzitzis all the time, but with the fringes tucked in. One Shabbos, a few months into my fieldwork, I noticed that he had the fringes out but tucked into his pants pockets. One Shabbos two months later, he wore the fringes completely out. That night, after Shabbos, Andrew went home to change out of his suit, and when he returned to Ner Tamid in casual clothes for a concert, the tzitzis were not showing at all. At that point he wore his tzitzis out only on Shabbos. A few months later, Andrew went to study and live in a yeshiva community in the New York area, where he likely encountered explicit teachings about tzitzis. In response to my e-mail question, he reported that he now wore his tzitzis "always out (except when I'm lazy)! If the whole point of tzitis [*sic*] is to remind us of the mitzvas [commandments], what is the point of wearing them in." I noticed this type of progression among several BTs: a gradual implementation of cultural practices and then a sense that it could not be otherwise.

While following the laws about modest dress, some BTs attempt to maintain fashion sensibilities from their pre-BT days. Michelle says she can often spot BT women by their dress, which she considers "a little hipper." She continues, "A lot of the FFBs, they do their shopping in Brooklyn, in Monsey, in Lakewood. I do my shopping here [in Philadelphia] and hope that I can find something modest." This is not only for the sake of convenience but also because she finds that a lot of the clothes manufactured for Orthodox women are not made in the contemporary styles she prefers. This means that she makes more visits to the tailor to lengthen skirts or shorten slits, while the clothing sold in the Orthodox stores never needs to be modified to meet the standards of modesty.

Some BTs question the stringencies that Black Hat Jews have applied to the laws of dress. One newly Orthodox woman continues to sleep in pajama pants (rather than long nightgowns) and wear sandals without socks, and it bothers her that some community members have criticized those practices. She reports having asked one FFB woman, "Do you think 10,000 years ago they wore socks in the desert?" Although the response was "yes," this BT was not convinced and continued to wear sandals. Similarly, a longtime BT man in his sixties has not assumed the view that Orthodox Jews should always look distinguished and conservative in dress. Although he wears dark suits on Shabbos, he continues to sport sweats or jeans during the week.

Many FFBs recognize that BTs differentiate themselves in dress—sometimes consciously, sometimes not. Rabbi Nussbaum, an FFB who wears his tzitzis tucked in, says he can often tell which men are BTs by the way they wear their tzitzis with the four tassels conspicuously hanging out. "Somebody who was always frum [an FFB] will generally not wear the tzitzis on four corners, but they'll actually bring the two from one side together and put the two from the other side together. Also, they'll generally—they'll take the tzitzis and they'll put it under their belt. It will come from under their belt as opposed to on top of their belt." I cannot comment on this, as I did not think it was appropriate to stare at men's belts trying to make sense of the semiotics of tzitzis. However, Rabbi Nussbaum's statement highlights the intricacies that BTs need to learn if they want to dress like natives. It also points out that BTs are not expected to learn all the details; they are expected to have a slightly different style. While some BTs do what they can to disprove this expectation, many are happy to distinguish themselves from FFBs, especially when it involves more conspicuous display of halachic observance.

In short, BTs conform to many of the norms of Orthodox dress, especially those mandated by halacha, but also continue to distinguish themselves in some ways. In a Black Hat community, a woman wearing a fashionable skirt outfit with sandals or a man wearing a sweatshirt or a brown blazer is much more likely to be a BT.

Hair, Head Coverings

Among Orthodox men, head coverings indicate subtle differences in religious identity. One of the most recognizable symbols of Orthodoxy is a kipah (Hebrew, skullcap), otherwise known as a *yarmulke* or, in Hasidic circles, a *kopl* (both Yiddish). Small groups of non-Orthodox Jews also wear a kipah all the time, but most do so only when participating in Jewish rituals, especially in synagogue. In the Milldale Black Hat community, most men wear large black kipahs, often made of velvet. Most men also wear black hats on Shabbos, some also during the week when they leave the house. Modern Orthodox Jews tend to wear colorful knit kipahs.

Underneath their kipahs, Milldale Orthodox men's hair is usually short and neatly trimmed, yielding a conservative look. Most have beards—some short, some full. Those who do not have beards have noticeable sideburns, in accordance with Jewish law. Some parents choose not to cut their boys' hair until they turn three, when they have a ceremonial haircut called an *upsherin* (literally "shearing off"). From age three, boys usually have short *peyos* (sidelocks). Some keep their peyos until they get married, and others cut them when they go to yeshiva. A few adults in Milldale have peyos—usually a sign that they have Hasidic affiliations or leanings.

For women, hairstyles and head coverings are also important symbols. In her introduction to a collection of essays on the subject by Orthodox women, Lynne Schreiber states, "Hair covering has become, for many women, more an issue of who one wants to associate with than actual law."[4] Although halacha requires married women to cover their hair, how they do so varies. Modern Orthodox women may wear a hat, kerchief, or some other covering or leave their hair uncovered when not in synagogue. In Milldale, most women wear a sheitel (wig), usually shoulder-length, straight, curled under, with bangs. When it is not Shabbos, women sometimes wear a sheitel, but sometimes they tuck all of their hair into a flimsy hat or the less formal snood—a thick hair net. Girls and unmarried young women generally keep their long hair tied back in a pony- tail. Young girls usually have medium-length or long hair with bangs, perhaps approximating the style of their mothers' sheitels.

BTs in Milldale generally conform to the norms regarding hair and hair cov- ering. At the beginning of my fieldwork, Mark had recently taken on Orthodox observance. He wore a colorful knit kipah or a small black suede one, sometimes with a baseball cap on top of it. Several months later, he was wearing a large black velvet kipah, sometimes with a black hat over it. At the beginning of the year he was also beardless, and by the end he had a short, well-kept full beard. He started growing the beard during the period known as *Sfira*—also known as the *Omer*—between two spring holidays when shaving is prohibited for about a month, and, rather than shave it off at the end, he decided just to trim it. He pointed out to me that his current style is quite different from the long-haired hippie look he gave up a few years ago.

An Orthodox Jew with an unconventional hairstyle is almost always assumed to be a BT. Jacob told me of an experience he had when he was first becoming Orthodox and still had long hair. He and a male friend, who wore his long hair in a ponytail, were invited to spend Shabbos with the Schwartzes. At shul, a friend of Mr. Schwartz criticized him for hosting these two young men, "especially the one with the really long ponytail." Mr. Schwartz replied, "There's more *yiras shomayim* [fear of heaven] in his ponytail than [pointing to the man leading services] in his white socks." Similarly, when Jacob was studying at a BT yeshiva, the administration liked to introduce him to visitors and say, "He has tzitzis hanging out of his ponytail," which Jacob interpreted to mean that on the inside he is very religious, despite his unconventional appearance. Eventually Jacob adopted a much more conventional Black Hat look: short hair, full beard, and black velvet kipah.[5]

For female BTs, hair covering is also a topic of much discussion and delib- eration. Even BTs who are very committed to Orthodoxy and really want to fit in to the community sometimes feel uncomfortable about the sheitel. A few months before Devora was to be married, she told me that she was looking forward to covering her hair with a hat or a fall (a half-wig that is worn with a hat or kerchief). She was reluctant to wear a sheitel, "because I'm not going to stick one that looks like a mop on my head." She did eventually get a sheitel she likes, and she wears that for Shabbos and special occasions, using various hats and kerchiefs, sometimes with a fall, the rest of the time.

Some women are able to maintain elements of their pre-Orthodox style in their sheitels, although custom-made human-hair sheitels cost thousands of dollars. One BT woman wears her sheitel curly and styled, and another keeps hers long with no bangs, usually tied back with a barrette. These sheitels stand out in contrast to the recognizable Haredi style of most FFB wigs, and, as a few BTs report, they are sometimes mistaken for real hair.

While most Milldale women wear their sheitels on Shabbos and sometimes other head coverings during the week, Julia does the opposite. When she got married, about a year after she became Orthodox, she bought a stylish blond sheitel, similar to her own hair. She wears this for special events, such as when she and her husband were honored at a Ner Tamid event. She also wears the sheitel every weekday to her non-Jewish workplace, where most of her colleagues assume it is her own hair. But on Shabbos she puts her hair up and covers it with a hat. She feels strange about wearing the sheitel and would prefer to wear it only on rare occasions, but she feels that, at her workplace, her natural-looking wig is more appropriate than a hat or other hair coverings.

BTs also distinguish themselves through details of their hats and kipahs. One day I noticed that Paula, an artistic grandmother who became Orthodox about ten years ago, had a small embroidered butterfly on the side of her beret, which was otherwise indistinguishable from the hats that many other Milldale women wear. That same day, her husband wore the same type of black velvet kipah that other men wear, but his had a thin band of blue trim around the edge. Although it is possible that some FFBs also distinguish themselves like this with details of their appearance, I have never noticed it or heard about it.

Whether or not BTs intentionally distinguish themselves, head wear is often a giveaway of religious background. A few FFB interviewees mentioned that BTs—both men and women—can sometimes be spotted "a mile away" by the way they wear their hat: too far forward, too far back, too much hair showing, not enough hair showing, or just awkward. Rabbi Nussbaum, claiming he can tell if a man is a BT, said: "Another giveaway will be wearing a black hat, I'll just say, inappropriately, either the way they're wearing it, or they'll wear it but without a jacket: so they're wearing sneakers, a T-shirt and a black hat. That's a giveaway. Small things like that." When BTs do not want to stand out, "small things" like hairstyles and hair coverings can make a big difference.

Food

At the Ner Tamid outreach center there is a framed poster: a large black-and-white photograph of a bagel with lox and cream cheese. The caption reads, "Is this the culmination of 3500 years of Jewish heritage?" Even though, as this poster implies, many Orthodox Jews have disdain for cultural Judaism devoid of any religious content, food also serves as an important marker of Orthodox Jewish identity.

Meals in Ashkenazi Orthodox homes like those in Milldale, especially on Shabbos, often include a combination of Eastern European classics and American standards, similar to the dinner I had at the Greenbaums' home. Of course, Orthodox Jews observe the laws of kashrus, prohibiting certain animals and requiring the separation of dairy and meat products and the utensils that touch them. In addition, special ritual foods are served on holidays, including wine for every festive meal, braided challah on Shabbos and holidays, apples and honey for *Rosh Hashana*, cheesecake and other dairy foods for *Shavuos*, and *matzah* (unleavened bread) and *charoses* (a mortar-like mix of fruit and nuts) for *Pesach*.

These holiday foods are also common among non-Orthodox Jews, and Eastern European dishes like gefilte fish and kugel are also served in non-Orthodox homes and institutions. In addition, Eastern European foods have made their way to other Jewish communities around the world. Anthropologist Shari Jacobson points out that the Syrian-origin BT women she observed in Buenos Aires made frequent use of English-language cookbooks from North America as they replaced their Middle Eastern cuisine with European foods. She analyzes this transition as a specifically Argentine reverence for Europe.[6] In addition, I argue that it represents the hegemony of Eastern Ashkenazi culture as the most respected form of Orthodoxy, spread by a number of Hasidic and Yeshivish institutions. The Syrian-origin BTs likely learn to revere Ashkenazi cultural practices through their classroom- and home-based interactions with Ashkenazi Orthodox Jews.

In Milldale, it is rare to find FFBs who are vegetarians or who experiment with world cuisine (at least this was the case in 2001–2002, when I did my research). This is a cultural domain in which BTs tend to distinguish themselves, as they often come into the community with more eclectic culinary sensibilities. A few FFBs and BTs told me they can tell when they are in a BT home by the food they are served. According to FFB Moyshe, if sushi, Indian spices, or fake shellfish are involved, or if dinner includes no meat, it is clearly a BT home. Another FFB stresses that it is a mitzvah (commandment) to eat meat and says he is surprised that some BTs do not give up their vegetarianism when they take on Orthodoxy. An otherwise worldly FFB woman said she is tipped off that people are BT when they discuss certain foods. "They talk about burritos and tacos. Do I know about this? Burritos and tacos? No, I know about gefilte fish."

In 2002, the three kosher restaurants in Milldale were a *milchik* (dairy) pizza place that also has Israeli and Eastern European food, a grill serving *fleishik* (meat) American standards, and a fleishik Chinese restaurant. Even then, French, Thai, Indian, and other world cuisine was gaining traction in Manhattan, Los Angeles, and other large Orthodox communities with many upper-middle-class members. These restaurants tend to serve a largely Modern Orthodox crowd, but they also cater to Black Hat BTs, who are accustomed to a diverse gourmet menu and do not want to give it up after becoming Orthodox. In the past decade, the taste for sushi seems to have spread around the Orthodox world, including Milldale, perhaps influenced by BTs. For example, a kosher sushi restaurant in Lakewood, New Jersey, advertises: "SAY MAZAL TOV—WITH SUSHI! There's nothing like a customized sushi platter to add that extra pizzazz at your next simcha [joyous occasion]!" Notwithstanding such changes in kosher cuisine, at a Friday night dinner in an Orthodox home in Milldale and elsewhere, it is still common to find chicken soup, kugels, and other Ashkenazi standards.

One strategy BTs use in adapting Orthodox cooking is to add their own worldly touches to traditional dishes. At one Shabbos lunch, the Kramers served gefilte fish with a unique flavor. A BT guest asked what made it so good, and Mrs. Kramer responded, "Curry and turmeric," words that I never heard in an FFB home. Another BT woman adds a "secret ingredient" to her challah (tasted like nutmeg to me). Of course, many BTs do stick to the meat and potatoes (Ashkenazi style) and even take informal cooking lessons with longtime community members. That is the best way to learn to make a kugel that is both fluffy and large enough to serve eighteen people for a Friday night dinner.

A few BTs expressed negative views about what they see as oily, heavy meals that lack variety and take too long to make. Orthodox outreach professionals know that food can be a sticking point. One event geared toward non-Orthodox Jews (prospective BTs) advertised "delectable international cuisine," a phrase that likely would not have drawn too many FFBs in 2002. The culinary influence of BTs—and Modern Orthodox Jews—is spreading throughout frum communities, adding healthy, diverse options to menus in strictly kosher restaurants and homes around the country.

Home Decoration

When a newcomer first enters an Orthodox home in Milldale, she likely notices two focal points of the decor: a large dining room table and prominently displayed bookshelves filled with religious books. These items are important because large festive meals and text study are two centerpieces of Orthodox life.

Since Orthodox Jews often have several children (eight or ten is not uncommon, and a few families in Milldale have twelve or thirteen), family members alone can fill up a table and a half. In addition, families of all sizes tend to have guests most Shabboses and holidays. Some, especially outreach professionals, host dozens of visitors on a regular basis. Others host smaller meals. On any given Friday night, Shira and Levi Light and their three young children might invite a local couple for dinner, in addition to the single woman from downtown spending the night in the guest room. Then they might host a different couple and their two children for lunch the next day. It is no wonder that large tables are the norm. Once I saw an advertisement on the synagogue bulletin board: "Free—large dining room table—60 x 40 plus 2 extension leaves." The next week, the flyer was gone.

Tables in Orthodox homes also have another distinctive feature: a tablecloth, generally white, covered by a plastic protective covering. The coverings are left on not just in families with young children and not just during meals but all the time, even on a Tuesday afternoon when the table is covered with piles of mail. Of the dozens of dining room tables I saw in Milldale, I only noticed one without a plastic covering, at the home of an FFB family with grown children. One BT in another city told me that his rabbi made a joke about the how people in their community "look too much into potential *shidduchim* (matches), even checking if their parents use plastic on their Shabbos tablecloths." While plastic coverings serve a functional purpose and are certainly not unique to Orthodox homes, they seem to have become a marker of Orthodox identity.

Orthodox Jews own dozens or hundreds of seforim, books of biblical and rabbinic literature written in Hebrew and Aramaic. Most families choose to display these books prominently in the living room or dining room, rather than in the basement or other less public rooms. For example, one FFB family has a few bookshelves visible from the dining room table, which are filled with seforim plus a few children's books. In the study (which doubles as a guest room), there are many more seforim, but there are also secular books, including a full set of *Encyclopaedia Britannica* and the Advanced Placement English literature review book (several of the children are avid readers). I only noticed a handful of Jewish books written in English.

I mentioned to one BT woman, who has three shelves of seforim in her small living room, that I have often noticed centrally located bookshelves in Orthodox homes, and she said, "Isn't that halacha—to display them prominently?" According to a local rabbi, it is not halacha but merely a widespread custom. I believe that it serves a symbolic purpose: allowing Orthodox Jews to display their attachment to Jewish texts. But this BT's understanding points to the interplay—and sometimes blurry boundary—between halacha (law) and minhag (custom), religion and culture.

Another distinctive feature of Orthodox homes is the collections of Jewish-themed art and Jewish ritual objects. Non-Orthodox Jewish homes often have a similarly large assortment of Judaica, but they are also likely to display secular art, including abstract paintings and trinkets from around the world. Aside from a few pictures of flowers, I rarely saw secular art in Milldale or other Orthodox communities. Secular art is not prohibited; its scarcity in the community merely points to the importance of Jewish symbols.

Common types of paintings and prints in Milldale include a man with a beard and black hat praying at the *Kosel* (the Western Wall in Jerusalem), a depiction of a biblical scene in micrography (tiny words used to create an image), and a lit Chanukah *menorah* (candelabrum). Liturgical selections are sometimes made into art: I saw several decorated versions of "Birkas Habayis" (a blessing for the house), "Eishes Chayil" (a hymn of praise sung to women on Friday night), and quotes from *Pirkei Avos*. I also saw many photos of famous rabbis—of both local and international fame—and a few black-and-white photos of great-grandparents from the "old country" (Eastern Europe).[7]

When Jews become Orthodox, they often take on many of these home decoration practices. BT homes usually include large tables with plastic covers, prominently displayed bookshelves, and Jewish-themed art. But, as we might expect, there are some differences. For practical reasons, BTs usually have different books than FFBs. They rely heavily on English books to learn about Orthodox observance and *hashkafa* (worldview), and they often use prayer books with English translations and explanations.[8] Some also keep secular books from their pre-Orthodox days, but they often store them in less conspicuous parts of the house.

One BT family chooses to keep most of their books in the study rather than in the living room. The study is lined with bookshelves, most of which contain seforim. Prominently displayed books include several volumes of an Aramaic-English edition of the Talmud, an entire set of an all-Aramaic Talmud, *Mikraos Gedolos* (Bible with several rabbinic commentaries), the *Mishneh Torah* (Maimonides' twelfth-century compendium of Jewish observance), a few dictionaries, and a number of English Orthodox books by Aryeh Kaplan, Lawrence Kelemen, and other authors popular among BTs. But a closer look reveals that there are a number of secular books stored on the bottom shelves, partially concealed by grated doors. Through the grates I saw *Influence: the Psychology of Persuasion*, *The Closing of the American Mind*, and *Men Are from Mars, Women Are from Venus*. Rather than discard these books or store them in a more private area, this BT family chose to keep them in the same room as their seforim—only in a less prominent location.

BTs in Milldale generally do have Jewish-themed art and photographs of prominent rabbis, but, as with books, they also sometimes keep art they collected before they became Orthodox. In some BT homes, I noticed that the walls of the main level were decorated with Jewish-themed art but the basement featured secular paintings, often modern or abstract. As we might expect, BTs avoid displaying art that could be considered offensive. One BT mentioned that he still has from his youth a Caribbean-themed painting of a woman in a bikini. He plans to sell it on eBay eventually, but for now he keeps this souvenir of his pre-frum days hidden in the basement.

Samantha has a poster that she bought in Berlin, where she visited just after the fall of the Berlin Wall, before she became Orthodox. An FFB once told her that it is not appropriate to have art from Germany, because of the Holocaust. But she considers this poster such an important part of her past—and likes the fact that she got it in Germany at a historic moment—that she keeps it on her hallway wall. Another BT displays a symbol of his secular past, but in a distinctly BT way: one of the Beatles wearing a black hat.[9]

Cecile enjoys modern art and wishes that she could find more Jewish-themed paintings she likes. For now, she prominently displays one modern secular piece and a few Jewish pieces. Next time she goes to Israel, she plans to look for some Jewish art that is more in line with her aesthetic sensibilities. BTs are constantly making decisions about what elements of Orthodoxy to incorporate into their lives and what elements of their pre-Orthodox past to display publicly. Art is just one resource they can use to strive for a sense of individual equilibrium.

Another element that distinguishes BTs from FFBs is pets. I saw only four pets—three dogs and one cat—during my study, and they were all in BT homes. Moyshe, a young FFB, said that he assumes a family is BT when he sees they have a pet. Owning dogs is considered particularly *goyish* (non-Jewish-seeming), and they arouse fear among many Orthodox Jews, a sense that may stem back to Eastern Europe. There are some restrictions about caring for animals on Shabbos, but it is possible to keep a pet within the confines of halacha. Therefore, some BTs have pets even if they recognize that it is not a common Orthodox practice. Ironically, some even use their pets to indicate their own Jewish/Orthodox identity—by giving them Hebrew or Yiddish names.

Names

Even more important for the performance of Orthodox identity are the names that people choose for their children—and for themselves. Most Orthodox names come from Hebrew; a common source is biblical characters, especially patriarchs and matriarchs. But rather than use the English translations as most non-Orthodox and some Modern Orthodox Jews do—Abraham, Isaac, Jacob, Sarah (rhymes with Farrah), Rebecca, Rachel, and Leah (rhymes with Mia)—Black Hat Jews use Ashkenazi Hebrew versions: Avrum, Yitzchak, Yakov, Sara (using the vowel in "bus"), Rivka, Rochel (using the "ch" sound), and Layah (rhymes with pray-uh).

Not all biblical names are popular in Orthodox communities; names of non-Jewish characters tend not to be. Even though Adam, Seth, and Ruth are

common names among non-Orthodox Jews, they are rarely heard in the Orthodox communities I have visited. Adam and Seth existed before Abraham became
the first Jew, and Ruth was a Moabite woman who married into a Jewish family
and converted to Judaism. An exception is the name Chava (Eve), which is common among Orthodox Jews.

In addition to biblical characters, some boys' and girls' names are taken
from Hebrew words relating to nature and positive qualities: Tzvi (deer), Dov
(bear), Menachem (one who comforts), Tzipora (bird), Shoshana (rose), Ahuva
(beloved), and Chaya (living being). Some of these Hebrew names are translations of Yiddish names, like Hersh (deer), Feyge (bird), and Reyzel (rose). Some
Orthodox Jews, especially those toward the Black Hat end of the continuum, still
use non-Hebrew Yiddish names, such as Sheindy, Goldy, Hindy, and Mendy. In
Milldale, I met children with Hebrew names like Yaffa and children with Yiddish
names like Sheindy.

Ashkenazi Jews tend to name children after deceased relatives. Non-
Orthodox Ashkenazim often give their children different but related English
and Hebrew names, such as naming their baby Max in English and Moshe in
Hebrew after his great-grandfather Morris/Moyshe, Hannah/Chana after her
grandmother Anna/Chana, or Sophia/Sarit after her great-grandmother Sara.
But Orthodox Jews, especially those toward the Black Hat end of the continuum,
usually use just a Hebrew or Yiddish name, generally in memory of a relative
with that same name. Of course there are exceptions. One FFB woman wanted
to name her daughter after her great-grandmother Sheyndel (meaning pretty),
but she was uncomfortable using such a Yiddish-sounding name. After getting
a rabbi's approval, she named her daughter Yaffa, which is the Hebrew equivalent.[10] But even this woman gave her daughter just a Hebrew name to be used
both in secular and religious settings.

Orthodox Jews tend to say names with the Jewish English diminutive/hypo-
coristic (nickname) suffix -y/-i, rather than the Yiddish correlates -el(e) and -ke,
although these are also still used. Examples include Rivky for Rivka/Rivkele,
Rochy for Rochel/Rochele, Avrumy for Avrohom/Avremele, Yitzy for Yitzchak/
Itzikl, and Chamy (rhymes with tummy) for Nechama/Nechamke. Hypocoristics
like these are used for children and some adults, and they are used not just
among relatives or close friends but even among strangers. I once went to an
FFB yeshiva to deliver a package and asked a few of the teenage boys if they knew
Zalman Felder. They said they did not, but one boy asked another, "Do you know
Zalmy Felder?" Even though he did not know him, he still used the hypocoristic
form of his name.

Another common Orthodox naming practice is to use double names.
Whereas many Americans have a middle name they rarely use, Orthodox Jews
are often referred to as Sara Layah, Chaya Miriam, or Shmuel Yisroel. I once met

a longtime BT named Yakov Tzvi and asked him what his first name was. Always a comedian, he replied by mimicking a famous Lenny Bruce routine: "You need two names to be frum. Yakov, Dov, Tzvi: not frum. Yakov Tzvi: frum."

As with dress and food, Orthodox Jews exhibit great variation in naming practices: Jews toward the Black Hat end of the continuum exhibit more Yiddish influences, and Modern Orthodox names are often similar to non-Orthodox Jewish names. Even within a given Black Hat community we see diversity. A prominent rabbi advises parents to give their children only one name, such as "Chaya" rather than "Chaya Sara." One FFB in Milldale feels it is important for Jews to have secular English names in addition to their Hebrew ones, so he gave each of his five children both. Some Orthodox Jews are partial to Yiddish names like Kreyndl and Frumky, and others consider them old-fashioned.

Newcomers to the Orthodox community face the decision of whether to continue going by their given name or to introduce themselves with a more Orthodox-sounding name. Many do take on a Hebrew name, either the one that was given to them at birth or one they chose during the BT process.[11] Charity, a woman who grew up Catholic, changed her name to Chaya when she converted to Judaism. Donna started going by her Hebrew name, Devora, when she went to Israel to spend a few months in a seminary. When she returned to the United States, her community quickly got used to her new name. About a year after becoming Orthodox, Will started asking people to refer to him by his Hebrew name, Yisrael. Within weeks, several of his BT friends were accustomed enough to calling him Yisrael that they no longer marked it as a new name. When I saw him a few months later, I accidentally addressed him as Will. He said, "Didn't I tell you I changed my name to Yisrael?"

Some BTs take on not only a Hebrew first name, but also a Hebrew middle name, sometimes the one given to them at birth. As we might expect based on his Lenny Bruce routine, Yakov Tzvi, formerly known as Jacob, did this. Some who were given only one Hebrew name at birth (or none) invent a second one, as Rebecca did. She liked the name Bracha (blessing), so she appended it to her name. When a new student at Ner Tamid introduced herself as Rebecca in the presence of Rebecca Bracha and Max, Max said "Another Rebecca," nodding toward Rebecca Bracha. She corrected him: "I'm Rebecca *Bracha*." Eventually, she Hebraicized the pronunciation, in line with the norms of the community, and went by "Rivka Bracha."

Name changes are, of course, a classic way of fitting into a new community. We see this with immigrants and their children and with individuals who want to identify more or less with an ethnic group. Even so, not all BTs feel comfortable changing their names. Andrew chooses to go by his English name rather than his Hebrew name, Aryeh. Francine tried going by her Yiddish name,

Fraidel, for a while, but she felt she was giving up too much of herself and eventually switched back to Francine.

BTs are faced with the name decision not only because Orthodox Jews tend to have Hebrew names, but because FFBs ask new BTs what their Hebrew names are and often refer to them that way. Long before Will had decided to go by Yisrael, some of the rabbis referred to him with this name, honoring him once when he gave a dvar torah by calling him "*Reb* Yisrael" (*Reb* is Yiddish for "mister" but in this community is used mostly to address rabbis). Similarly, although Marissa and Mark usually introduce themselves with their English names, many community members address them and refer to them with their Hebrew names, Menucha and Simcha. For example, when entering Mark's phone number into his cell phone, Rabbi Hollander used Simcha rather than Mark. Even I was not immune to name judaization—although I always introduced myself with the English name Sarah (rhymes with Farrah), several FFBs pronounced my name the Ashkenazi Hebrew way, Suh-ruh or Sore-uh.

The pressure for new BTs to use Hebrew names comes not only from FFBs but also from their fellow BTs. Rivka Bracha always referred to Marissa as "Menucha," even though she often heard her introduce herself to others as Marissa. And when Mark/Simcha was entering Mitch/Mordechai's phone number into his cell phone while chatting with a few BTs, he asked, "How do you spell Mordechai?" An onlooker started to spell it, but Mitch said, "My English name is Mitchell, if that makes it easier." Another BT said with a smile, "Use Mordechai."

BTs also face pressure from another side: their pre-Orthodox communities. Parents often refuse to call their BT children by their Hebrew names. And non-Orthodox friends sometimes feel uncomfortable using new names for their longtime friends. Joan's childhood friend made fun of her for choosing the name Yocheved Chaya, which is too long and guttural for his taste. Even so, she continues to use her new Orthodox name, even in his presence. To deal with conflicting pressures like this, some BTs choose to use different names for different audiences. Yossi showed me his business card, and it said, "Joe the Handyman." I asked, "Why not Yossi?" "Because I give my card to all kinds of people," he said. Similarly, Yisrael still goes by Will at work, because he thinks it would be "too hard" to change there. When Boruch signed his name as "Barry" on the consent form for my study, I was surprised, as I had never heard anyone refer to him that way. He said that he grew up as Barry and still uses it in his law practice.

When deciding what to name their children, BTs in Milldale almost always choose Hebrew names with Ashkenazi Hebrew pronunciations. For example, the newsletter of one BT yeshiva has a "mazel tov" (congratulations) section that lists the marriages of current and former students and the births of their children. All the babies have Hebrew names, even though some of the parents do not. One BT couple pointed out that the names they chose for two of their three children are hard for their nonreligious and non-Jewish relatives to pronounce because the names are unfamiliar and have the [ch] sound. Luckily for the grandparents, this couple uses common nicknames that do not include [ch].

Hebrew names are such a strong marker of Orthodox identity that an Orthodox person who becomes secular is likely to change his name. Once I telephoned an Orthodox family in which the oldest son is no longer observant. A voice unfamiliar to me answered the phone, saying, "This is Jack." I figured out that this must be the oldest son, whose parents and siblings still call him Yechiel.

An issue related to names is the use of titles. In the Milldale Orthodox community I heard many more people introduced and referred to as "Mr.," "Mrs.," "Rabbi," "Rebbetzin," and "Dr." than is common in non-Orthodox circles. For example, I had only heard people refer to Joseph Ilikoff as "Dr. Ilikoff" (he is a scientist) until I visited him at his office and heard him called "Joseph." Similarly, a young BT woman lived with the Fefer family for several months and still called the middle-aged parents Rabbi and Mrs. Fefer. Titles are more commonly used for people with advanced degrees or rabbinic ordination and for older married people. First names are usually used when the speaker, hearer, and referee all have a similar status in the community. Children are expected to refer to adults with their titles, even close family friends. As a young married graduate student, I was usually referred to as Sarah or Sorah, but sometimes people introduced me to young children as Mrs. Benor.

Some rabbis garner so much respect that they are not only referred to as Rabbi X but are addressed in the third person. In yeshivas, students generally address their rabbis this way, as in "How does the *rav* [rabbi] hold on that?" (rather than "What is your opinion about that?"). An FFB woman told me that in her Bais Yaakov primary school the students addressed the teachers like this: "Does the *morah* [teacher] want our homework now?" This same woman reports that she addresses a few rabbis in the third person at the yeshiva where she works. I heard several Milldale residents—BTs and FFBs—address respected rabbis in the classroom and at home, and a few times they used the third person.

"Learning" (Jewish Text Study)

Partly based on halachic obligation, Orthodox Jews attach great value to learning biblical and rabbinic principles through oral presentations and text study.[12] In synagogue, the rabbi usually gives a dvar torah, which connects the weekly portion of the Bible to moral lessons about contemporary life. At Shabbos and holiday meals, the man of the house often gives a dvar torah as well. Sometimes guests (usually male) and even children are asked to do the same. As one BT told me, "They say when you have a meal, if you don't have words of Torah, it's like eating *treif* [not kosher]. . . . That's why you always have a dvar torah when you sit at the meal. It sanctifies the meal."

Shomrei Emunah, the synagogue in Milldale, offers three different shiurim (lectures, classes) every day and eight others once a week. Most are for men only, but a few are co-ed and one is for women only. The schools teach general studies part of the day and *limudei kodesh* (holy studies) the rest of the day. This includes laws and customs, Hebrew language, *Chumash* (Torah/Pentateuch, also known as the Written Law), *Navi* (Prophets) for boys and girls, and Talmud (the Oral Law, consisting of Mishnah and *Gemora*) for boys.

Men spend much of their leisure time learning on a daily or weekly basis with a *chavrusa* (study partner), explicating the Gemora and other rabbinic texts. This act of studying traditional texts is referred to as "learning," based on the Yiddish cognate *lernen*. Although women in Milldale sometimes attend classes, they rarely study with a chavrusa. When they do, it tends to focus on laws pertaining to women, and they usually do not delve into the original Hebrew/Aramaic texts (another area of distinction from Modern Orthodox Jews).

The importance of learning for Orthodox males is illustrated by two speeches I heard at the *bris* (baby boy's circumcision celebration) of Yehuda and Rachel's first son. Yehuda thanked the guests for coming and said he hopes his son will have "a bright future in learning. [Smiling] He should *shtayg* away." *Shtayg* is a Yiddish word meaning "ascend, advance," and it usually refers to advanced Gemora learning. After Yehuda's speech, one of his learning partners stood up and made some comments, mentioning the *nachas* (pride) the parents should get from this boy, especially in his learning.

BTs need time to get used to the "learning" practices common in Orthodox communities. It takes a good deal of knowledge, skill, and/or preparation to be able to present a solid dvar torah or explicate a rabbinic text written in Hebrew or Aramaic. To acquire these skills, BTs attend regular classes at Ner Tamid and Shomrei Emunah, not only on texts but also on Hebrew language. BT males in Milldale tend to set aside regular times for learning, as FFB males do, but it often takes years before they are competent enough to study Gemora without help. Some BT men spend months or years in yeshivas in Israel or elsewhere to hone their text skills. One recent BT, Yisrael, a relative beginner in text study, said there is nothing he would rather do on vacation than learn. He spent his ten-day vacation at a men's BT yeshiva in the New York area. Some people even quit their jobs to learn full-time.

At Ner Tamid events, and at meals where several BTs are in attendance, the rabbis often ask a relative newcomer—someone who has been attending classes and events for a year or so—to prepare and present a dvar torah. This milestone serves to indicate the rabbi's confidence that the BT has learned enough to participate in this speech act. Usually the ritual is limited to men, but the rabbis at Ner Tamid sometimes ask a woman to give a dvar torah, as well.

As BTs begin to spend more time in an Orthodox community, they feel even more pressure to be knowledgeable about Torah and proficient in Hebrew. One BT, Daniel, never spent time in yeshiva but nonetheless felt a need to demonstrate learnedness in the speeches he made during his two-year term as president of the synagogue. He told me, "I felt a sense of responsibility when I spoke to have some words of Torah in what I said. So if I were addressing the congregation, I would have some . . . relevant statement that maybe referred to this week's parsha or to something I just learned, just to tie it into the thought that I was doing."

This is another instance of a BT using a common Orthodox practice—Torah learning—as he integrates into the community. But because Daniel did not have many years of experience studying texts in the original Hebrew/Aramaic, the quotes he included in his speeches were usually in translation. This served as a regular reminder to the audience that Daniel did not grow up Orthodox. Similarly, some BT men who have not spent significant time in yeshiva still participate in regular learning sessions, often with a chavrusa. But they generally focus on Torah or English books about halacha, while FFBs and more learned BTs spend their time explicating Gemora.

Leisure Activities

While frum Jews spend much of their leisure time reading and hearing about ancient texts, they also read contemporary Orthodox periodicals. Most popular in Milldale in 2002 were the English-language weeklies *The Jewish Press*, *HaModia* ("The Herald"), and *Yated Ne'eman* ("Foothold of the Faithful"), as well as the monthly magazine *The Jewish Observer*. I often saw one or more of these periodicals on coffee tables in Milldale, and I even noticed children reading them.

The most common leisure activity is hosting or attending a social gathering centered around food and drink. Non-Orthodox Jews and non-Jews often throw a party for no reason at all, but Orthodox entertaining tends to center around Shabbos and holidays and the many simchas of lifecycle events: the bris, the bar mitzvah, and the events marking a marriage—the *l'chayim* and *vort* ("toast" and "speech" parties to celebrate an engagement), the *ufruf* (when the groom is "called up" to the Torah the Shabbos before the wedding), the *Shabbos kallah* (Shabbos celebration for the bride before the wedding), the *chasuna* (wedding) itself, and the *sheva brachos* ("seven blessings"—daily celebrations during the post-wedding week). The parties to honor these occasions range from a small informal meal at home to a lavish party in a formal catering hall.

Between parties, Orthodox Jews socialize informally, of course. Women and teenagers often spend time chatting at each others' homes or on the phone, and men catch up with friends before and after prayer services and learning sessions. Although some men and older boys discuss professional sports, and the primary school in Milldale does have an eighth-grade basketball league, professional and amateur sports are not a locus of major activity.

Among frum Jews in Milldale, American popular culture is not very popular. I hardly ever heard community members talking about movies, and I only saw a few televisions; if a family does own a TV, it is usually kept in the basement, not in the more public spaces of the home.[13] One FFB family borrowed their neighbor's TV-VCR to watch their son's wedding video. And a BT family borrowed the TV-VCR from Ner Tamid so that the children could watch some educational videos they had checked out from the library. Of course, there are exceptions, like the FFB man who told me he grew up on *The Brady Bunch* and had a crush on Marsha, or the FFB woman who scheduled our interview for 7:30 P.M., "right after *Jeopardy*."

Many of the BTs I met in Milldale have given up movies, sitcoms, and secular night life. One woman has taken this to an extreme: she no longer plays secular games. She said she recently saw the game Life when babysitting, and it bothered her that it was "filled with secular values," like the accrual of money. Another recent BT, who still enjoys popular culture and has a sizeable collection of recent films on video, said, "I'm nervous to say I went to the movies." She wonders how community members would view her if they knew she hasn't given up secular activities.

Because most BTs grew up deeply immersed in popular culture, references to TV shows and movies often serve as an identifier of a non-Orthodox childhood. One Shabbos afternoon when I was lounging around with Levi and Shira and a few of their BT friends, Levi made a reference to a *Saturday Night Live* skit and then said, "But that's from a past life." The last part allowed him to assure his audience that he no longer partakes in frivolous activities like watching late-night television. But his decision to reference a TV show that most of his FFB friends would not be familiar with highlighted the fact that he is a BT. When BTs are together (and generally not in the presence of FFBs), they sometimes bond by nostalgically discussing movies and shows they grew up with. For example, telling me about her interactions with her BT friends, Michelle said, "It's not that we sit there and discuss major things from our past that aren't appropriate to discuss, but we'll talk about a movie here and there. We'll talk about stuff, or we'll say 'Oh, remember this?'" This kind of communal bonding among BTs is common, as social researcher Roberta Sands found in her interviews with BTs in three East Coast cities.[14]

Not all FFBs grew up sheltered from popular culture. Many Modern Orthodox Jews do watch TV and movies, and a few decades ago many Orthodox Jews farther to the right of the continuum did so as well. Rabbi Hollander, a widely admired FFB teacher in his forties, often alludes to American culture in his lectures, such as a comedy routine by Bill Cosby or an episode of *I Love Lucy*. Although he may not be up on more recent phenomena like Conan O'Brien or *American Idol*, these references still allow him to connect to non-Orthodox students and draw them into the conversation. With an FFB crowd, he probably would not make the same references, both because there would be less comprehension and because some people might take offense. The one time I heard him speaking to an audience that included several FFBs, as well as several BTs, he joked, "And then we go to the chasuna [wedding], have a great time, dance to some rock and roll [pause]—*chas v'sholom* [God forbid]." This line made the BTs (as well as the FFBs) laugh, but it also reinforced the fact that their new community looks down on the secular culture of their childhood.

Music

As Rabbi Hollander's remark points out, secular vocal music is rarely heard in homes or parties in the Milldale Orthodox community, partly because its lyrics are considered inappropriate. Orthodox composers, producers, and performers have filled the gap left by this taboo by creating, performing, and marketing a large array of new songs.[15] Orthodox popular songs usually deal with religious themes and are sung in Hebrew, Jewish English, or sometimes Yiddish. The unique musical style blends synthesizer-based American pop with some Eastern European and Middle Eastern influences. Because men are prohibited from hearing women sing, most of the music produced in Orthodox communities is performed by men or boys.

Almost every time I went to the Ner Tamid outreach center, I heard music playing. Except for the time one of the BT rabbis was in a Louis Armstrong mood, the chosen selections were Orthodox singers like Shlomo Carlebach and Mordechai Ben-David. At the Hollander home in Milldale, I often enjoyed watching three-year-old Mendy dancing and singing along to Orthodox music. And when the FFB Silverberg boys—home from yeshiva on a two-week break—spent a day building the family's *sukkah* (outdoor booth for the autumn Feast of Tabernacles), they blasted Hebrew tunes on the stereo for hours.

BTs generally become fans of Orthodox music, buying albums and singing along and dancing at weddings and other simchas. In a speech about the accomplishments of Ner Tamid, Samuel—a BT who became frum in his forties—said, "Ba'alei teshuva go from listening to the Grateful Dead to Mordechai Ben-David." The Grateful Dead hold a mythic place in the Orthodox community, as many former Deadheads are attracted to the Orthodox lifestyle. For many newly Orthodox Jews, the Dead—with all of the associated culture—have become a symbol of their pre-BT days. In his long-haired youth, Zev used to follow the

Dead around the country. Now he does not even know where his Dead tapes are, and he listens only to "Jewish music."

Some BTs do maintain contact with their previous musical loves. Yael, who used to spend much of her spare time drumming in a hard-rock band, still has some albums from her favorite group, Rush, and she does listen to them from time to time. Levi, a longtime BT, is familiar with the Orthodox music scene. But he is also proud of his former Deadhead identity and does not want to give it up completely. Although he has changed his e-mail address from LeviBear@pseudonym.com (a nickname given to him by a BT friend: his Hebrew name plus a Grateful Dead reference) to Teshuvah@pseudonym.com (repentance), he still has Grateful Dead teddy bear stickers on his windshield and even plans to get new ones for his next car. He does occasionally listen to his old records, but not when his young children are around. He wants to wait until they are older to introduce them to the Grateful Dead.

One musically talented BT family in Milldale satisfied their desire to perform while maintaining observance of *kol isha*, the law against men hearing women sing. The mother and two daughters started an all-women's band that performs only for female audiences. Their songs are influenced by American musical genres like the blues and show tunes, but they all have Orthodox themes, like preparing for Shabbos and "men in tzitzis." The older daughter referred to the group as "a BT band," saying that FFBs would never sing songs like these.

One of the few times I heard Milldale Orthodox Jews listening to non-Orthodox music was in the Kramers' van on the way to New York for a wedding. The Kramer parents both became BTs in their twenties, and their teenage children have grown up as FFBs. For part of the trip, they listened to an Orthodox band. When the tape ended, they turned on the radio, which was set to a classic rock station. When "American Pie" started, the children got excited. They sang along for the chorus and some of the verses. But just as the singer was about to say, "The three men I admire most, the Father, Son and the Holy Ghost," the mother turned the volume all the way down. One of the sons asked why, and she answered, "It's words you don't want stuck in your head." The older daughter said, "Probably something about Yoshke" (the Yiddish diminutive form of Jesus and the name I generally heard applied to him in Orthodox communities). After "American Pie" was over, the mother put in another Orthodox tape, which happened to start with "*Ani ma'amin*," a Hebrew song stating a "full belief" that the Moshiach (Messiah) will come. I couldn't help but smile about the ironic contrast.

The Kramers are unusual in that the children are allowed to listen to rock and roll and even watch television. Most Black Hat Orthodox children would not know any of the words to "American Pie." But the Kramers are typical in that the children sing along with the Orthodox tapes and the parents try to shelter them from Christian imagery. Twenty years ago, when the Orthodox recording industry was much smaller, it was more common for FFBs to listen to secular music. One older BT said she thought a few FFBs seemed like BTs because of their knowledge of rock and roll. But she recognizes that these FFBs grew up at a time when Black Hat Orthodoxy was less strict in such matters.[16] Even so, most Black Hat FFBs today (and many BTs) would not find themselves listening to a classic rock station in the first place.

Marriage and Children

Within the Orthodox community, marriage is highly valued. It is extremely rare for FFBs to be single after their mid-twenties. This is illustrated by an advertisement in an Orthodox periodical for a free computer training program for "Women Coping on Their Own (Widowed, Divorced, Separated)." The Haredi organization sponsoring this course assumes that "women coping on their own" are limited to those who have once been married. It does not include women who have never been married and certainly not women who identify as lesbians (homosexual activity is forbidden in Orthodoxy, and those who identify as homosexual often leave the fold). The organization that placed this ad might assume that women who have never been married have careers and can cope on their own. Even so, this ad illustrates how Orthodox communities expect women to get married, whether or not they have a career.

Orthodox communities toward the Black Hat end of the spectrum have strict standards of gender separation, stemming partly from the laws of *negia* (which forbid touching members of the opposite sex outside marriage). Unmarried males and females have little opportunity to socialize outside of their families, and dating is limited.[17] The norm is for Orthodox men and women in their early twenties to be set up by a professional shadchan (matchmaker) or a mutual acquaintance.[18] The couple ultimately makes the final decision, but it is not acceptable for individuals or couples to initiate courting independent of a third party. Because physical contact and even being alone together are prohibited before marriage, a prospective couple meets for dates in public places.

The BTs I have met seem happy to participate in the matchmaking system. As soon as they become involved in an Orthodox community, they often feel pressure to begin the dating process. Rabbis and families who help the BTs integrate into the community recommend potential matches or matchmakers. Once they are set up, BTs seem to have more dates and telephone conversations than FFBs before deciding to get married. Even so, the courting period tends to be relatively short. It is not uncommon for a couple to become engaged a month after meeting and be married three months later.

The Ner Tamid outreach center helps single people of all ages find each other with its social events, lectures about relationships, and officially advertised "matchmaking services," offered by the wife of one of the teachers. When I started my fieldwork at Ner Tamid, there were twelve regulars who were interested in getting married in the near future, four of whom had previously been married and divorced. Two years later, ten of them had found other BTs and gotten married in Orthodox ceremonies. Except for one couple that came to Ner Tamid together, all the spouses came from other Orthodox communities—in New York, New Jersey, and as far away as California.

One reason that outreach organizations like Ner Tamid are so eager to help people find their *bashert* (predestined match) is that marriage helps to solidify a BT's observance. A man who works for a BT yeshiva explains:

> You really don't know where someone is [in religious observance] until they marry and walk out. And that's one of the greatest things about seeing them marry is that you know they're locking in. Once they've married, it's harder for a person to just drop it and to walk away, because you've got a commitment to another person who's also seriously holding a certain level in Judaism. So . . . it's like a graduation day for us when we see a wedding. We know the students have really locked in. And there are rare exceptions to that, but that is a good outward sign that they're really committed.

BTs tend to marry other BTs, for a number of reasons. From the BT perspective, it is nice to share common experiences, including having transitioned to greater observance and continuing to deal with non-Orthodox family and friends. From the FFB perspective, there are at least three problems with a "mixed" (FFB and BT) marriage. One is a fear of recidivism—that the BT might change his mind and decide to drop his observance—all the more harmful when an FFB spouse is involved. Another is the potential confusion that children of a BT might face when interacting with their non-Orthodox grandparents. A third issue is that the BT likely does not have yichus, or good lineage, an issue to which FFBs attach great importance.[19] A woman who became Orthodox in her twenties may have a good pedigree according to secular American norms, but she is missing an important element of yichus: a father who is a well-respected Orthodox rabbi. I observed the emphasis on yichus at the sheva brachos (post-wedding week celebration) of Rabbi Hollander's FFB son Shmuel. When Shmuel gave a dvar torah, he spent several minutes praising his bride's FFB father for being a *godol hador* (important man of the generation) and a *talmid chacham* (learned scholar). In addition, some FFBs are bothered by the prospect that their grandchildren would be descended from a couple (the other grandparents) who presumably did not observe *taharas mishpacha* (literally "family purity," a set of laws forbidding sexual contact between husband and wife during part of the menstrual cycle and requiring a woman to immerse in the mikveh monthly).

Although the dozens of couples I encountered during my fieldwork were mostly both BTs or both FFBs, I did meet at least seven "mixed" couples. The FFBs who marry BTs are usually somewhat more independent-minded, have been unsuccessful on the FFB matchmaking scene, or have previously been married and divorced. When a BT marries an FFB, it is often considered a sign of successful integration into the Orthodox community. One divorced BT woman I met in Israel was elated when a matchmaker set her up with an FFB.

Whether or not they are paired with an FFB, BTs often feel more assimilated into the community when they get married. As one rebbetzin said, once they are married, "they're not just guests by people [at others' homes]," meaning they are now expected to host their own Shabbos dinners. While single people can also host dinners, this is a rare occurrence in the Orthodox community. Single people and even newlyweds are usually invited to join families for Shabbos and holiday meals. But after *shana alef* (the first year of marriage), they are expected to host others. As Heilman writes in his study of Modern Orthodox Jews: "Only the married members seem to be full-fledged members of the . . . community."[20]

I was regularly reminded of the importance of marriage during my fieldwork, especially when I visited the large Black Hat community of Monsey, New York, three months before my baby was due. The woman I was staying with was calling her friends to help me arrange interviews, and she added her endorsement: "She's a very nice lady. She's married, and she left her husband for three days to visit Monsey." Once she said, "She's married, and she's expecting." It was clear that being married added to my legitimacy in the Orthodox community and being pregnant multiplied it.[21] At age twenty-seven, if I had not been married and at least on the way to motherhood, I would have been seen as flouting the norms of the community, and I would have been offered matchmaking services frequently.

The norm is not only to marry young but also to have many children. Although some Orthodox rabbis permit the use of birth control in certain circumstances, others do not. Children are considered a blessing, and BTs often have just as many children as FFBs. However, since many BTs do not become Orthodox until their thirties or even later, they miss out on valuable childbearing years. One BT said that she can often tell who is BT by their age and the number of children they have. If a woman is twenty and has kids, she is probably FFB. If she is thirty with one kid, she is probably a BT.

Having children often makes a BT feel more integrated into the Orthodox community. When I was pregnant during my fieldwork, I had more in common with community members and, therefore, more potential conversation topics. Since at least seven other women were due within a few months of me, my visits to the community included many pregnancy- and baby-related conversations.

Several BTs expressed joy in the fact that they have children who are frum from birth and whose friends and classmates are children of FFBs. This often has an equalizing effect on the parents. Shira's involvement with the parent-teacher organization of her children's school allows her to interact with FFB mothers on equal footing, even though she had no knowledge of Judaism until about ten years ago. Rochel, a learned FFB rebbetzin who teaches classes on women's observance, often comes over to chat with Shira while their kids play together. Although they come from very different backgrounds and might be seen as differing in status, they somehow seem on a par when they are standing together in Shira's living room, each holding a baby and keeping an eye on the toddlers at their feet.

Similar to the yeshiva staff member's explanation above, having children also serves to solidify a BT's observance. One BT told me that she has changed for the better since she had children, because she feels the need to serve as a role model for them. Even if a BT was previously flawless in her halachic observance, having children may push her to improve her *midos* (character traits).

Eventually, BTs learn from their own children. The kids come home from school using Hebrew words the parents are not familiar with or ask for help on homework the parents do not understand. The BT parents are likely to look up words or seek help from more knowledgeable friends. While this adds to the parents' knowledge of Orthodoxy, it is also somewhat demoralizing and infantilizing. At the same time, the child's knowledge and performance can help BT parents feel more accepted. Bracha Sara said she really felt assimilated into Orthodoxy one day when she was driving her four children home from school in a huge station wagon and one of her sons said, "I'm shmoiling!" (a made-up word: "boiling" with the Yiddish *shm*-cluster). She recalls thinking, "Here I am driving my 'yeshiva-mobile,' and my kid is making up Yiddish-sounding words. I've made it into the mainstream."

Conclusion

In this chapter, I have described elements of Orthodox culture as I observed them in Milldale and elsewhere.[22] A common theme is that there is a good deal of variation within Orthodoxy. One BT said, "I feel like any Orthodox community is a carbon copy of another Orthodox community—on the surface." To an outsider or newcomer, the long skirts, dark suits, Shabbos meals, large dinner tables, and shelves of seforim may look the same in any Orthodox community. But once the observer spends more time in the Orthodox world, the variations between and within communities shine through. Cultural practices like dress, food, and music indicate individuals' location along the Modern Orthodox to Black Hat continuum, as well as ancestral origin, geography, Hasidic versus non-Hasidic, and other social and religious dimensions.[23] For example, Jews from the Middle East have different hand-washing rituals, and Jews of German origin wait less time between eating meat and milk. In some neighborhoods of Brooklyn, a dvar torah over dinner would be in Yiddish, while in others the entire conversation would be in Yiddish.

Some of the practices discussed above are dictated by a strict interpretation of halacha, Jewish law. Women must cover their elbows and knees (and hair if they are married), and men must cover their heads. Food must be eaten according to the laws of kashrus, and women may not sing in the presence of men. But some practices have no basis in halacha and are merely influenced by Orthodox ideologies. For example, the reverence for the recent Eastern European Jewish past influences the foods, the connection to the biblical Children of Israel influences the names, and the high value attached to Jewish textual learning influences the prominence of books in home decor. These ideologies are maintained partly through discourses about them and partly through cultural practices.

The forms of dress, music, food, and home decoration described in this chapter serve as "cultural capital" in Orthodox circles. Social theorist Pierre Bourdieu brought attention to the importance of cultural practices, including preferred classical composers, favorite artists, table setting techniques, and leisure reading materials, in the perpetuation of social class differences.[24] According to Bourdieu, cultural capital can exist in three states: embodied, objectified, and institutionalized. Although the Orthodox situation is different in many ways, all three of these forms of capital are also important. Embodied cultural capital, characterized as "long-lasting dispositions of the mind and body,"[25] includes knowledge of biblical and rabbinic literature, ways of covering the hair and tucking in tzitzis, and the linguistic practices described in the next chapter. Objectified cultural capital includes seforim (holy books), artwork depicting Jerusalem, and the *blech* (a metal stove covering that allows observant Jews to warm food on Shabbos, when cooking is prohibited). Orthodox day schools and FFB-dominated yeshivas and seminaries offer institutionalized cultural capital in the form of traditional education.

When newcomers enter Orthodox communities, they tend to lack all or most of these forms of cultural capital, and many work hard to acquire them. This even applies to institutionalized cultural capital: while they cannot attend an Orthodox elementary school, they can acquire credentials and competencies by taking time off from their career or secular education to study in a BT yeshiva or seminary. An FFB child must expend little in exchange for the religious and cultural competence she acquires at home, school, and play. In contrast, for a BT adult, the acquisition of frum cultural capital comes at the expense of time, money, and feelings of inauthenticity, infantilization, and in-betweenness.

On the other hand, BTs have access to other forms of cultural capital that many FFBs lack. FFBs and longtime BTs often talk about new BTs' refreshing and contagious enthusiasm surrounding belief and observance. For example, a rabbi writing on an Orthodox outreach center website (likely read mostly by BTs) tells a joke about BTs going overboard in their observance and comments: "It's easy to make fun of the seeming obsession of the newly observant with not doing 'the wrong thing'—but those of us who are not FFF (frum-from-Friday) could well take a lesson or two from those who are."[26]

BTs also have alternative cultural capital outside of the religious sphere. BTs with musical talent (such as Matisyahu), juggling skills, or karate moves can be the life of the party at weddings and public gatherings. BTs who are already accomplished in their careers are appreciated for the skills they can contribute to the running of Orthodox communities, such as finance, administration, and web design. And of course BTs with disposable income are highly valued for their financial contributions to Orthodox institutions.

The notion of cultural capital also helps us understand why BTs do not always conform to Orthodox cultural norms. In some cases, BTs' distinctive cultural practices are due to a lack of skill, such as when they study from English how-to books and rabbinic translations rather than the Hebrew and Aramaic originals. But in many cases, BTs purposely distinguish themselves in order to preserve elements of their previous selves, connect with non-Orthodox friends and relatives, and/or align themselves with BT peers. They do this by maintaining stylish dress, modern art, and world cuisine, even as they follow halacha and many cultural norms common in their new communities. An example of this selective accommodation and deliberate distinctiveness is the BT who keeps two decals on his car: a bumper sticker that says "Moshiach is coming!" and the Grateful Dead teddy bear stickers on his windshield. There is also the young man who wears his black hat with trendy sunglasses and the woman who prepares her Eastern European gefilte fish with curry and turmeric.

When FFBs use unusual cultural practices like these, they may be seen as Modern Orthodox, from "out of town," or just bizarre; trim on a kipah or a black-hat Beatle poster may serve as negative cultural capital for FFBs. When BTs do these things, the primary (and intended) perception is likely that they are BTs (although they may also be perceived as Modern Orthodox, from "out of town," or bizarre). BTs complicate the notion of Orthodox cultural capital. And through hybrid cultural practices, BTs are able to present themselves not only as Orthodox Jews but also as ba'alei teshuva.

4

"This Is Not What to Record"

Yiddish, Hebrew, and the English of Orthodox Jews

When I told Orthodox Jews in Philadelphia and around the country that I was interested in Orthodox language, a common response was, "Have you heard the Journeys song 'Yeshivishe Reid'?" This song begins:

> In the hallowed halls of *yeshivos* [yeshivas] far and wide
> Our young men have discovered a new way to verbalize.
> With Yiddish, English, Hebrew—it's a mixture of all three,
> And a dash of Aramaic—a linguistic potpourri!
> That's called: *yeshivishe reid* [yeshiva speech], *yeshivishe shprach* [yeshiva language]:
> *Takeh* [really], *eppis* [something], *gradeh* [in reality], a *gevaldike zach* [remarkable thing].
> It's called: *yeshivishe reid, yeshivishe shprach*:
> It's the talk of the town, *mamish* [really] *tog un nacht* [day and night].[1]

This song points to the widespread understanding that American Orthodox Jews, especially men who study in yeshiva, speak a unique combination of four languages: English, Yiddish, Hebrew, and Aramaic. In this chapter, I explain the role of these four languages in Orthodox communities, I give details about how they are mixed together, both inside and outside the study hall, and I describe competing language ideologies. This discussion will help the reader understand the linguistic landscape that ba'alei teshuva encounter as they are immersed in Orthodox communities.

Languages of American Orthodoxy

First, some historical background. Throughout history, Jews have tended to be multilingual. Their communal linguistic repertoire usually included some variety of the local vernacular and—depending on education—various degrees of knowledge of Hebrew and Aramaic for reciting prayers and reading biblical and rabbinic literature. The use of the vernacular in combination with the holy languages of the texts is a special case of multilingualism referred to as diglossia or multiglossia.[2] In addition, because of Jews' history of migration, their linguistic repertoire sometimes included an additional language or vestiges thereof—the language used before the migration, such as Judeo-French among early Yiddish speakers. All these languages—textual Hebrew and Aramaic and in some cases a pre-migration language—influenced the vernaculars of Jews around the world, yielding Yiddish, Judeo-Spanish (also known as Ladino or Judezmo), Judeo-Arabic, Judeo-Italian, and many more Jewish languages.[3]

Jews in America are no exception to this historical trend.[4] They speak some variety of American English, and those who are engaged in religious life have various degrees of skill in Hebrew and Aramaic. The main pre-migration language, Yiddish, still plays an important role in American life, often in humorous or nostalgic contexts like e-mail jokes and souvenirs.[5] And today there is an additional linguistic influence: Modern Israeli Hebrew, which Americans encounter in their visits to Israel and their interactions with Israelis in America, especially in the Hebrew school classroom. In short, the English spoken by American Jews is influenced to varying degrees by textual Hebrew/Aramaic, Yiddish, and Israeli Hebrew.

While American Jews of all denominations use at least some Yiddish and Hebrew words, the most distinctive language can be found among Orthodox Jews.[6] They tend to have more knowledge of textual Hebrew/Aramaic, Yiddish, and Israeli Hebrew due to the communal emphases on religious observance, text study, and connections to Eastern Europe and Israel.

Textual Hebrew

Textual Hebrew is central to the lives of Orthodox Jews. On a given day, Orthodox men recite several blessings surrounding their dressing, washing, and eating, recite the three daily prayer services, and study biblical or rabbinic texts, mostly in Hebrew (with some Aramaic). Women recite most of the same blessings, and they may say some of the same prayer services, but they tend not to study the same texts. In addition, many women regularly recite psalms in the original Hebrew, especially when they know of people in need of healing. On Shabbos, Monday, Thursday, and certain holidays, anyone who attends synagogue hears a public reading of a Torah portion, with an additional reading from Prophets on Shabbos and holidays (*haftorah*). At festive meals on Shabbos and holidays, families sing Hebrew songs around the table. If all the men present are family members, women may sing aloud; otherwise, they might follow along in a book as the men sing. Even children know dozens of Hebrew songs.

As Orthodox life is filled with Hebrew recitation, it is not surprising that most community members are able to read Hebrew and understand at least some of what they are reading. Children are taught the Hebrew alphabet by kindergarten, around the same time they learn the English alphabet. Both boys and girls study the Bible and rabbinic commentaries in the original Hebrew, and boys also study works of Jewish law written in Hebrew (and Aramaic).

According to halacha, Jews are allowed to study the bible and pray in translation. Jewish communities throughout history have offered vernacular translations for this purpose, and contemporary America is no exception.[7] Even so, traditional Jews continue to use Hebrew when praying or reading the Bible, because it is considered *loshon kodesh*, the "holy language." Rabbinic literature predicts the ultimate reward for using Hebrew: "Whoever speaks in the sacred tongue has a place in the world to come."[8] One rabbi at Ner Tamid, in teaching the biblical story of the Tower of Babel, explained that Hebrew is the only objective language, because it "is the language with which God created the world." Hebrew words describe the very essence of the objects they refer to, he said, while all other languages are subjective. To read the Bible or pray only in translation would be to live a life that is that much less holy.[9]

Textual Aramaic

Aramaic, a close Semitic cousin of Hebrew, was the lingua franca among Jews when parts of the Bible and the Gemora were written. Millennia later, traditional Jews still use Aramaic, but only for limited purposes: to study rabbinic literature and to recite and sing certain prayers and songs. On Shabbos, Passover, and in every daily prayer service, Aramaic makes brief appearances. Since Orthodox men are expected to study Gemora regularly, boys learn talmudic Aramaic in elementary or middle school. With some exceptions in Modern Orthodox communities, frum women generally have limited comprehension of Aramaic.

Textual Hebrew and Aramaic are considered the most important non-native languages for Orthodox Jews to know, even over other languages that appear in the rabbinic texts. Jacob, a longtime BT, illustrated this when he was reading Gemora with Rabbi Nussbaum, an FFB. As Jacob struggled through the Hebrew and Aramaic, trying various pronunciations and translations, Rabbi Nussbaum helped by responding with "yes" or—more often—"no." Jacob almost always made several attempts to understand each word before he finally gave up and asked Rabbi Nussbaum for help. On one occasion he was reading Rashi, an influential eleventh-century French rabbi who sometimes included in his commentary words in French, also known as [*b'*]*laaz*, an acronym for [*b'*]*loshon am zar* ([in] the language of a foreign people). Rather than make several efforts to translate one such word, Jacob said, "This is in *b'laaz, b'loshon am zar*, in Old French." After he tried twice to pronounce it, he said blithely, "I don't know that French word. Sorry." If French had been as important in his mind as Hebrew and Aramaic, he likely would not have "apologized" insincerely for not knowing the word. This episode highlights the significance of Hebrew and Aramaic over other languages Jews have spoken and written.

For BTs who are integrating into Orthodox communities, learning to recite Hebrew and, to some extent, Aramaic is very important. Even those who do not lead prayers, recite from the Torah, or study with a partner are still expected to recite Hebrew or Aramaic in public—as they bless candles and children on a Friday night, sing songs around a Shabbos table, or say the mourner's kaddish. A person's rendering of textual Hebrew and Aramaic is often a sign of his or her religious background. As one FFB put it, "When a man is a *chazen* [cantor, or one who leads prayer services], you can pretty much tell" whether he grew up frum, based on the comfort with which he uses Hebrew/Aramaic, as well as the consistency of his pronunciation (more on this below).

Yiddish

Unlike some more insular Yeshivish and Hasidic communities, most Orthodox Jews in Milldale are not fluent in Yiddish.[10] The only people who use Yiddish as an everyday language are some older speakers who grew up with it. Several of the men in the community learned Yiddish in yeshiva and speak it on occasion to elderly immigrants or to friends or relatives in New York or elsewhere. To my knowledge, none of the young people raised in Milldale today has speaking or reading ability in Yiddish, beyond the words and phrases that are used within English.

Even so, Yiddish phrases are maintained for a few ritualistic functions, such as in some songs and in the auctions of the Torah honors (some synagogues auction off each *aliyah*, the honor of being called to say the blessings surrounding the Torah readings). On the holiday of *Simchas Torah*, I heard Yiddish used for both of these at Ner Tamid. One song praised Torah study in very simple Yiddish: "*Toyre iz a gute zakh, a gute zakh, a gute zakh*" (Torah is a good thing, a good thing, a good thing). Rabbi Fischer was leading the service, and he started off the auction for the third aliyah. He started at eighteen dollars, the numerical value of *chai*, Hebrew for "life." Several BTs in the crowd bid on the aliyah, and the price went up to eighty dollars. When nobody else bid, Rabbi Fischer ended the auction: "Eighty dollars *ershtn mol* [first time], eighty dollars *tsveytn mol* [second time], eighty dollars *dritn mol* [third time], sold: eighty dollars."

In Milldale, Yiddish is not associated with men to the same extent as it is in some Black Hat communities in Brooklyn and elsewhere.[11] Jacob, a Milldale BT, used to visit Brooklyn frequently. An elderly man there would speak only Yiddish to Jacob, even though he had limited comprehension and always responded in English. But the man spoke English to Jacob's wife. Although he could clearly speak English, he insisted on using Yiddish with Jacob because of his view that men should converse in Yiddish. In Milldale, the use of Yiddish is apparently associated more with generational proximity to immigration than with gender.

I found conflicting attitudes about Yiddish. For example, several BTs spoke about Yiddish as a warm, *heimish* (homey, relaxed; sometimes used to refer to people toward the Black Hat pole, especially Hasidim) language. But one recent BT said, "Yiddish is a strange language. In Europe that was how everyone spoke, but our language is English. Yiddish doesn't seem alive to me, so I don't know why we need it. . . . I want to learn Hebrew, loshon kodesh. *Nebach* [pity] is not religious. It's purely cultural." This BT feels that the religious aspects of Orthodox linguistic practice are more important than the cultural ones. But she herself uses non-Semitic Yiddish words like frum, shul, and heimish and even some of the same Yiddish grammatical influences she criticizes. Similarly, an FFB woman told me that she does not like Yiddish names like Bryna and Frumky.[12] She mentioned someone she knew who "named her daughter [Shprintza], nebach"—ironically using a Yiddish word in the act of criticizing her friend's choice of a Yiddish name.

Modern Israeli Hebrew

In addition to these languages that flourished in the recent or distant past, Orthodox Jews are sometimes exposed to the Hebrew of contemporary Israel, referred to as Modern Hebrew, Israeli Hebrew, or Ivrit. Some spend time studying in Israel (often in English-language programs in yeshivas and seminaries), and others visit for brief vacations. Even those who have not been to Israel tend to have some interactions with Israelis in the United States. There are a few Israeli families in Milldale, and some Israeli *aniyim* (poor people) go door-to-door asking for donations in Hebrew. I did not hear much Israeli Hebrew spoken in Milldale, but many of the residents have some speaking ability.

Orthodox Jews tend to recognize that Modern Hebrew is different from the language of the traditional texts. The rabbi who said that loshon kodesh is the only objective language contrasted "loshon kodesh, Classical Hebrew," with Modern Hebrew, which is "very, very subjective." Even so, community members see the two types of Hebrew as mutually intelligible for the most part; some outreach rabbis even counsel BTs that living in Israel will help advance their comprehension of rabbinic literature.

Orthodox Jewish English: The Distinctive Frum Repertoire

It is clear that Orthodox Jews tend to have more knowledge of textual Hebrew/Aramaic and Yiddish—and sometimes of Israeli Hebrew—than most non-Orthodox

Jews.[13] Because of this knowledge and because of the tight-knit nature of frum communities, their English is much more distinct from general American English than that of other American Jews. Indeed, when outsiders hear Orthodox Jews speak, several distinctive features stand out. As with any speech style or ethnic language variety, it is impossible to define any one "Orthodox Jewish English" that all Orthodox Jews use.[14] Instead, it is more accurate to describe a repertoire of distinctive linguistic features that Orthodox Jews may (or may not) use as they construct their complex identities.[15] By using Yiddish influences and certain Hebrew/Aramaic words with specific pronunciations, they can align themselves with some people and distinguish themselves from others. They can position themselves along the social axes discussed in chapter 1—Modern Orthodox to Black Hat, BT to FFB, geography, gender, and more. And through the variable use of these linguistic features they can present themselves differently to different audiences and in different situations.

The following sections describe many of the features in the Orthodox linguistic repertoire. Note that some of these features are not unique to Orthodox Jews but are also used by non-Orthodox Jews (especially those highly engaged in religious life and those closer to the Yiddish-speaking generation of immigration) or even non-Jews. Even so, the use of several of these features in combination generally indicates Orthodox Jewish identity. The combination of textual and ancestral influences also points to the interplay between religion and culture in Orthodox communities. If Orthodoxy were strictly a religious dimension, Yiddish would play less of a role in the distinctive Orthodox repertoire. The centrality of this ancestral language underscores the role of culture in being—and becoming—frum.

Because most of my fieldwork for this book was conducted in Philadelphia, the question arises: how widespread are the linguistic features discussed below? Are the Yiddish influences in English also found in Orthodox communities in New York, Detroit, Dallas, and Los Angeles? Do frum people in Atlanta, Baltimore, and Cleveland also use hundreds of Hebrew words? The answer is yes. Based on my previous research among Modern Orthodox Jews in New York and Chabad Jews in Northern California, others' research on communities in Maryland and elsewhere, several periodicals, and the wide world of Orthodox cyberspace, I believe that the linguistic phenomena discussed in this chapter can be found around the country and beyond.

To add quantitative evidence to the picture, I include data from a web-based survey I conducted in 2008 with sociologist Steven M. Cohen. Because it is very difficult and expensive to obtain a random sample of American Jews, the survey used the nonrandom "snowball sampling" method, meaning we sent it to several hundred people and asked them to forward it to others. Over 40,000 people responded, and the analysis is based on 30,053 respondents who grew up and live in the United States and who spoke only English as children. This sample consists of 25,179 Jews, including 1,811 Jews who identify as Orthodox, as well as 4,874 non-Jews. We asked respondents whether they know and use several Hebrew, Aramaic, and Yiddish words, as well as a number of Yiddish grammatical constructions. The results offer more evidence of the importance of language in distinguishing Orthodox Jews from others and from each other.[16]

Of course, there are regional differences. Like other Americans, Orthodox Jews display elements of regional accents. I heard many locally born speakers using Philadelphia vowel pronunciations. And those from elsewhere maintained elements of their New York, Midwest, and Southern accents. But overlaid on their regionally inflected American English were the many features of the distinctive Orthodox linguistic repertoire.

Loanwords from Hebrew, Aramaic, and Yiddish

In his research on Yiddish, Max Weinreich makes a useful distinction between different types of Hebrew: the *Whole Hebrew/Aramaic Element* (WHE) and the *Merged Hebrew/Aramaic Element* (MHE).[17] The WHE is the whole sentences of Hebrew and Aramaic that Jews read or recite while praying, learning, or participating in other rituals. The MHE is the Hebrew and Aramaic words that are integrated into the spoken or written language. This dichotomy is similar to the distinction made in research on language contact between code switching and loanwords.[18] *Code switching* occurs when a bilingual speaker alternates between two languages in entire conversations, sentences, or parts of sentences. A *loanword* is a word from one language used within another language, even by people who cannot speak its source language. The following example, from a written dvar torah by Rabbi Heshy Grossman, includes both loanwords (the MHE, italicized) and a code switch, in this case a biblical quote (the WHE, underlined): "In the *Bais Medrash* [study hall], a good question merely begs a response. The more difficult the problem, the deeper the understanding when the answer is found. The words of Bil'am may have conquered the rest, but the *Bracha* [blessing] still echoes in the one place that's ours: 'Mah Tovu Ohaleicha Ya'akov Mishkenoseicha Yisrael [How good are your tents, Jacob, your dwelling places, Israel (Numbers 24:5)].'"[19]

Both the WHE and the MHE are important in traditional Jewish circles. In this section, I explain how the MHE, or loanwords, is used among Orthodox Jews in America. In earlier work, I have demonstrated how it is often impossible to determine which language a loanword comes from: textual Hebrew, Aramaic, Yiddish, or Israeli Hebrew.[20] Many of the loanwords that derive originally from textual Hebrew or Aramaic were also incorporated into Yiddish and are now used in English with Yiddish influences in meaning and pronunciation. Textual

Hebrew and Aramaic contribute to the maintenance of many words, and Israeli Hebrew provides some pronunciation norms and some new words. Because it is often impossible to point to just one origin of a given word, I use the generic term "loanword" for a word used within English that derives from any combination of textual Hebrew, Aramaic, Yiddish (including its Germanic, Slavic, and Romance components), and Israeli Hebrew.

How many loanwords are there in Orthodox Jewish English? Based on non-overlapping words in several Jewish English lexicons—minus those unique to non-Orthodox religious life—plus my own list of additional words, I estimate 2,000 to 2,500.[21] Orthodox Jews use loanwords to refer to concepts and items that have no simple English equivalent, such as *blech* (a metal stove cover that allows observant Jews to warm food on Shabbos, when cooking is prohibited) and *dafka* (specifically, really, to make a point of), but they also use them even when an English equivalent exists, as in *chap* (understand), *yid* (Jew), *licht* (candles), and *sakana* (danger). The following quote, from a rabbi teaching a class on Passover, is an example of how loanwords are integrated into English sentences (loans are italicized; other distinctive features are underlined): "The *mitzvah* of the *matzah-by* [at] the *seder* should be—We're *machmir* [strict], it's a *chumra* [stringency] to have *shmura mishas haktsira* [(matzah) that is watched from the time of the harvest], that the wheat that is harvested for *Pesach* [Passover] should be already watched from the time of the harvest."

Another example is the following excerpt from a flyer I found on the Shomrei Emunah bulletin board. It advertises a *gemach* (*gimel-mem-chet*, a Hebrew acronym for *gemilus chasadim*, acts of kindness), a free lending service common in Orthodox communities. In Milldale there are gemachs for wedding dresses, medical equipment, and toys. The flyer read (italics and translations are mine): "Are you planning a *Kiddush* [reception following Shabbos services], *L'chaim* [reception with alcohol to celebrate an engagement], or *Bris*? Do you know a *Choson V'Kallah* [groom and bride] who need *Sheva Brochos*? Let our new *G'mach*—'*Simchas* [*Rochel Tova*]' help you. . . . May we share many *simchos* together."

Several areas of meaning are well represented by loanwords in Orthodox Jewish English, including religious rituals and objects, holidays and lifecycle events, food, laws, values, and text study. In addition to loanwords that refer to specific items or concepts, Orthodox Jews use a number of loanwords and phrases for greeting and parting (table 4.1).

Several Hebrew and Yiddish phrases are used when talking about future events or positive or negative things, phrases that linguist James Matisoff refers to as "psycho-ostensives."[22] In Orthodox Jewish English, these are borrowed from Yiddish/Hebrew or used in English translation. In table 4.2, I enumerate some of them using Matisoff's categories. These psycho-ostensive phrases are

---

TABLE 4.1

Phrases of greeting and parting in Orthodox Jewish English

Greeting	Occasion (and translation)
Good *Shabbos*	On Shabbos
Good voch, *Shavua tov*	After Shabbos on Saturday night (good week)
Good *Yontif*/*Yomtov*	On holidays (good holiday)
Sholom aleichem	After not having seen someone in a while (peace be upon you) (mostly men)
Aleichem sholom	Response to "Sholom aleichem" (mostly men)
Mazel tov	When greeting other guests (not just the honored family) at a wedding, birth celebration, or bar mitzvah
Parting	**Occasion**
Zay gezunt	Any time (be healthy)
Be well	Any time (translation of *zay gezunt*)
Kol tuv	Any time (all goodness)
Good *Shabbos*	Before Shabbos, as early as Wednesday if you might not speak again before Shabbos
Good *Yontif*/*Yomtov*	In the days preceding a holiday
Shana tova	On Rosh Hashana (the New Year) and in the preceding few weeks (good year)

Hebrew-origin words are italicized

---

extremely common in Orthodox communities and important for BTs to learn during their process of integration.

Up to this point, it may seem that all loanwords in Orthodox Jewish English are used for specific religious or cultural reference. However, this is not the case. There are several words for silliness or nonsense, including *leytsanus* (clowning around), *shtus* (nonsense), *meshugas* (craziness), and *narishkeit* (stupidity, silliness). There are also several loan adverbs, including *takeh* (indeed, actually), *kimat* (almost), *bichlal* (entirely, in general), and *avade* (certainly).

Another area in which loanwords are common is child-directed speech, also known as baby talk. The majority of the loanwords used in Milldale baby talk are from Yiddish, although not to the same extent as among Hasidim in Brooklyn.[23] Mothers, older sisters, and female relatives and friends call young children *bubby* or *bubbale* (little doll), *kinderlach* (children), or *shefelach* (lambs).[24] Children are instructed to "go *shlofy*" (go to sleep), and if they disobey they might

TABLE 4.2
Orthodox Jewish English phrases related to positive and negative events

Phrase	Meaning (and use)
Acknowledging good things	
Baruch Hashem	Blessed [be] God (appended to positive statements, said as a response to "How are you?")
Thank God	(similar to Baruch Hashem)
Shkoyach / Yasher koach	Good job, thank you, lit. strength to you
Mazel tov	Congratulations, lit. good constellation
Acknowledging bad things	
Nebech	What a pity
Oy / oy vey / oy vey iz mir	Oh, no / lit. woe is me
Avoiding bad things	
Kaynahora / keyn *ayn hara*	No evil eye (appended to positive statements)
Bli ayin hara	No evil eye (similar to kaynahora)
Chas v'sholom	God forbid (appended to negative statements), lit. sparing and peace
(*Chas v'*)*chalila*	God forbid
Future hedges	
Bli neder	Without a vow (appended to statements of personal intent)
Im yirtse Hashem / *mertsishem*	God willing (appended to future statements)
B'ezras Hashem	With God's help (similar to Im yirtse Hashem but can also be appended to past statements)

receive a *patsh* ([playful] smack). Some body parts are often referred to with loanwords in child-directed speech: *tuches* (rear end), *keppy* (little head), *pupik* (belly button), and *hentelach* (little hands).[25]

Several kinship terms are loanwords from Yiddish or Israeli Hebrew. Grandma and grandpa are usually called *bubby* and *zeidy*, and aunts are sometimes *tanty*. Children call their mothers *Mommy* (which can be seen both as English and as Yiddish *mame* with the Jewish English [-i] ending), *Ma* (short for Mommy/*mame*), or *Ima* (Israeli Hebrew), and they call their fathers *Tatty* (Yiddish *tate* with the Jewish English [-i] ending), *Ta* (short for Tatty), or *Abba* (Israeli Hebrew).[26] Some children use different kinship terms at different life stages, but generally Mommy and Tatty are used among people closer to the

Black Hat side of the spectrum, and Ima and Abba are used in families that are more Modern Orthodox or have a strong connection (experiential or emotional) to Israel.

How Loanwords Are Integrated into English

A whole chapter could be written on how Orthodox Jews integrate loanwords into their English. Do loan nouns get their plural suffix from English (e.g., *shiurs*, *tallises*), from Israeli Hebrew (*shiurím, talitót*), or from Ashkenazi Hebrew/Yiddish (*shiúrim, taléysim*)? Are Yiddish-origin adjectives used with the Yiddish suffix (a *choshuve* man) or without (a *choshuv* man) (*choshuv*: "important")? In this section I focus on one aspect: how loan verbs are used within English.

In Yiddish, Hebrew-origin verbs are integrated in two ways: directly (as in *taynen*, "to claim") and with a helping verb like *zayn* (to be, as in *maskim zayn*, "to agree"). This second type is known as a *periphrastic verb*. In Orthodox Jewish English, both of these Yiddish verb integration types have been maintained. In non-Orthodox Jewish English, directly integrated verbs like "to *kasher*" (to render kosher) are often used, but periphrastic verbs are generally not. Among Orthodox Jews, especially those immersed in traditional text study, periphrastic constructions like "to be *zoche*" (to merit) are quite common. An example from the Orthodox press is the use of three periphrastic verbs in one article written by a woman (italics in original, underlined mine, translations mine): "Gratitude that the *Ribbono Shel Olam* [God, Master of the Universe] was *mezakeh* [favored] us with changing their views of Torah *Yidden* [Jews] in some small way. . . . We were privileged to be *mekadesh* [sanctify] *Shem Shamayim* [God, Name of the Heavens]. . . . May we be *zocheh*, very soon, to bring home all the multitudes of *Yidden*."[27]

This construction is used frequently in spoken language as well. Here are some examples that I heard during my fieldwork:

1. "There's no reason to be *maarich* [take a long time]; we'll let Rebbetzin [Markovich] be *maarich*" (a BT woman introducing Rebbetzin Markovich before a lecture)
2. "The *pasuk* [verse] is *meshabeyach*, praises, the wine for being red" (an FFB man teaching a class)
3. "Being *shomer* [minding, guarding] my *dibur* [speech]" (a BT woman telling me what she has changed about her speech, that is, avoiding loshon hora)
4. "Don't be *mevatel* [nullify/waste] my *zman* [time]" (an FFB man teasing another FFB)
5. "It might be *meorer* [arouse] the *tayva* [lust]" (an unmarried FFB man explaining to me why he planned not to hold hands with his future wife in public)
6. "That's another way we're *mekayem* [fulfill] the *mitzvah*" (an FFB man teaching a class)

To BTs and others who did not grow up with it, the periphrastic verbal construction sounds strange, perhaps even ungrammatical. But for many FFBs, saying these Hebrew verbs without a helping verb sounds like a grammatical mistake. For example, I asked an FFB man about the Yiddish-influenced phrase "He was *mekarev* me" (He brought me closer to religiosity) and its more Anglicized version, "He *mekarev*ed me," which is common among BTs. He said he uses the former and that the latter does not sound right to him.

Variation in Loanword Use

There is a great deal of variation in who uses which loanwords and in which situations. We find major differences in loanword use when we compare Orthodox Jews of different ages, genders, levels of learnedness, and religious backgrounds. And individuals use different loanwords when they talk or write about different topics, in different settings, and with different audiences.

Older people and those with more exposure to Yiddish are more likely to use Whole Yiddish phrases like *Zol zayn shtil* ([You] should be quiet), *Lomir geyn* (Let's go), and *Tshepe nisht* (Don't make an annoyance). They are also more likely to use some Yiddish loanwords that are not also from Hebrew/Aramaic, such as *eyniklach* (grandchildren), *greps* (burp), and *in mitn drinen* (in the middle of things, suddenly). Young children know and use many Hebrew and Yiddish loanwords, especially those related to rituals in which they take part, like *bracha* (blessing), *chasuna* (wedding), and *negl vaser* (literally "nail water," poured ritually over the hands in the morning)—even young children are expected to say blessings, celebrate at weddings, and participate in morning ablutions. Children use loanwords when they discuss certain religious concepts, like tznius, midos, and *muktza* (items that should not be handled on Shabbos). And they are certainly familiar with the Yiddish loanwords said to them in child-directed speech. But just as most young children do not talk about advanced concepts like materialism and worldview/weltanschauung, Orthodox Jews do not discuss *gashmius* and *hashkafa* until they are old enough to understand them. It is often not until children study about certain concepts in school that they learn the loanwords associated with them. This makes for an interesting contrast between FFB children, who use many non-philosophical loanwords, and BT adults, who learn words like *gashmius* and *hashkafa* early in their Orthodox education but might never pick up some of the words that FFB children use on a day-to-day basis.

In my research on a different Orthodox group, a Chabad Lubavitch Hasidic community in California, I found that boys and young men used more loanwords than girls and young women, especially words associated with traditional text study.[28] The same appears to be true in this non-Hasidic Orthodox community. Since women here do not study Gemora, they generally do not use loans like *kal vachomer* (all the more so, *a fortiori*), *tayn* (claim), and *svora* (justification). Men, on the other hand, use words like these regularly in their learning sessions, and they sometimes transfer them to everyday speech, as well.[29] Men who are less involved with learning are less likely to use some of these words.

The use of loanwords varies greatly according to setting, topic, and audience. Two men learning Gemora together use many loanwords, and the same men fixing a car use fewer. A mother uses several loanwords when talking to her daughter about the laws of *taharas mishpacha* (family purity), but she uses fewer when talking to her about potential *shiduchim* (matches). When Orthodox Jews speak to outsiders or newcomers, they generally use fewer loanwords and often translate those they use. For example, the word *frum* is commonly used in the Orthodox community. I heard BTs and FFBs use this word frequently in conversations with me and with each other. I also heard a few instances of "Orthodox" and "religious," but only in conversations with me or other outsiders. Similarly, Orthodox Jews talk about *Hashem* frequently, but they tend to use the word "God" when speaking to outsiders. Exceptions include the phrases "God willing," "God forbid," and "thank God," which are sometimes used even in in-group conversation.[30]

The gender of the audience also affects the use of loanwords. In Milldale, Rabbi Passo gives many classes to both single-sex and mixed audiences. I observed his co-ed class, which was attended mostly by young men, and his all-women's class, which was attended mostly by older women. In the mixed class, Rabbi Passo used many loanwords and only a little translation, and in the women's class he used fewer loanwords and more translation. Another FFB rabbi was teaching a class at Ner Tamid and regularly complimented students for insightful comments. He praised Marissa for a "beautiful" idea and said Mike had come up with "*mamish* an excellent thought." Both Marissa and Mike had been involved with Orthodoxy for a similar amount of time, but the rabbi apparently considered it more appropriate to use a loanword with a man than a woman in this instance.

Ideology about Loanwords

Many Orthodox Jews feel it is important to use loanwords, rather than their English equivalents. Lexicographer Sol Steinmetz cites the following statement by an educator writing in the Orthodox press: "Although students should know how to refer to these items in English, the norm should be *Motzaei Shabbos*—not Saturday night; *daven*—not pray; *bentsch*—not recite Grace after Meals; *Yom Tov*—not holiday."[31] I heard an FFB rabbi in Northern California express a similar sentiment when I asked him about his use of loanwords in his third-grade Orthodox class. He said, "These people should not ever come to a *Pesach seder* and talk

about Moses taking the Jews out of Egypt. It should not be heard. It should be
'*Moyshe* took them out of *Mitzrayim*.'" These statements appear to be fueled by
an ideology of Jewish/Orthodox distinctiveness, as well as by a reverence for
Hebrew and Yiddish.[32]

Another indication of the importance of loanwords is when people are corrected for not using them. In Philadelphia, I observed a few instances of BTs or
FFBs correcting new BTs' use of English words when they could have used loanwords. For example, Amira saw a picture of a recently married woman wearing
a sheitel and asked Rabbi Fischer, "Is that a wig?" Rabbi Fischer answered, "A
sheitel." Some BTs also correct themselves. In the following exchange between
two recent BTs, Mitch invites Andrew to help him think of the Hebrew word for
"tradition":

MITCH: There's a saying: if you do an *aveyra* [sin] three times, it becomes *halach*—
    it becomes, uh, um, not tradition, that Hebrew for tradition—
ANDREW: *Mínchag* [tradition, should be pronounced *min(h)ag*].
MITCH: Your *mínhag*! It becomes your *mínag* . . .

Clearly Mitch felt that using this Hebrew loanword was important enough to
request assistance and delay the end of his sentence.

Another way that Orthodox Jews demonstrate the importance of loanwords
is in their reading practices. Rabbi Tovin was reading Bible passages aloud to
a class in English translation, and he rendered the English personal names in
the Hebrew original, with mostly Ashkenazi pronunciation. Where the text read
"David," Rabbi Tovin said "Dóvid," and where the text said "Ishmael," he said
"Yishmóel." I observed a similar practice in Rebbetzin Passo's lectures about
taharas mishpacha to Miriam, a BT who was about to be married, and me.
Mrs. Passo read passages from a Jewish English book on the subject, and when
she came to a word that could have been in Hebrew she usually changed it to
Hebrew: "God" to *Hashem*, "the Ninth of Av" to *Tisha B'Av*, and Mount Sinai to
Har Sínay.

Not everyone feels the same way about loanwords. Some frum Jews are
concerned about what they see as linguistic incompetence. Take, for example,
a comment on a blog post about yeshiva *bochurs* (boys) using the word "*matzav*"
(situation) as in this sentence (italics and translations are mine): "So d'*matzv*'s
like this, my button fell off, the *zach* [thing] is somewhere in the *oilam* [world/
vicinity] of my room, could you, ah, be *metakain* [fix] it?" The comment was as
follows: "(read with British Accent and channel Henry Higgins . . .) 'Why can't
the English teach their children how to speak?.' Seriously though, we are raising a generation of frum young people who can't string together enough words
for one full English sentence. How sad."[33] Despite comments like these, posts

and comments on blogs like this regularly include loanwords from Hebrew and Yiddish.

There are several reasons that Orthodox Jews attach a high value to the frequent use of loanwords. One is the holiness of Hebrew, discussed above. Another reason is the sense of community it fosters: when people speak English with many loanwords, it makes some people feel like part of the group and others feel excluded, as I heard especially from Prospective and Peripheral BTs. The communal boundaries that language creates are, of course, much stronger in Orthodox communities where Yiddish is the main spoken language, such as Kiryas Joel (a Satmar Hasidic village in Orange County, New York) and parts of Brooklyn. There, monolingual English speakers would be excluded to a much greater degree. In places like Milldale, even people with little knowledge of Hebrew/Yiddish loanwords (such as many new BTs) would still be able to participate in most realms of communal life. However, the frequent use of loanwords can make them feel like outsiders, just as it makes others feel in the know. Many community members recognize the distancing effects of loanwords, and, when speaking to outsiders or recent BTs, they sometimes avoid them or use them with English translations. In the classes at Ner Tamid, teachers could easily avoid words like *nisoyon* (test) and *mabul* (flood). But they choose to use the loanwords—often with their English equivalents. As some teachers explained, this is partly because they feel that learning Hebrew words is an important part of the socialization process of newly Orthodox Jews.

In addition to these reasons, some loanwords are used because of what I call the *l'havdil* factor, based on Max Weinreich's research on Yiddish. "In principle," Weinreich wrote, "the distance between Jewishness and the [non-Jewish] culture of the environment was signified by the expression *lehavdl* (to discern)."[34] He points out that in Yiddish, certain Hebrew or Romance loanwords are used to distinguish Jewish from non-Jewish referents.[35] An example of this in Yiddish is the use of *bentshn* (to bless), a derivative of Latin *benedicere*, rather than the expected Middle High German *sëgenen* (to bless). As Weinreich explains, *sëgenen* was avoided because it still carried connotations of the Latin word it derived from: *signare* ([to bless by] making the sign of the cross). Instead of this word that seemed "too Christian," Yiddish speakers used the word maintained by their ancestors who moved to Germanic lands from Romance lands.

The l'havdil factor is active in the lexical choices made by many Orthodox Jews in America. Words like *neshama* (soul) and *malach* (angel) are preferred over their English equivalents, which are associated with Christianity. Some Orthodox Jews call San Jose "S. Jose" and Santa Monica "Simcha Monica," rather than verbalize the saintly origins of these city names.[36] One rabbi who works in outreach told me about the lexical practices of one of the organization's most popular lecturers. He said this man uses very few loanwords when teaching newcomers. But he insists on using *Tanach* instead of "Bible" (he includes a translation the first time he says it), because he thinks people associate the word "Bible" with Christian preachers.

Orthodox Jews often avoid words associated with Jesus and Christian holidays. A common name for Jesus is *Yoshke*, a diminutive Yiddish form of his Hebrew name, *Yeshu*.[37] Some Orthodox Jews refer to "Christmas" as *kratsmach*, a pun that sounds like Christmas and means "scratch me" in Yiddish (although non-Yiddish speakers tend not to know the literal meaning). An article in *The Jewish Observer* bemoans the Christmasization of the Jewish holiday Chanukah. The author avoids the word Christmas all together: "I'm feeling a bit confused these days. Shopping days, holiday season, gifts for everyone on your list—those were things I associated with their holiday. You know the one that comes on December 25. The non-Jewish one. The one, in fact, that represented the beginning of a new religion."[38]

Even so, words associated with Christianity are not completely absent in frum speech. One way people use words like these is to mark them as non-Jewish through humor. For example, a Modern Orthodox FFB said that a retreat was scheduled "right before [sarcastic tone] The Holy Christmas." And he called December twenty-fourth "*Erev* Christmas," *erev* being Hebrew for "the night leading into [usually a Jewish holiday]." It is not only the avoidance of Christian terms that constitutes l'havdil language, but also the use of Hebrew loanwords and a distancing tone.

Other Distinctive Lexical and Grammatical Features

While loanwords are by far the most salient feature of the Orthodox linguistic repertoire, several other features are also important in indicating Orthodox identities. English word use and word order are influenced by Yiddish in a number of ways.

Phrasal Verbs

English has many phrasal verbs—phrases that include a main verb and a particle, such as "lay off" and "eat up." Many of these phrasal verbs have different meanings than one might expect based on the words that form them. Yiddish also has a large number of phrasal verbs, and a number of these are transferred into Orthodox Jewish English (table 4.3).[39]

An example of two of these phrasal verbs used in one sentence is from an FFB rabbi teaching a class about the Passover seder: "If you have children by the seder, it's a time to go ahead and focus on the children, to *tell* them *over* about *emuna* (faith), trust and belief in Hashem, and to *give over* the seder."

TABLE 4.3

A sample of phrasal verbs in Orthodox Jewish English

Phrasal verb	Meaning	Cognate phrasal verb in Yiddish, meaning
answer up	counter, retort	*entfer op*, counter, retort
bring down*	cite, mention, declare to future generations based on past wisdom	*breng arop*, bring from afar (but it may have similar connotations in the language of Gemora study)
fall out	land [on a date]	*fal oys*, land [on a date]
give over*	communicate, impart	*geb iber*, communicate, impart
learn out*	deduce	*lern op*, deduce
leave over	leave behind	*loz iber*, leave behind
read over	read (perfective) (*not* peruse)	*leyen iber*, read (perfective)
say over*	recapitulate, recount	*zog iber*, repeat
speak out*	say aloud, utter (*not* protest or speak one's mind)	*red oys*, utter, reprimand; or *red aroys*, pronounce
tell over*	recount, retell	*dertseyl iber*, retell

*Included in Weiser, *Frumspeak*, with the same meanings

"Should"

Another area of Yiddish influence is in the use of the English word "should," which mimics the syntax of Yiddish *zoln* (should):

"I would want *that a zeidy should have* a beard."
Yiddish: ". . . *az a zeydi zol hobn* . . ."
Standard English: ". . . a grandfather to have . . ."

"I want *that you should take* her number."
Yiddish: ". . . *az du zolst nemen* . . ."
Standard English: ". . . you to take . . ."

"My wife had dropped him off at shul, *that he should come in* and get me"
Yiddish: ". . . *az er zol araynkumen* . . ."
Standard English: ". . . so he could come in . . ."

"I do it *that they should see* that . . . there's a different way"
Yiddish: ". . . *az zey zoln zen* . . ."
Standard English: ". . . so they will see . . ."

I heard this construction among some FFBs and BTs, both men and women, especially people closer to the Black Hat end of the continuum who speak Yiddish or who are children of immigrants. According to my 2008 survey, Jews who identify as "Black Hat / Yeshivish or Chassidish" are significantly more likely to report that they use this construction (20 percent) than other Orthodox Jews, non-Orthodox Jews, and non-Jews (11–14 percent).

"By," "To," and Omitted Prepositions

In Orthodox Jewish English, a number of prepositions are used with influences from their Yiddish correlates, especially "by" and "to." "By" is influenced by Yiddish *bay*, which is similar to German *bei* and Israeli Hebrew *etsel* (which is influenced by *bay*). Uriel Weinreich's dictionary translates Yiddish *bay* as: "(A) at, beside, near, by; (B) with, at the house of; (C) on (the person of); (D) in the mind of; (E) about, around; (F) on (coincidence); (G) in the eyes of."[40] Most of these uses are transferred to Orthodox Jewish English, as in these examples from FFBs and BTs in Philadelphia:

(A) at [a location]: "by the mikveh," "by the table," "by the restaurant," "by the bus station"

(B1) at the house of: "Are you eating by Rabbi Fischer?" "I'll stay by them."

(B2) with, among: "By Chabad, it's different," "Things they've seen by their parents," "By us, monarchy, unity did not mean individuals losing their individuality."

(D, G) according to the opinion of, in the mind of: "Who's Reb Yehuda holding by?" "I *pasken* [rule halachically] by him."

(F) at [an event, time of year], on (coincidence): "If you have children by the seder," "by the rehearsal."

The Yiddish-influenced "by" is quite common among Orthodox Jews of all ages, genders, and religious orientations. I heard all the usages above from longtime BTs, both male and female. The most common usage of "by" among BTs in the early stages of integration is (B1), as in "I usually stay by one of the rabbis" or "I spent Shabbos by them." The 2008 survey asked about this use and found that it is an important marker of Orthodox identity: over half of all Orthodox respondents report using it, compared to less than a quarter of non-Orthodox Jews (table 4.4).

The other Yiddish-influenced preposition commonly heard among Orthodox Jews is "to." Examples include "Would you like to come to us for lunch?" and "We're going to Rabbi Hollander." Yiddish allows the cognate preposition, *tsu*, in constructions like these, while Standard American English would render them as "come to our house for lunch" and "going to Rabbi Hollander's (house)." This influence from Yiddish is not very salient to most Orthodox Jews, even BTs. This

TABLE 4.4

**Percentage of survey respondents who report
using Orthodox Jewish English phrases**

	Non-Jews (N=5,809)	Non-Orthodox Jews (N=22,951)	Modern Orthodox (N=1,078)	Orthodox [unspecified] (N=492)	Black Hat (N=239)
"She's staying by us"	10	21	50	54	62
"Are you coming to us for dinner?"	8	31	68	71	71

Note: N = number of respondents in each category

may be because the same preposition is used in the same slot in Standard English; the only difference in Orthodox Jewish English is the mention of a person as opposed to a person's house. In some sentences the only difference between Standard and Orthodox English is an apostrophe—inaudible, of course: "I'm going to the Hollanders(') for lunch." The survey found that Orthodox Jews are much more likely than non-Orthodox and non-Jews to use this construction (table 4.4).

Another Yiddish influence common in the English of Orthodox Jews is not using a preposition with statements of time (Ø indicates omitted preposition):

Her bus gets in Ø 10:15. (FFB woman)

Ø *Chol hamoed* I'm not going to work, *bli neder* [without a vow]. (FFB woman)

Next year Ø *Tisha b'Av* [mournful summer holiday], we will have another one. (FFB man)

I'm already frum Ø twenty years. (BT woman)

What are you doing Ø *Sukkos* [Feast of Tabernacles]? (BT man)

In general American English sentences like these would have prepositions. Of course there are other expressions of time that do not require a preposition, such as "I'll see you Wednesday" or "Next Thanksgiving we'll get a bigger turkey." But the sample sentences above would take prepositions; other people who discuss plans for these Jewish holidays—religious non-Orthodox Jews—would likely use prepositions: "during *chol hamoed*," "on *Tisha b'Av*," and "for *Sukkos*" (or *Sukkót*, the pronunciation based on Modern Hebrew that is more common among non-Orthodox Jews).

"Hold," "Learn"

I have identified five distinctive meanings of "hold" or "hold by" in Orthodox Jewish English, all of which are influenced by Yiddish *halt*:

1. hold/*halt* (be located along the spectrum of religious observance): "Who am I to judge where they're holding religiously?" "Where are you holding [in your trajectory toward greater religious observance]?"
2. hold/*halt* (be located in a text): "Where are we holding?" "We're holding here."
3. hold/*halt* (opine, practice [according to a legal opinion]): "He holds that, if it goes out, you don't have to relight it."[41] "The shul holds like that." "He holds like Reb Yochanan."
4. hold by/*halt bay* (accept, believe [in]): "We don't hold by the eruv." "If you hold by Reb Aron, . . ."
5. hold by/*halt bay* (be on the verge of): "With all that handshaking, I guess they're holding by an agreement."[42]

Similarly, the English word "learn" is used with one of the meanings of Yiddish *lern*: "study traditional texts," as in "Are we going to learn next week?" Both "learn" and "by" are commonly used by BTs.

Present Perfect Tense and "Already"

I heard a few frum men and women use the present tense where general American English would use the present perfect: "*I'm a BT* [I have been a BT] fifteen years, and I don't say that" and "I know someone *who's already frum* [who's been religious] for twenty years." This could be an influence from Yiddish, Israeli Hebrew, or both. Since I only heard a few BTs use this construction, I was surprised to read it in an e-mail from a recent BT who had just started studying in yeshiva: "I'm still struggling with the vocabulary, but I remind myself that it takes time, and *I'm only here* [I've only been here] a little over a week."

This construction is often used with the word "already," since in Yiddish *shoyn* (already) with a present-tense verb indicates the present perfect:[43]

Ikh	voyn	do	shoyn	akht	yor.
I	live	here	already	eight	years

I have lived here for eight years.

In addition, I noticed several speakers—BTs and FFBs, men and women—using "already" in other instances where Yiddish would but general American English would not. For example, one FFB rabbi used the following sentences in lectures, both of which would likely not include "already" in general American English:

That was *already* like a big thing *already*.

It's *already* considered conquered *already*.

Even someone speaking Yiddish would likely not use *shoyn* twice in sentences like these. This would indicate that the frequent use of "already" has become a marker of Orthodox identity. Therefore, it is not surprising that a few BTs do acquire this feature, as in a BT woman's "I came to it with more already" and a BT man's statement that pronouncing [o] as "[oy] is already like the next level."

Word Order: Adverbs, "For Sure"

Yiddish influence is also evident in Orthodox Jewish English word order. The following sentences place an adverbial phrase between a verb and its object, which is grammatical in Yiddish but sounds unusual in English:

You'll be stuck studying *all day* Torah. (FFB man)

I was able to pick up *pretty well* the lingo. (BT man)

The adverbial phrase "for sure" is also sometimes used in slots where general American English would likely not use it. In these examples, general American English would likely use "definitely" in the slot where "for sure" is or would place "for sure" at the end of each of these sentences.

If I were to go [to] a meeting at the yeshiva, I would *for sure* put stockings on. (BT woman)

If it's warping, it's *for sure* kosher. (FFB man)

You think he's *for sure* Orthodox? (FFB girl)

These sentences are emulative of Yiddish word order, as the adverbial phrase directly follows the verb.

"So"

Orthodox Jewish English uses the word "so" in environments where general American English does not:

"If I see someone who's using the wrong language, *so* I'll realize that they're just becoming frum"

"Since we don't have a Temple nowadays, *so* we don't do that."

This feature may be an influence from Israeli Hebrew, in which sentences like the following are quite common:

Im	*at*	*ohevet*	*oto,*	*az*	*tagidi*	*lo.*
If	you	like	him,	*so*	tell	him.

The extra connective "so" has become fairly common among BTs and FFBs—both those who have spent time in Israel and those who have not.

As the title of this chapter suggests, these are not the only distinctive grammatical structures and phrases in Orthodox Jewish English (e.g., "what to eat" means "something to eat").[44] The current list conveys a sense of the large role of Yiddish and secondary role of Israeli Hebrew in distinguishing the English grammar of Orthodox Jews, the subject of much discussion, especially among BTs (more on this below). Now we turn to English pronunciation.

English Pronunciation

For the most part, Orthodox Jews pronounce English like other Americans from their cities and regions. However, there is some influence from New York pronunciation around the country, based on familial and social ties with New Yorkers. For example, among Jewish survey respondents who are not from New York, Orthodox Jews (25 percent) are slightly more likely than non-Orthodox Jews (20 percent) to pronounce "horrible" and "orange" with an "are" sound (rather than "ore"). In addition, the Orthodox linguistic repertoire includes a number of distinctive pronunciations.

Devoicing of Consonants at the End of Words

If the vocal cords vibrate in the production of a consonant, that consonant is voiced. Voiced consonants include [g], [d], [b], [v], and [z], and their unvoiced correlates are [k], [t], [p], [f], and [s]. Some languages, including some dialects of Yiddish, change voiced consonants to their unvoiced counterparts ([g]=>[k], [d]=>[t]) when they come at the ends of words. This phenomenon is called word-final devoicing. In English, some Orthodox Jews devoice some of their consonants, yielding words like these:

round => rount

liarz => liars

big => bik

wrong => wrongk

The devoicing of [ng]—probably representing influence both from ancestral Yiddish and from more recent New York speech—is especially common, as in words like "eatingk," "shiningk," and "harvestingk."[45]

Release of [t] at the End of Words

In American English, a [t] at the end of a word can be released with a burst of air or can be cut off in the throat, or glottalized. While the glottalized version might sound normal, or unmarked, to most Americans, the released version is also common. Previous research on other populations—including girls who consider themselves nerds, gay men, science fiction fans, New York Reform Jews, and a Martha Stewart impersonator—shows that frequent [t] release is used by individuals who wish to be seen as intelligent, precise, or adamant.[46] In my quantitative study of [t] release among Orthodox Jews, I found that both men and women used higher rates when taking stances of authority or adamancy and that men released their [t]s more frequently overall, as they are expected to be more learned. Even though frequent [t] release is not unique to Orthodox Jews, it seems to indicate Orthodox identity, especially among men.[47]

Distinctive Pronunciation of Short [a]

Another distinctive feature is the pronunciation of short [a] when it occurs before [m] or [n], as in "Sam," "camp," and "candle." Most Americans pronounce this [a] higher in the mouth and more tense than when the same vowel occurs before other letters, as in "sag," "cap," and "caddy." This phenomenon, known as pre-nasal short [a] raising and tensing, is common among Americans, in contrast to English in Great Britain and elsewhere. However, some Orthodox Jews do not raise short [a] at all.[48] This Orthodox pronunciation seems to be centered in New York but is also common among the younger generation in other parts of the country.

Intonation: Chanting, Rise-Fall

When people study Talmud, they come across a problem: the text has little punctuation. A common remedy, practiced by Jews around the world, is to use pitch when reading aloud to indicate where phrases and sentences start and stop. The resulting patterns of intonation often sound like chants.[49] When American Orthodox Jews study Talmud, they tend to translate the Aramaic text into (Yiddish or) English, often carrying the chanting intonation over into the translation. Here is an example from FFB Rabbi Nussbaum's study session (capital letters indicate chanted high tone, italics indicate chanted mid tone, regular type indicates spoken intonation): "K'gon she'OY*rach shtey hashuros min hamizrach u*'MAY *riv*. The length of the two rows was from *east to* WE-*est*."[50] He starts saying the Aramaic phrase in spoken intonation, and then he begins chanting at the word *oyrach* (length). The beginning and end of the chant have high-to-mid contours, and the rest is chanted in a mid-tone monotone. The high-to-mid contour on the word *mayriv* (west) serves as a comma, indicating a phrase boundary. Rabbi Nussbaum then translates the Aramaic phrase with spoken intonation until "*east to* WE-*est*," which he chants with the same rise-fall contour as "*hamizrach u*'MAY*riv*." When he finishes reading the sentence a few minutes later, he ends it on an even lower pitch: the chanting correlate of a period.

As linguist Uriel Weinreich points out, chants like this, "deprived of their singing voice quality, are easily transferred by scholars from the reading of the Talmud to oral discussions about it, and thence to ordinary conversation, especially pilpulistic [hair-splitting] arguments on intellectual subjects."[51] Rise-fall chanting is especially common in if-then sentences that are intended as important points, such as the following from Rabbi Roseman: "He says that HAD *they not been rushed out of* EGypt, *they would have made their matzahs in Egypt it*SELF." Rabbi Roseman, a longtime BT teaching a class about Passover, renders the first three words in spoken intonation and chants the rest of the sentence. "Had," "Eg-," and "-self" are all given high tones ("self" also has a slight fall), while the rest of the words are chanted in a mid-monotone.

Although I rarely heard chanting intonation used outside of the study domain (except in imitations and performances of Orthodox speech), I often heard a remnant of it: "rise-fall" intonation. This contour is used at the end of introductory phrases and embedded clauses to indicate a "dramatized transition" between phrases.[52] Here are some examples from Orthodox Jews in New York and Philadelphia (capital letters indicate rise; italics indicate fall):

The yeSHIva, which is on [Harris] RO-*oad*, is . . .

By SAYING *that*, that would make other groups feel uncomfortable.

Years BA-*ack*, they would have maybe just had one video . . . So NO-*ow*, they make it a point to make . . . two videos.

Sometimes, especially in women's speech, the rise in pitch occurs over several words, or even the whole phrase, and the fall in pitch occurs only on the last stressed syllable of the phrase:

AS I WAS BECOMING *frum*, I got more interested in it.

IF YOU'RE GOING TO THE *store*, get me some milk.

Intonation is among the most salient features of Orthodox Jewish English. Several BTs, FFBs, and non-Orthodox Jews mentioned "tonality," "the lilt," or the "sing-song quality" when I told them I was researching Orthodox language. Imitations of Orthodox speech often involved chanting or other manipulations of intonation. And one FFB in New York said that he can often "spot a *frummie*" who calls into a radio talk show, based mostly on his or her intonation.

Speech Rate

Another linguistic feature many people mentioned is fast speech rate. Non-Orthodox Jews, BTs, and FFBs said that Orthodox Jews, especially FFBs, speak more quickly. One FFB said, "We think quickly" and noted that his non-Orthodox relatives talk more slowly. Related to this, there is an ideology that Orthodox speech—especially among young men in yeshiva—is more slurred and harder to understand. One BT described people she met from a yeshiva community: "You don't understand half the things they're saying, they talk so fast." And an FFB mother said that her sons came home from yeshiva speaking in a more "slurred" way, which annoyed her and her husband. She says, "It's become the style today for yeshiva boys to mumble. This has definitely been an issue for us." While I did not include speech rate in my analysis of recorded speech, it is clearly a topic of conversation in the community—and a potentially fruitful area for future research.

Hesitation Click

At the other end of the spectrum of salience is a linguistic feature I refer to as a *hesitation click*. It is used for self-repair, to express a negative reaction to the previous or current statement, or as a general hesitation marker. The click derives from Israeli Hebrew and is similar to the practice called "suck-teeth" or "kiss-teeth" in African diaspora communities.[53] I heard this click in all the Orthodox communities where I conducted research, as well as among some non-Orthodox Jews who have spent significant time in Israel. Here are some examples:

Self-repair:
"It's not common, but it's—[click] there are other subjects."
"But sometimes it's more—[click] I don't know how to explain it."

Disapproval:
"No, but it's not—[click] no, you don't understand."
"We just do. [click] It's not that girls can't."

Hesitation:
"What if there were—[click] If there were snakes and scorpions, they would have found them."
"It's not as, [click] you know, as choshuv."

I believe that the click is picked up by Americans who spend time in Israeli yeshivas, and when they return to the United States their friends and relatives pick it up from them. The click seems to be a very "contagious" linguistic feature, as many Orthodox Jews who have never spent time in Israel use it frequently. Aside from loanwords, this was the feature that I heard from the most speakers, FFBs and BTs.

Subtractive Features: Profanity and Loshon Hora

Orthodox speech styles differ from general American English not only in additive features such as loanwords, distinctive intonation, and Yiddish grammatical influence but also in features that are avoided. Aside from the prohibition
against loshon hora (gossip), Orthodox tradition, especially the Black Hat variety, also restricts curse words and sexual innuendoes. When I ask recent BTs
if they have changed the way they talk, they tend to discuss these subtractive
features before any additive ones, probably because of all the lectures they have
heard about "guarding the tongue" (see more on this in chapter 6).

Discourse of Distinctiveness

It is clear that a researcher can point out dozens of distinctive linguistic features
common in Orthodox communities. But are Orthodox Jews without linguistic
training aware of these features? What about BTs? Is "Orthodox Jewish English"
something people talk about?

Inside and outside the Orthodox community, there is a discourse about Orthodox language, generally referred to as "Yeshivish," but sometimes called "Yinglish" (a term also used by non-Orthodox Jews for the Yiddish-influenced English
of immigrants) or a "jargon."[54] In addition to the song "Yeshivishe Reid" (quoted at
the beginning of this chapter), community members mentioned Chaim Weiser's
scholarly and humorous book *Frumspeak: The First Dictionary of Yeshivish.* Women
told me that their brothers or sons speak Yeshivish, men said they sometimes
use Yeshivish, and BTs complained that they do not understand enough Yeshivish. People told me they associate a distinctly Orthodox English with men, with
yeshiva students, and with New Yorkers. People compared it to a medical jargon, to
the specialized terminology of lawyers, and to other ethnic dialects. An Orthodox
journalist in Lakewood wrote an article comparing Yeshivish to African American
English, citing my academic research on Jewish American English.[55] Similarly, one
rabbi said in a class at Ner Tamid, "I don't understand the people in the 'hood,
and they wouldn't understand my English, especially when I use a lot of Yiddish
words. . . . We have Yeshivish, and the people in the 'hood have Hoodish."

To help me better understand how Orthodox Jews view individual linguistic features, I investigated some of them with the experiment known as the
matched guise test (explained in chapter 2). For example, I tested BTs' and FFBs'
reactions to an instance of slang and mild obscenity using the word "sucks."
Participants in the experiment heard these sentences said by the same person,
mixed up with several other sentences:

A: This is really bad.
B: This totally sucks.

They were asked to indicate in writing whether the speaker of each sentence sounded Orthodox and FFB. This feature yielded very dramatic responses, larger than any of the other features tested: respondents felt that the speaker of sentence B is not likely to be Orthodox, although a few mentioned that she could be Modern Orthodox. Indeed, in my research among Modern Orthodox FFBs, I did hear "sucks," "screwed over," and other words that are considered obscene among Jews closer to the Black Hat end of the spectrum.

Although I learned a lot from participants' written responses, I sometimes learned even more by observing their reactions as they listened to the excerpts. While most respondents were familiar with the slang use of "sucks," a few FFBs asked me to replay that excerpt and seemed unaware of the word. When an FFB woman asked for clarification, her FFB husband repeated, "This totally sucks," apparently not knowing the obscene connotations. Their teenage daughter giggled and did not repeat the word. In discussions with me after the matched guise test, most respondents avoided saying "sucks," referring to it instead as the "curse word" or "bad word." A few BTs did say it, which is not surprising considering their responses on the matched guise test. (BTs ranked the "sucks" stimulus more likely to be BT at a slightly greater rate than FFBs did.)

Another feature I tested with this experiment is the Yiddish-influenced "hold":

A: OK, so where are we holding?
B: OK, so where did we leave off?

The experiment showed that many people do consider this "hold" to be an Orthodox marker. For the question "Do you think the speaker is Orthodox?" many BTs and FFBs rated A higher than B, but BTs (69 percent) were more likely than FFBs to do so (43 percent).[56] As I explain below, BTs tend to notice "hold" and often consider it bad grammar, while some FFBs do not realize its nonstandard status.

A feature that turned out to have low salience on the matched guise test is the "so" that is likely influenced by Israeli Hebrew:

A: Since they were here early, so they can start now.
B: Since they were here early, they can start now.

Some respondents noted that A was more likely to be Orthodox than B, but the percentage was much lower than for other features. The average difference in responses between A and B was not significantly different from the dummy questions, and there was no significant difference between BTs and FFBs. These experiment results are corroborated by my observations: I rarely heard people discuss this sentence-internal "so" as an Orthodox feature (although some did mention frequent use of "so" at the beginning of sentences).

TABLE 4.5
Distinctive features of Orthodox Jewish English

Distinctive feature	Likely source	Survey results: reported use greater among Orthodox	Do people discuss it or use it in imitations?	Matched guise results: Higher numbers = more awareness
Loanwords	Textual Hebrew, Aramaic, Yiddish	yes**	yes	
Phrasal verbs	Yiddish	yes**	no	0.12
"should"	Yiddish	yes*	no	
"by"	Yiddish	yes**	yes	0.39*
"to"	Yiddish	yes**	no	0.51**
Preposition Ø	Yiddish		no	
"hold"	Yiddish		yes	0.63**
"learn"	Yiddish	yes**	yes	
Present perfect	Yiddish	yes**	no	
"already"	Yiddish	yes**	no	
Adverb order	Yiddish		no	
"for sure"	Yiddish		no	
Connective "so"	Israeli Hebrew		no	0.25
Devoicing	Yiddish		no	0.04
Release of [t]	Learnedness		no	0.25
Low short [a]	New York		no	
Rise-fall intonation	Yiddish, Talmud		yes	0.25
Hesitation click	Israeli Hebrew		no	0.12
Avoid gossip	Jewish law		yes	
Avoid obscenity	Jewish law		yes	0.91**

Note: Significance is based on chi-square tests (column three) and paired samples two-tailed t-tests (column five).

* = significant at the *p*<.05 level; ** = significant at the *p*<.01 level; blank = not tested

In determining how aware people are of individual linguistic features, we can learn a good deal from observations and interviews, as well as from the matched guise experiment. Table 4.5 lists all the features discussed above, including their likely sources, data from the 2008 survey comparing reported use by Orthodox and non-Orthodox Jews, and awareness of the features based on discourse/imitations and the matched guise test.

As the survey results in column three indicate, Orthodox Jews are more likely than non-Orthodox Jews to report using all features tested. The fourth and fifth columns focus on awareness of the linguistic features. Column four, based on my ethnographic observations and interviews in Milldale, indicates whether BTs and FFBs discussed features overtly or used them in performances and imitations of Orthodox speech. Column five presents results from the matched guise test about whether the speaker sounds Orthodox when using each of these features.[57] For the most part, these two columns correlate with each other: features people talk about are more likely to be noticed in the matched guise experiment.[58] These differences in salience are important to the analysis of BTs. If some features are noticed and discussed more, then BTs may have stronger views about them, as well as greater ease learning them.

In addition to differences in salience, ethnographic observation indicated that there is a wide range of attitudes about these linguistic features. When I mention Orthodox language to BTs and FFBs, reactions include both smiles and grimaces, sometimes from the same people. Orthodox Jews express fondness for this distinctively Jewish language variety and embarrassment about the use of what some call "bad grammar." Variation in attitudes, as well as in language use, is related to several factors, including BTs' feelings of pride or shame about their non-Orthodox past, as I explain in chapter 6. Another factor, perhaps more significant, is how individuals wish to position themselves along the Modern Orthodox to Black Hat continuum, the subject of the next chapter.

5

"*Torah* or *Toyrah*"

Language and the Modern Orthodox
to Black Hat Continuum

When Orthodox Jews create a profile on the popular online matchmaking service Frumster.com, they must select a category that describes their religiosity. These categories include four that are seen as existing on a continuum from least to most strict in observance and least to most distinct from general American society: Modern Orthodox Liberal, Modern Orthodox *Machmir* (strict), Yeshivish Modern, and Yeshivish Black Hat. One of the questions Frumster participants are asked is: "What does [this category] mean to you?" Responses vary widely, mentioning individuals' practices of kashrus and negia, specific yeshivas in Israel, New York, Baltimore, and elsewhere, and attitudes toward secular education. Some on the Black Hat end of the spectrum mention *daas torah*, the notion that rabbis with expertise in traditional texts have a high level of wisdom on life matters. And some on the Modern Orthodox end of the spectrum mention the importance of being part of the secular world by attending concerts and movies.

In all categories a common response includes something about serving God or following commandments. For example, a woman who identifies as Modern Orthodox Liberal defines that as "Shomer Shabbat, Kashrut, Baal Chesed" (observing Sabbath, dietary laws, and doer of good deeds). And a man who identifies as Yeshivish Black Hat defines that as "Toras Chaim and Ahavas Chesed" (living Torah and love of good deeds). These two responses are similar in content, but they differ in form. The Modern Orthodox respondent, a woman who identifies her ethnicity as Ashkenazi, uses Sephardi or Israeli pronunciation (Shabbat, kashrut), while the Black Hat respondent, a man who identifies his ethnicity as "Sephardi (Moroccan/North African)," uses Ashkenazi pronunciation (Toras, Ahavas). These two Orthodox Jews may have some similarities in their views of religious observance, and they both decided to use Hebrew loanwords in their response. But they made different choices in how to render the Hebrew letter ת (thaw/tav). These choices were not in line with their ancestral origins but rather with their self-reported location on the continuum from Modern Orthodox Liberal to Yeshivish Black Hat.

This small example shows the importance of language—in consort with beliefs, observance, and other cultural practices—in the presentation and perception of Orthodox identities. FFBs use subtle differences in pronunciation, word choice, and grammar to indicate their location along the Modern Orthodox to Black Hat continuum. When newcomers become Orthodox, they also participate in this system of linguistic self-identification.

The Orthodox Continuum

The continuum is well known not only in community discourse, as the Frumster example indicates, but also in scholarhip.[1] Researchers explain how Orthodox Jews compare themselves to other Orthodox Jews based on the stringency of their observance and their openness toward non-Orthodox and non-Jewish society and culture. Ayala Fader explains how the continuum figures prominently in the discourse of Hasidic Jews: "The use of modern as a marker of difference focuses on activities or objects which blur the borders separating Jews from gentiles. This is particularly relevant for and evident in the presentation of bodies and exposure of minds. It is, thus, particularly around issues of modest dress and access to certain types of media, literature or other forms of knowledge that different kinds of Jews may be located on a continuum which spans modern to the most *frim*, religious."[2] The Bobov and other Hasidim she worked with position themselves not quite on the right end of the continuum: they see themselves as more "with it" than the "*nebby*" (nerdy) Satmar Hasidim.[3] We also see similar discourse on the other end of the continuum. Samuel Heilman's study *Synagogue Life* details how members of a Modern Orthodox synagogue use this spectrum to compare themselves to the other Jews in their neighborhood. They see themselves as more "frum" than Reform and Conservative Jews and less "crazy" than more traditional Yeshiva Jews.[4]

The Orthodox Jews I met in my various research sites also referenced this continuum. In the (mostly Modern) Orthodox group at Columbia University, students talked about marginal community members being toward the right end of the spectrum by using the term "black hat," or just "black": "Sometimes we get a few black-hatters" or "They were more black than Modern Orthodox." A principal of a school in which teachers and administrators are Chabad Hasidim contrasted his community with a Modern Orthodox one. He said, "We've been referred to in the press as Ultra-Orthodox," marking that label as a term he would not use on his own, but also indicating that he wished an outsider to associate his community with the Black Hat end of the spectrum. Many non-Hasidic Jews see Hasidim as more strict and farther to the right within the continuum. For example, one frum blogger describes a particular school as "super right wing/yeshivish/no denim out of school/a step away from chassidish."[5]

In the Milldale community of Philadelphia, most people see themselves as somewhere in the middle of this continuum. One man says he is "not Modern Orthodox, not Yeshivish, but somewhere in the middle," and a woman says she is "between Modern Orthodox and frummer." Another woman says that neighborhood X is "too Modern," neighborhood Y is "too Yeshivish," and Z, where she chose to live, is in the middle. In short, the ends of the Modern Orthodox to Black Hat spectrum are poles of reference, even if some people are reluctant to use them as labels for themselves. If members of the Milldale community had to select a category on Frumster.com (some of them have!), I suspect that most would select Yeshivish Modern, and a few might select Modern Orthodox Machmir or Yeshivish Black Hat.

Two major factors in how this continuum is constructed are halacha and gender separation.[6] All Orthodox Jews consider halacha to be binding, but Black Hat Jews interpret many laws more strictly. The more *chumras* (stringencies) a Jew follows, the closer he or she generally is to the Black Hat pole. For example, Modern Orthodox Jews tend to drink any milk, whether or not it has a *hechsher* (rabbinic seal of kosher food), while many Black Hat Jews drink only milk that is certified as *Cholov Yisroel* (literally "milk of Israel," supervised by Jews from cow to carton). Similarly, Jews toward the Black Hat end of the continuum are stricter about gender separation: men and women are divided by a mechitzah not only at shul (as among Modern Orthodox) but also at weddings and other public events.[7]

In addition to halachic and gender issues, the continuum also manifests in cultural practices. Heilman points to differences in how people move their bodies during prayer: Modern Orthodox Jews *shuckle* (also spelled *shokel*), or sway, less vigorously than Haredim.[8] In the early 1970s, when Heilman conducted his fieldwork, the young sons of Modern Orthodox synagogue members—educated by more traditional teachers—shuckled differently than their fathers: "It is not surprising to see, next to a slowly swaying father, a rapidly rocking son." However, he goes on to say, "as the boy matures and locates himself on the spectrum of Orthodox life," his shuckling may change in intensity. "For the boy who does not leave home for a life in the yeshiva, the shokeling soon approximates that of his father. The boy who does leave home for the yeshiva, however, may establish for himself a pendulation much more vigorous than his father's."[9] Those closer to the Black Hat side of the continuum who shuckle more intensely indicate not only their fervor in prayer but also their distinctness from Orthodox Jews closer to the Modern pole.

Another difference that has received attention in previous literature is appearance.[10] Men on the Black Hat end of the spectrum tend to wear dark suits (long *kapotes* [caftans] for Hasidim), white collar shirts, black velvet yarmulkes, black hats, and (especially among Hasidim) long beards—a look influenced by the norms of traditional Jews in prewar Eastern Europe. Men on the Modern Orthodox end tend to appear more American, wearing more casual clothing, sporting short beards or clean shaves, and covering their heads with the less conspicuous knit yarmulke or baseball cap. Women in Black Hat communities tend to wear high necklines, long sleeves, long skirts, and socks or stockings, while Modern Orthodox women are less strict about these requirements, sometimes even wearing pants. The situation is similar with hair coverings for married women: many Black Hat women cover their hair with a sheitel, while Modern Orthodox women are more likely to cover their hair with a hat or scarf or sometimes not at all. Those who identify somewhere in between the two poles use various combinations of these visual manifestations of tznius (modesty) and tradition to indicate their location along the Orthodox spectrum. The results are that Black Hat Jews tend to look more distinct from general American society, while Modern Orthodox Jews can often blend in with their non-Orthodox neighbors.

Some quantitative evidence for the importance of appearance in the construction of the continuum comes from my study of Frumster.com. With permission from Frumster staff, I gathered information on two hundred

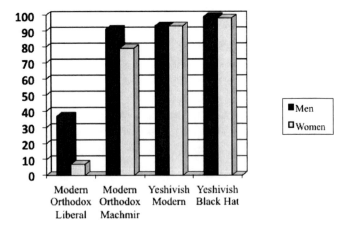

FIGURE 5.1. Percentage of Orthodox men who wear *tzitzis* daily; percentage of Orthodox women who plan to fully cover their hair when they marry

Source: Author's analysis of responses on Frumster.com: 795 men, 787 women.

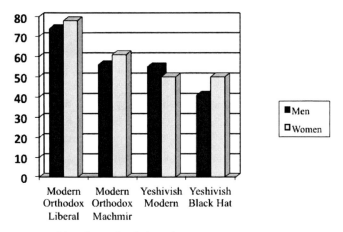

FIGURE 5.2. FFBs with at least a bachelor's degree

Source: Author's analysis of responses on Frumster.com: 464 men, 489 women

participants in each of eight categories: men and women who are Modern Orthodox Liberal, Modern Orthodox Machmir, Yeshivish Modern, and Yeshivish Black Hat. I correlated their self-selected categories with their responses to various questions. As figure 5.1 shows, men toward the right end of the continuum are more likely to wear the ritual fringes known as tzitzis, and women toward the right end of the continuum are more likely to plan to cover their hair when they marry.[11]

In these instances, the major difference is between Modern Orthodox Liberal and the other categories. This is the case in several areas of distinction. A teacher in a Modern Orthodox yeshiva high school in Riverdale, New York, writes: "Whenever I ask my students whether they feel that they are more fundamentally like a non-Jewish Horace Mann student a few blocks away, or a Hasidic teenager in Williamsburg, they invariably tell me that they are much more like a non-Jewish prep school student whose concerns and pressing issues are most similar to their own than they are to their fellow Orthodox Jew."[12]

Another important aspect of this continuum is orientation toward secular education.[13] Those toward the Modern Orthodox pole tend to attend secular universities, especially ones that have kosher facilities and opportunities for Orthodox prayer and study. The number of Black Hat Jews who pursue secular education is much smaller, as figure 5.2 demonstrates among Frumster participants (a group probably skewed toward secular education). Among those who identify as Yeshivish Black Hat, women are more likely than men to pursue higher education. This is because of the greater tendency among Black Hat men to be full-time learners in a yeshiva or kollel, supported in part by their working wives.[14]

Frumster.com cannot burden site users with a comprehensive list of questions that relate to differences between Modern Orthodox and Black Hat Jews. But if it did, it might also ask about many of the practices described in chapter 3, such as preferences for names, cuisine, music, art, and leisure activities like TV and movies. Those closer to the Black Hat pole tend to prefer distinctly Jewish practices (often with Eastern European influence), while those closer to the Modern Orthodox pole tend to participate more in secular American culture.

Despite these tendencies, location along the continuum does not always match cultural practices. As figures 5.1 and 5.2 suggest, there are Jews who watch TV and have advanced degrees but still consider themselves Black Hat, and there are some who identify with the label Modern Orthodox Liberal but always wear tzitzis or cover their hair when they marry. In addition, some people participate more in Black Hat cultural practices when they are with their Black Hat friends and less elsewhere, such as in their non-Jewish workplace.[15] Finally, many frum Jews reject labels like these and would not feel comfortable being boxed into a section of a continuum (for this reason, Frumster.com created a catch-all category, "shomer mitzvot"). Even so, people in the know tend to make assumptions about Jews' religiosity and identity based on how they dress, interact with secular culture, and otherwise present themselves to the world.

Language and the Continuum

In addition to these religious and cultural practices, language plays a major role in the construction of the Modern to Black Hat continuum. As sociologist Charles Liebman found in the 1960s, "modernist" and "sectarian" Orthodox schools differed in their language of instruction (Yiddish, Hebrew, or English) and in their pronunciation of Hebrew (Ashkenazi or Israeli).[16] These trends continue today. In my research on Frumster.com, I found that participants toward the Black Hat pole are more likely to report Yiddish knowledge, and this trend is starker among men (figure 5.3). The gender differences in Yiddish knowledge relate to differences in education, as many men's yeshivas use Yiddish for translation of texts or general instruction, while many women's seminaries do not. The gender differences in Yiddish knowledge and use are even greater in Hasidic communities.[17]

There is also a difference in attitudes toward Yiddish. Many Orthodox Jews who see themselves as closer to the Modern pole consider Yiddish to be old-fashioned, while many closer to the Black Hat pole (especially but not only those descended from Yiddish speakers) consider it warm and heimish. As discussed

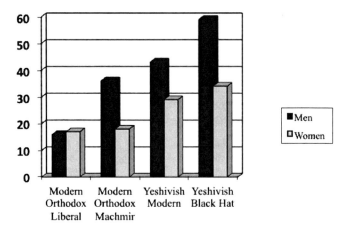

FIGURE 5.3. Percentage of respondents who list Yiddish as one of the languages they speak

Source: Author's analysis of responses on Frumster.com: 758 women, 751 men

in chapter 4, conflicting ideologies about Yiddish exist in frum communities, even within individuals. But in general, those who have more negative attitudes toward Yiddish tend to align themselves closer to the Modern Orthodox pole.

A combination of exposure and attitudes leads to a continuum of language use (figure 5.4): those closer to the Modern Orthodox pole use more Israeli Hebrew pronunciation and English that sounds more like that of other Americans, and those toward the Black Hat pole use more Ashkenazi Hebrew pronunciation and Yiddish influences, leading to speech sometimes referred to as "Yeshivish." Community members discuss this continuum, referencing specific linguistic features, such as "I want that you should . . ." and the pronunciation of [o] as [oy]. For example, Shana, a recent BT who wears short sleeves and low necklines and aligns herself closer to Modern Orthodox than Black Hat, teased her friend Tamar for using the word *tzniusdik* ("modest"; many Orthodox Jews, especially BTs and those toward the Modern Orthodox pole, use *tznius* without the Yiddish adjectival suffix -*dik*). Shana shook her by the shoulders playfully and said, "You're starting to sound Yeshivish!" Shana's response was based on

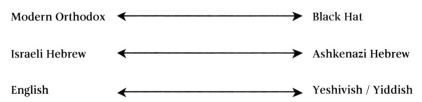

FIGURE 5.4. Linguistic manifestation of the Orthodox continuum

her sense that Tamar was moving toward the Black Hat pole, evidenced not only by her language but also by her concern with Haredi notions of modesty.

In the survey I conducted with Steven M. Cohen, we asked several questions about Hebrew, Aramaic, and Yiddish loanwords, Hebrew pronunciation, and Yiddish grammatical constructions. For several of the variables, respondents who identified as Modern Orthodox differed significantly from those who identified with the survey's category "Black Hat / Yeshivish or Chassidish" (table 5.1). Some of these variables differ most between Orthodox and non-Orthodox (such as "chas v'shalom"), and others differ most between Black Hat and everyone else (such as "I'm living here ten years already"). But they all

TABLE 5.1

Percentage of survey respondents who report using
Orthodox Jewish English loanwords and phrases

	Reform (N=8,986)	Conservative (N=8,305)	Modern Orthodox (N=1,083)	Orthodox [unspecified] (N=494)	Black Hat / Yeshivish or Chassidish (N=239)
chas v'shalom (God forbid)	7	16	65	76	78
takeh (really)	18	27	36	43	55
l'chatchila (before the fact)	2	5	27	45	49
PAY-sach (vs. PEH-sach or Passover)	56	61	65	74	79
gmar cha-SEE-mah TO-vah	1	2	14	32	42
"She's staying by us"	18	25	50	54	62
"I'm living here ten years already"	21	24	29	27	44
"What do we learn out from this?"	6	8	21	29	40
"She has what to say"	9	12	23	27	28

show that language is an important element in how Orthodox Jews indicate to others their location along the Modern Orthodox to Black Hat continuum. As Orthodox journalist Jerry Hellman puts it, "Any fluent Yeshivish speaker will automatically be able to discern from a person's intonation and accent in pronouncing Yeshivish words which 'label' he is associated with and which community he stems from."[18]

To further illustrate this linguistic continuum, I present a case study of the language of "learning," or the study of traditional texts, especially Talmud. This activity, which many men participate in weekly or even daily, offers a fine opportunity for a researcher to record and analyze Orthodox language use among pairs and small groups of men. While I did not analyze women's language in this systematic way, qualitative data presented in others chapters indicates that they also contribute their linguistic variation to the construction of the Modern Orthodox to Black Hat continuum.

At the Talmud learning circles that Heilman observed in the United States and Israel, the men shift among Hebrew, Aramaic, Yiddish, English, and combinations thereof. Their language choices show their simultaneous connections to various communities: the American or Israeli societies where they live, the Eastern Europe of their recent ancestors, and the ancient and medieval rabbinic society whose texts they are reading. Heilman shows how the Haredi circle in Israel uses much more chanting from the Gemora and less translation, and the little discussion they do have is mostly in Yiddish. The Modern Orthodox circle in the United States uses some chanting but much more explanation in Yiddish-laced English.[19]

In my fieldwork among Orthodox Jews, I observed a similar alternation among the four languages and a similar spectrum of textual chanting and English use. In addition to these larger differences in language use, I found that men use subtle variation within these languages to position themselves along the Modern to Black Hat continuum. In this section, I present data from several chavrusa (one-on-one) learning sessions I recorded in Philadelphia. First I discuss FFBs, and then I discuss recent and longtime BTs.

FFBs and the Language of Learning

Avrum grew up attending a Modern Orthodox yeshiva, and he still wears a knit kipah and no black hat or beard. Now in his twenties, he lives in the downtown area, where the small Orthodox community is quite modern and there is not yet an eruv (boundary enabling observant Jews to carry on Shabbos). He attends services at the Ner Tamid Center and learns there weekly with Andrew, a recent BT, partly to volunteer in a teacher role and partly to keep up his own learning. Mr. Weisman and Rabbi Nussbaum are both middle-aged FFBs who live in Milldale and daven and learn at the Black Hat congregation Shomrei

Emunah. They both wear black velvet kipahs and black hats. Based on their facial hair—Nussbaum has a long beard and Weisman is clean-shaven—we would expect that Nussbaum identifies closer to the Black Hat pole than Weisman does. While I did not ask them to classify themselves according to the Frumster labels, based on their choices, we can speculate about which labels they would select: Avrum—Modern Orthodox Liberal, Weisman—Yeshivish Modern, and Nussbaum—Yeshivish Black Hat. By analyzing their linguistic performance, we can see a correlation with their choices in appearance and residence (table 5.2).

Yiddish-Influenced English

In chapter 4, I enumerated a number of Yiddish grammatical influences that Orthodox Jews use within English, including "We *learn out* from this," "We're eating *by* them," and "He *holds* like Reb Meir." When we count the three FFBs' Yiddish grammatical influences and divide by their total word counts, we see an ascending pattern that correlates with their other practices (table 5.2).

Hebrew Pronunciation

The second area of analysis is the pronunciation of Hebrew and Aramaic—in both the WHE (stand-alone Hebrew) and the MHE (loanwords used within English). American Jews draw primarily from two major systems of pronunciation, the Israeli system and the Ashkenazi system. The Ashkenazi system was used by Yiddish-speaking Jews in Eastern Europe, and the contemporary Israeli system

TABLE 5.2

Self-presentation of three FFBs

	Avrum	Weisman	Rabbi Nussbaum
Community they live in	Non-Orthodox	Milldale	Milldale
Kipah	Knit	Black velvet	Black velvet
Beard	No	No	Long
Black hat	No	Yes	Yes
Percentage of Yiddish grammatical features / word count	0.24	0.50	0.62
Percentage [th] pronounced [s]	63	100	100
Percentage [o] pronounced [oy]	0	0	78

TABLE 5.3

Pronunciation differences between Israeli and Ashkenazi Hebrew

	Israeli	Ashkenazi
1. Biblical [th]	[t]	[s]
2. Stressed [o]	[o]	[oy] ~ [uhy]
3. Stress	Generally ultimate	Generally penultimate
4. Kamats vowel	[a]	[o] ~ [uh]
5. Tsere vowel	[eh]	[ey]

is based on Sephardi norms with some influence from Ashkenazi pronunciation. Table 5.3 shows the five major differences between these systems.

American Jews make choices (at varying levels of consciousness) between these two systems, and these choices are influenced by educational institutions. Most American Jewish schools used the Ashkenazi system until the birth of the State of Israel in the mid-twentieth century. Gradually over the next few decades, most non-Orthodox schools and some Zionist Modern Orthodox schools switched to the Israeli pronunciation norms, either through an ideologically driven policy change or because of an influx of Israeli-born Hebrew teachers.[20] Today, Modern Orthodox schools tend to teach Israeli Hebrew pronunciation, and other Orthodox schools generally teach the Ashkenazi system. This split is influenced by divergent ideologies about Israel and Eastern Europe. The close connection Modern Orthodox Jews have to the State of Israel results in a sense that Israeli pronunciation is a norm to strive for, and the close connection that (Ashkenazi) Black Hat Jews have to prewar Europe results in their preference for Ashkenazi pronunciation. Of course, many Black Hat Jews also have strong ties to Israel, and many Modern Orthodox Jews also have strong ties to Eastern Europe. But the association between Eastern Europe and traditionalism leads Black Hat Jews, with their traditionalist orientation, to value Ashkenazi variants over Modern Israeli ones.

One of the most salient aspects of Orthodox variation is the realization of the Hebrew letter ת (thaw), which was pronounced [th] in antiquity. The contemporary Israeli Hebrew variant is [t], and the Ashkenazi variant is [s], as in words like *Sukkos/Sukkot* and *gashmius/gashmiut*. The use of [s] or [t] is by no means categorical. Sociolinguist Aliza Sacknowitz compared members of two Orthodox congregations in suburban Maryland, "Torah Congregation," which is closer to the Modern Orthodox end of the continuum, and "Darchei Shalom," which is closer to the Black Hat pole. She found that members of Torah

Congregation used the Ashkenazi [s] 40 percent of the time, compared to 72 percent among members of Darchei Shalom.[21] Similarly, I found that Modern Orthodox students at Columbia University often alternated between [t] and [s]. Examples include *Shabbos* ~ *Shabbat, shacharis* ~ *shacharit* (morning prayers), and *chossen* ~ *chatan* (groom), often spoken by the same person, sometimes even in the same conversation. Many of these Modern Orthodox Jews expressed an ideology that Israeli pronunciation is the norm to emulate but recognized that they sometimes used Ashkenazi [s].[22]

On the other hand, those to the middle and right of the Orthodox continuum are expected to and generally do say [s]. In the Black Hat-leaning Milldale community, I heard very few people express a desire to emulate Israeli phonology. The norm is [s], and I even heard people correct the use of [t], such as an FFB woman suggesting that a BT say "*gmar chasíma tóva*" rather than "*gmar chatimá tová*." Another woman teaching a small class in Milldale was reading aloud from a Jewish English book that included transliterated Hebrew words written with the [t]. But she read them with [s], as in "*taharas*" when the book said "*taharat*" (purity). Among the FFBs whose study sessions I recorded, only Avrum—the one closest to the Modern Orthodox pole—used some [t]. Weisman and Nussbaum both used only [s] (table 5.2).

Another salient phonological variable is the stressed [o] vowel in Hebrew and Aramaic words. This vowel can be realized as [o] or [oy], as in the title of this chapter, *Torah* versus *Toyrah*, or in *bodek* versus *boydek* (inspect) and *machloket* versus *machloykes* (disagreement). The [oy] variant is strongly associated with Jews near the Black Hat pole, especially Hasidim, as well as with FFBs and men. Aside from the word *shkoyach* (good job/thank you, as opposed to *shkoach* or the less reduced form *yasher koach*), most of the tokens of [oy] I heard in all my studies were from FFB men on the Black Hat side of the spectrum. In the FFB chavrusa data, the only speaker to use the [oy] vowel was Nussbaum, the one with the long beard (table 5.2).

This very small sample of Modern Orthodox and Black Hat FFBs shows how language variation helps to constitute individuals' location along the Orthodox continuum. A question that arises, however, is to what extent individuals say *Toyrah* or *Shabbat* because those are the forms they learned as children or because they are making active choices as adults. While I cannot answer this question for individuals who remain in the same location along the continuum, I can offer data on how Jews who shift over time, including BTs, change their linguistic performance.

All Orthodox Jews have some sense of where they stand along the continuum between Modern Orthodox and Black Hat. For many, their location changes over time as they proceed through life stages. A number of the Modern Orthodox Columbia University undergraduates in my study in the 1990s were in the process of moving to the left or right religiously. Some who expressed a desire to move away from the Modern pole transferred to Yeshiva University (Yeshiva College for men or Stern College for women) after a year or two at Columbia or even dropped out of college in favor of full-time yeshiva study. Others shifted in the opposite direction: they came to Columbia wearing long skirts and planning to cover their hair when they marry, and a few years later they switched to pants and now keep their hair uncovered except when they attend their Modern Orthodox synagogues. In Milldale, there are formerly Modern Orthodox Jews who shifted toward the Black Hat pole. And while some parents are concerned about their children becoming less frum, others complain about their children rejecting their home traditions in favor of their more "Yeshivish" teachers' textually based traditions.[23]

Ba'alei Teshuva and the Language of Learning

If Jews who grew up Orthodox change their location along the continuum, then BTs make even more dramatic changes. As these newcomers join the ranks of Orthodoxy, they tend to learn that they necessarily position themselves along the Modern to Black Hat continuum—whether they want to or not—through their religious observance, social interactions, affiliations, and cultural practices. What do BTs change about their language, and how do those changes relate to their desired location along the continuum?

The data in this section come from the recorded study sessions of five BT men who have been Orthodox for varying amounts of time, ranging from one and a half to thirty-two years (table 5.4). The visual practices and living choices of these five BTs correlate with the amount of time they have been Orthodox. This is partly because some BTs take on new practices gradually. At the time of this study, Andrew was a Peripheral BT living in the downtown area; since then he has attended yeshiva, moved to a Yeshivish community, and begun to wear a black hat on Shabbos. Similarly, Joseph was in graduate school during the time of the study and chose to live in the Modern Orthodox community near campus rather than commute over a half-hour from one of the Black Hat neighborhoods. It is important to note that the data presented here represent a snapshot in time, and these men's symbolic practices—including language—may have changed in the years since the study. Even so, at the time of the research, these five men had staked out at least temporary locations on the Orthodox spectrum. Using the data in table 5.4, including their linguistic variation, we might speculate about which Frumster categories each BT would select: Andrew—Modern Orthodox Machmir; Joseph and David—Yeshivish Modern; and Jacob and Rabbi Fischer—Yeshivish Black Hat.

TABLE 5.4

Self-presentation of five BTs

BTs	Andrew	Joseph	David	Jacob	Rabbi Fischer
Years Orthodox	1.5	5	7	10	32
BT stage	Peripheral	Yeshiva	Yeshiva	Yeshiva	Yeshiva
Community they live in	Non-Orthodox	Modern Orthodox	Mixed Orthodox	Milldale	Milldale
Kipah	black velvet	black velvet	black velvet	black velvet	black velvet
Beard	no	no	short	long	long
Black hat	no	no	only on Shabbos	yes	yes
Percent of Yiddish grammatical features / word count	0.18	0.37	0.34	0.40	0.73
Percent [th] pronounced [s]	36	100	100	100	100
Percent [o] pronounced [oy]	0	0	0	24	8

Yiddish-Influenced English (BTs)

The BTs' use of Yiddish grammatical influences within English varies even more than the FFBs', ranging from 0.18 percent to 0.73 percent of their total word count (table 5.4). This variable correlates not only with their location along the continuum but also with the time they have spent in the community. This is partly because the longer they have been involved with Orthodox Jews the more they have been exposed to these Yiddish influences. But another important factor is how comfortable they feel using constructions like "staying by them" and "Where are you holding?" Some BTs, especially recent ones like Andrew, consciously avoid phrases that they consider grammatically incorrect (more on this in chapter 6). Others, like Jacob and Rabbi Fischer, feel very comfortable using them. Note that Rabbi Fischer uses even more Yiddish grammatical influences than the FFBs discussed above. Many years ago, he made a decision to become a Black Hat Orthodox Jew. He gradually took on the religious and cultural practices of his community, and over thirty years later he looks, acts, and speaks so much like his FFB peers that many in his community assume that he grew up frum.

Hebrew Pronunciation (BTs)

When we turn to pronunciation, we see that ideology plays a similar role. Even though four of the five BTs grew up attending Hebrew schools where the letter *thaw* was pronounced [t] (Jacob grew up secular with no Hebrew education), all but Andrew now use only [s] (Andrew used 36 percent [s] in these recordings). These BTs seem to have made conscious decisions to switch from [t] to [s], because that is the norm in the communities they have chosen. Even Joseph, who lives among Modern Orthodox Jews who use both [t] and [s], used only [s] both in his study session and in his conversations that I observed. By choosing to use [s], and by wearing a black velvet kipah while some of his friends wear colorful knit ones, he indicates to others that he positions himself to the right of Modern Orthodoxy. The same is true for David, who lives in a mixed Modern and Black Hat community, where both variants are common. Both David and Joseph consider themselves in between Modern and Black Hat, and their use of only [s] signals to others that they are not Modern Orthodox.

At the time of this study, Andrew had been Orthodox for only one and a half years, but he had begun to transition from [t] to [s]. He chose to wear a black velvet kipah, like his Yeshivish friends in Milldale. But his low percentage of [s] would seem to indicate that he wanted to be seen as closer to the Modern Orthodox pole. The fact that he used any [s] at all—when just two years earlier he used only [t] when singing Hebrew prayers in his family's Reform temple—shows that he wished to identify to some extent with those to the right of Modern Orthodoxy. His mixed use of this variable was influenced by his learning partner, Avrum, who used 63 percent [s]. Several years after I recorded his study sessions, Andrew reports that he uses only [s]. His variable use of [s] and [t] in 2002 show not only his desired location on the spectrum but also a transitional phase in his acquisition of new ways of speaking.[24]

Even though Andrew and Avrum use both [s] and [t], they still refer to an ideology that [s] is more appropriate. Once Avrum was teaching Andrew the Aramaic word *hasam* (there), and he said, "*Hatam* or *hasam*. They'd never say *hatam*. It's *hasam*." "They" apparently refers to Orthodox Jews learning Gemora in a yeshiva, and by not using "we," Avrum distances himself from them. Interestingly, Avrum never says this about a Hebrew word, and both he and Andrew often use [t] in Hebrew words, especially in suffixes like "*ot*" and "*tam*." But Avrum clearly finds it more appropriate to use [s], the Yiddish variant, with Aramaic words.

The next variable shows a similar influence from ideology. In this sample, the only BTs who sometimes use [oy] are Jacob and Rabbi Fischer.[25] Jacob and

Rabbi Fischer are the two BTs who have long beards and live in Milldale. Using a combination of [oy] and [o] for this Hebrew vowel is part of how they indicate their location closer to the Black Hat side of the continuum. Andrew, Joseph, and David use only [o], never [oy]. All three of them grew up using the [o] variant in Reform or Conservative Hebrew school. When they became involved with Orthodox communities they were exposed to both the [o] and [oy] variants. Unlike Jacob and Rabbi Fischer, they chose not to use [oy], because, as they report, they associate it with Black Hat Orthodoxy and with FFBs.

David never used [oy] in his learning session or in other conversations, except when he spontaneously imitated Yeshivish speech for me. In this brief performance, he used the scratchy voice of an old man, a periphrastic verb (to be *mechabed,* "honor"), and the word *oylam* (in this case meaning "audience"). He associates [oy] with Yeshivish Jews, and he does not identify with that group. Similarly, I never heard Joseph use [oy] in his social conversations or study sessions. When I asked him if he ever uses [oy] in words like *Toyrah,* he said, "No, [oy] is already like the next level. . . . People who say *Toyrah* are really uh— either *ba'alei teshuva* who are really trying hard to look really Yeshivish, or [FFBs who have] a Chassidish or . . . very religious upbringing. Like most guys at YU wouldn't say *Toyrah.* They would say *Torah.*" YU is Yeshiva University, an institution that leans toward the Modern side of the spectrum with its focus on secular subjects in addition to religious learning. Although some people who attend YU wear black hats and beards and do say *Toyrah,* they do not identify with Black Hat Orthodoxy enough to shun secular education. Because of his desired location on the continuum, as well as his sense of what is authentic for a BT, Joseph uses [o] rather than [oy].

BTs often get a sense of what is appropriate from the FFBs and other BTs who serve as mentors during their transition to Orthodoxy. Andrew's study partner, Avrum, likely influences his variable use of [s] and the fact that he uses only [o], not [oy]. If Andrew had studied with Nussbaum instead (as Jacob did), he might have used a higher rate of [s] and perhaps even some [oy]. When BTs enter an Orthodox community, they often emulate the language and culture they encounter (in fact, they may have little or no knowledge of other parts of the continuum). However, like the woman who curries her gefilte fish and the man who framed a Black Hat–wearing Beatle, BTs sometimes make conscious decisions to differentiate themselves from their FFB friends.

Conclusion

Both FFBs and BTs use linguistic variation to claim a spot along the Orthodox continuum. While both groups may be aware of their linguistic performance, the choices of BTs tend to involve more consciousness. Most of them grew up using little or no Yiddish influence in their English, and those who learned Hebrew learned mostly Israeli Hebrew pronunciation. When they participate in Orthodox communities, they encounter a range of linguistic alternatives, along with dozens of other religious, social, and cultural options. As they decide where they want to locate themselves along the Modern to Black Hat spectrum, they choose among these options.

BTs' linguistic and cultural decisions signal more than their religiosity. They also indicate their desire to blend in with FFBs or to highlight their BT identity—in other words, their location along a BT–FFB continuum. BTs often diverge from FFBs by the same ideological differences that distinguish Modern Orthodox from Black Hat Jews—attitudes toward American society, prewar Eastern Europe, and Israel. Because BTs grew up integrated into American society and often with more of a connection to Israel than to Eastern Europe, they are more accustomed to the ideological stances common among Modern Orthodox Jews. As they become entrenched in Orthodox communities, they may alter their ideological stances. And their changes in ideology can affect and be affected by their linguistic and other cultural choices. But not all BTs fully adopt the ideologies and cultural practices of their FFB peers. As the next chapter explains, some of the BTs I met in Milldale avoid linguistic features associated with Black Hat Jews, not because they want to present themselves as Modern Orthodox but because they want to present themselves as BTs.

6

"Just Keepin' It Real, *Mamish*"

Why *Ba'alei Teshuva* Adopt (or Avoid) Orthodox Language

Rivka Bracha grew up known as Rebecca and had little exposure to Judaism. Two years ago, in her early twenties, she started attending classes at Ner Tamid. Since then, she has spent several months studying in a seminary in Israel, moved to Milldale, and married another Orthodox Jew. She got rid of her tank tops and bought a slew of long dresses and skirts. While she used to enjoy eating at all different kinds of restaurants, she now frequents only kosher establishments and has learned to cook brisket and potato kugel.

In the past two years, Rivka Bracha has changed the way she talks so dramatically that many find it hard to believe that only a few years ago she had never met an Orthodox Jew. She now uses Yiddish-influenced grammar, as in "You want that I should come?" and "This is not what to record." She often uses clicks, releases many of her [t]s, and incorporates many rise-fall intonation contours into her speech. She uses hundreds of Hebrew and Yiddish loanwords, including the stereotypical Orthodox *mamish* (really), and I rarely heard her use an English word when a loanword was common, as in *chas v'sholom* (God forbid), *mirtseshem* (God willing), *goy* (non-Jew), and *bracha* (blessing). She talks a lot about *Hashem*, and she often says *baruch Hashem*, especially in response to "How are you?" She pronounces her Hebrew loanwords in the Ashkenazi way—*Tsfas*, rather than *Tsfat* (Safed, city in Israel), and *Shvúes* rather than *Shavuót* (Feast of Pentecost). She uses Hebrew plurals—*gerim* (converts) and *hashkafos* (worldviews) rather than *gers* and *hashkafas*, and she even uses the Yiddish adjective suffix as FFBs do: "a *Chassidishe rebbe*" and "the *Yiddishe* statue of liberty."

When I asked Rivka Bracha what she has changed since becoming Orthodox, the first thing she mentioned was her language: "I don't speak the good King's English any more. I speak this Yinglish, Yeshivish stuff, which is fine by me." She went on to tell a story about standing with a BT friend and listening to an FFB mother use some Yiddish-influenced speech with her kids. The friend criticized the language, but Rivka Bracha said it sounded fine to her. She knows that features like "by them" are not standard, but she uses them because that's what frum people do. She says that she has learned the language just by spending time in the Orthodox community and that now she sometimes even thinks in Yeshivish. She considers herself Yeshivish, in contrast to Modern Orthodox, and she uses language to position herself along that continuum.

Rivka Bracha told me proudly that an FFB woman cast her as the "*Yiddishe bubby* from Boro Park" (Jewish grandmother from an Orthodox neighborhood in Brooklyn) in the women's Purim *shpil* (play). Perhaps the casting choice highlighted the ironic contrast between her newness and a Brooklyn grandmother's veteran frum status—part of the upside-down nature of the Purim holiday. Or maybe Rivka Bracha was able to sound even more frum than local FFBs. Either way, this BT was thrilled at the recognition of her successful acquisition of Yeshivish and the perception that she could sound FFB only a few years after becoming frum.

Samuel, a BT in his sixties who grew up affiliated with Conservative Judaism, observes the same commandments and customs as Rivka Bracha, but he has a very different way of being Orthodox. He and his wife moved to Milldale about eight years ago, when they just were becoming religious. Within four years he was asked to be on the board of the synagogue because of his business experience. His wife, Paula, became very involved with synagogue committees. Socially, Samuel and Paula are extremely well integrated into the Orthodox community of Milldale. They have close friendships with FFBs and other BTs, and they often host non-Orthodox Jews visiting the community. But when it comes to their symbolic practices, they maintain a degree of distinctness.

Like their neighbors, Samuel and Paula have decorated their home mostly with Judaic art. While many FFBs display a plaque with a Hebrew prayer or blessing, Samuel and Paula's entryway features an English plaque—a translation of a rabbinic quote from *Pirkei Avos*. Samuel dresses somewhat conservatively, wearing slacks and collar shirts even when lounging around the house. But, unlike many of his neighbors, he wears a black suit and hat only on Shabbos and other special occasions. At other times he covers his head with a black velvet yarmulke, distinguished by a thin band of blue trim along the outer edge.

In terms of language, Samuel has not made many changes. He does use a number of Hebrew and Yiddish loanwords, pronounced in the Ashkenazi way, such as *kehíla* (congregation), *kávod* (honor), *tznius* (modesty), and *daven* (pray). But I never heard him use Yiddish grammatical influences, clicks, distinctive intonation, or [t] release. Within his loanwords, he sometimes uses forms that FFBs would consider strange or incorrect: *from-keit* instead of *frumkeit* (religiosity); *bal tshuva* where the first part rhymes with "pal" instead of "doll"; "a *ba'alei teshuva*" (*ba'alei teshuva* is plural); "they *mekarev*ed us," rather than the periphrastic "they were *mekarev* us"; and "people that are very *chesed*," instead of "very involved in *chesed*" (*chesed* is a noun, meaning "kindness").

Samuel knows that his dress and language identify him as a BT, and he feels fine about that. He is proud of his BT identity; he even once considered starting a magazine by and for BTs. While language is an important element of the socialization process for many BTs, Samuel sees it as inconsequential. He told me about a well-known rabbi he admires who rarely uses Hebrew and Yiddish words in public presentations. Samuel said, "I don't see any reason that you have to load your language up with things like that. . . . Being able to communicate what the thoughts are behind it is what's important." In general he considered my research focus on language to be misguided. When I asked a follow-up question about language, he said, "Not to cast a damper on what you're doing, I don't really consider that to be really relevant." He went on to tell me what is important for a BT: "That you have a sensitivity to people and that you have a connection to God and that you live a life that's . . . connected to a value system."

Rivka Bracha and Samuel express their newfound Orthodox identities in very different ways. Although both have become strict in their halachic observance, they make differential use of language and other cultural practices to align themselves with some people and distinguish themselves from others. Rivka Bracha positions herself closer to the FFB and Black Hat ends of the spectrums, and Samuel highlights his BT identity and his location in the middle of the Modern to Black Hat continuum. They creatively use the religious and cultural resources available to them to construct their multilayered selves and present themselves as Orthodox Jews and as BTs.

As Rivka Bracha and Samuel illustrate, BTs take diverse approaches to Orthodox culture. Some change their wardrobe only as much as halacha demands, and others try to conform to Orthodox styles, often looking to FFBs as models to emulate. Some merely add a few dozen Hebrew and Yiddish words to their vocabulary, and others change the way they talk so much that they can pass as FFB. In this chapter, I use the lens of language to explore BTs' motivations for assimilating to or avoiding community norms.

Quantitative Portrait of BTs' Adoption of Orthodox Language

Speakers acquire the linguistic features described in chapter 4 to varying extents. Table 6.1 indicates what percentage of BTs used various linguistic features when I was observing them during my year of fieldwork. This analysis is based on my recordings and notes of the speech of twenty-nine BTs that I observed for at least three hours at Ner Tamid and/or in Milldale. All BTs used several loanwords, three-fourths of BTs used some Yiddish features (reflected in sentence structure or how English words are used, such as "eating by them," "tell over a story," or "it's for sure kosher"), and about half used the hesitation click and rise-fall intonation. I only heard a few BTs use word-final devoicing (pronouncing "going" as "goink," or "beard" as "beart"), and I heard no BTs use the distinctive pronunciation of short [a] in words like "candle" and "man."

Different BTs acquire different linguistic features and vary in their overall linguistic distinctiveness. I created an index to measure how distinct an individual's language is compared to general American English by assigning points for the use of each feature, and the results are presented in tables 6.2 and 6.3.[1] With minor deviation, the BTs' use of linguistic features correlates with their stages of integration (introduced in chapter 1): Peripheral, Community, and Yeshiva/Seminary.[2] Those who are only peripherally involved with Orthodox life use the least, those who have moved to an Orthodox community use more, and those who have spent time in a yeshiva or seminary use the most.

The pattern that emerges is in line with the "implicational scales" found in studies of sociolinguistic variation around the world, from Rochester to Guyana. As sociolinguist John Rickford explains, "Implicational scales depict hierarchical co-occurrence patterns in the acquisition or use of linguistic variables by individuals or groups, such that x implies y but not the reverse."[3] This means that speakers who use features lower down in the table also tend to use features above: a speaker's use of rise-fall intonation implies that he or she will also use loanwords, Yiddish grammatical influences, and the hesitation click. As tables 6.2 and 6.3 indicate, this is mostly the case among BTs.

Why are certain features acquired more than others? One reason is the extent of exposure. It is not surprising that loanwords—being the most common and salient feature in Orthodox Jewish English—are the most represented

TABLE 6.1

Percentage of twenty-nine BTs who used a linguistic feature in each category at least once during year of observations

Loanwords	100
A Yiddish-origin feature ("should," "by," "to," preposition absence, "hold," "learn," present perfect, "already," adverbial phrase placement, "for sure," or connective "so")	76
Hesitation click	52
Rise-fall intonation	45
Devoicing of final consonants	10
Distinctive short [a] pronunciation before [m] and [n]	0

TABLE 6.2
BT men's use of linguistic features according to BT stage

	Peripheral						Community						Yeshiva		
Pseudonym	Hank	Leonard	Will	Stuart	Mitch	Mike	Samuel	Mark	Fred	Andrew	Levi	David	Kalman	Jacob	Chaim
Loanwords	1	1	2	2	3	2	2	3	2	3	3	3	3	3	3
Yiddish features				2	1	1		1	1	1	3		3	5	7
Click									1		2		1		1
Intonation									1	1	1	1	1	1	1
Devoicing						1						1			
Short [a]															
Total points	**1**	**1**	**2**	**4**	**4**	**4**	**2**	**4**	**5**	**5**	**9**	**5**	**8**	**9**	**12**

TABLE 6.3
BT women's use of linguistic features according to BT stage

Pseudonym	Peripheral		Community							Seminary				
	Barbara	Rhoda	Sarah	Marissa	Paula	Shira	Shelley	Miriam	Cecile	Michelle	Marjorie	Dina	Devora	Rivka Bracha
Loanwords	1	1	1	2	2	2	3	3	2	2	1	1	3	3
Yiddish features		1	1	0.5		1	2	2	1	1.5	3	4	5	8
Click			1		2	2	2	1	1	2	2	2	2	2
Intonation				1					1	1	1		1	1
Devoicing												1		
Short [a]														
Total points	**1**	**2**	**3**	**3.5**	**4**	**5**	**7**	**6**	**5**	**6.5**	**7**	**8**	**11**	**14**

feature in the speech of newcomers. Similarly, devoicing is one of the least common features. But exposure is not the only factor influencing which features BTs acquire; individuals' ideology also plays a major role.

Language Ideology

Even if a speaker is aware of a linguistic feature and has the ability to use it, she might choose not to incorporate it into her speech. Shelley uses several aspects of Orthodox Jewish English, including many Hebrew words, clicks, and a few Yiddish grammatical influences. But I never heard her use "by." She spontaneously mentioned "the overuse of the word 'by'" as a distinctive feature of frum speech, and she even speculated, correctly, that it is a Yiddishism. Her conscious avoidance of this feature is based on her perception that it is incorrect speech. Similarly, Marissa did not use two of the features that she found salient ("hold" and "to"), according to her responses to the matched guise test and her comments to me. She explained that she avoids them because she thinks they sound strange—not only nonstandard but also old-fashioned, like the speech of her immigrant great-grandparents. Even though she is enthusiastic about her embrace of Orthodoxy and her desire to integrate socially into her new community, she chooses to avoid some linguistic features because she perceives them negatively.

These ideologies are probably influenced by these speakers' belief that grammar deviating from Standard English is incorrect.[4] However, negative language ideologies extend beyond concerns about standardness; some BTs also express opinions about Hebrew loanwords. For example, Andrew chooses not to say "baruch Hashem" as a response to "How are you?" even though this practice is common among his FFB and BT friends. He thinks it trivializes praise for God to use this phrase in mundane situations, and he prefers to reserve it for when he is especially thankful. Joseph has different reasons for avoiding certain linguistic features. As we saw in the previous chapter, he never uses the Ashkenazi [oy] vowel in Hebrew words because he thinks it sounds inauthentic, like someone imitating an identity not his own. Here we see the heightened self-consciousness inherent in adult language socialization. For these BTs, ideologies about what is correct, appropriate, and authentic have a strong effect on their language use (more on this in chapter 8).

Why do BTs have diverse ideologies about individual linguistic features? One factor is formal education. When BTs join an Orthodox community, they often alter their Hebrew pronunciation based on instruction they receive in synagogues, outreach centers, and yeshivas. If they grew up pronouncing the Hebrew letter *thaw* as [t], they often switch to [s] if their new teachers use [s] in the classroom. But formal education is not the full story. Outside the classroom they hear people talk about certain linguistic features: some say that "by" is bad grammar, and some opine that Ashkenazi pronunciation connects us to our ancestors. Ideologies like these are sometimes stated and sometimes implied. For BTs entering the community, the people they choose to spend time with and emulate have a major impact on their language ideologies and language use.

Although people's views about language do influence how they speak, the two do not always match. For example, Marissa said she does not like the Yiddish-influenced "by." While I did hear her use "at" several times when she could have used "by," I also heard her use "by" a few times in conversations with FFBs. Similarly, Shelley said she thinks it is important to pronounce Hebrew the Israeli way, rather than the Ashkenazi way, partly because of her time spent in Israel and her slightly more Modern Orthodox orientation. So she says *chidúsh* (innovation) rather than *chídish* and *chatimá* (referring to being sealed in the Book of Life) rather than *chasíma*. But she also uses many Yiddish pronunciations, especially in common words like "Shábbos" and "kósher" (rather than "Shabbát" and "kashér"), some of which she may have acquired before becoming frum. Marissa and Shelley's language ideologies do influence their language use, but the speech they are exposed to in their everyday lives sometimes trumps how they think they should talk.

While language ideology can have an impeding effect, it can also expedite a newcomer's adoption of linguistic features. If a BT considers a loanword religiously significant, she may be more likely to use it. This is especially the case with the many phrases that reference God. When I asked Miriam, a longtime BT, what she has changed about her language, she focused on theology. She feels that learning Hebrew words and phrases is a BT's key to understanding and acquiring the belief system of Orthodox Judaism. She decided early on to start using phrases like "baruch Hashem" even though she did not yet feel the presence of God in her everyday life. Soon she did develop that sense, in part, she says, because of her language use.

This phenomenon has been noted in other studies of BTs. In sociologist William Shaffir's study of newly Orthodox Jews in a yeshiva in Israel, he writes, "In light of the institutionalized context within which the conversion experience is situated, [BTs] quickly adopt the appropriate behavioral trappings of Orthodox Judaism, including dress, language, study, and prayer, hoping to eventually acquire the requisite attitudes which correspond to their behavior."[5] In another study of BTs, Lynn Davidman foregrounds the importance of social interaction: "Behavioral changes often take place first in the context of participating with other people; changes in feelings follow."[6]

The phenomenon of "say now, believe later" has also been found in other research on transformations of identity and worldview. For example, "some A.A. [Alcoholics Anonymous] members initially mimic the phrase 'I am an alcoholic,' and don't fully accept the identity until later."[7] And the anthropologist Susan Harding found that newcomers to a group of Falwellian fundamentalist Christians—herself included—would acquire the beliefs after taking on the religious language of the community.[8] In these instances of *na'aseh v'nishma* (the biblical quote "we will do and we will hear/understand"; see chapter 1), we see more evidence for the interplay between the spiritual and the cultural.

In short, ideologies of correctness and importance play a major role in newcomers' acquisition of Orthodox language. BTs are less likely to acquire features that they consider incorrect or inauthentic and more likely to acquire features that have high value for social and religious integration into frum life. This highlights the agency involved in adult language socialization, as well as the diversity of approach. Individuals have knowledge of various communal norms, and they often make conscious decisions about which ones to adopt and how to make them their own.

Locating Oneself within the Sociolinguistic Landscape

Another way that ideology affects the acquisition of new ways of speaking is that individuals perceive a connection between language and social categories. As newcomers integrate into their new community, they use language to align themselves with some individuals or groups and to distinguish themselves from others. This alignment and distinction are possible because of the ideology that certain groups speak in certain ways. As I discussed in chapter 1 (see table 1.1), community members hold recursive views about language and social categories. They believe (correctly) that Orthodox Jews use more Yiddish influences and other distinctive features in their speech than do non-Orthodox Jews, and they (correctly) project that opposition onto other social distinctions: Black Hat versus Modern Orthodox, men versus women, New Yorkers versus those from "out of town," and FFB versus BT.

The notion that BTs are less distinct from non-Orthodox Jews than from their FFB peers is often true within a given Orthodox community, especially toward the Black Hat end of the continuum. Sometimes intentionally and sometimes inadvertently, many BTs use fewer Yiddish influences than their local FFB peers and maintain aspects of their pre-Orthodox dress, music, and activities. The consequence of this cultural distinction is that BTs in Black Hat communities are often associated with other groups on the left side of table 1.1, especially Modern Orthodox Jews and non–New Yorkers. Several respondents to the matched guise test pointed out that some of the speech samples that they ranked low for Orthodoxy or for FFB-ness (and therefore that they assumed were spoken by non-Orthodox Jews or BTs) could have been spoken by Modern Orthodox Jews. And a few told me that they ranked speakers who sounded like they were not from New York as less likely to be Orthodox and less likely to be FFB, perhaps reflecting a Northeastern bias that would be less evident in Black Hat communities in the Midwest, South, and elsewhere.

These responses to the experiment were similar to statements I heard in interviews. One FFB rabbi, who might be described as Yeshivish Modern, talked about how BTs sometimes dress and talk more like Modern Orthodox Jews. A woman on the West Coast talked about how she assumed a Chabad rebbetzin she met was a BT, based on her creative cooking and lack of Yiddish linguistic influences, but later found out that she grew up in a Chabad community "out of town." The connection between the BT–FFB axis and other axes of Orthodox Judaism manifests not only in symbolic practices but also in community members' discourse about those practices.

Of course, nobody suggested that BT men talk like women, two other dimensions on opposite sides of table 1.1. But other conversations pointed to a feminizing discourse about BT men in the domain of text study. For example, in this exchange with Devora, I mentioned that I had recorded a chavrusa study session at Ner Tamid. Devora, a recent BT, incorrectly assumed that both of the male learning partners were BTs (emphasis added):

DEVORA: You recorded their chavrusa?

SARAH: Mm-hm, 'cause I'm interested in how people learn.

DEVORA: What were they learning?

SARAH: They were learning . . . Gemora.

DEVORA: Oh, they were learning a Gemora. That's always fun to—

SARAH: Yeah.

DEVORA: It's a shame that—You should try to—they won't let you, because you're a woman, probably, but, go into like a, you know—

SARAH: A yeshiva.

DEVORA: See how *the real people*—

SARAH: I'd love to. . . .

DEVORA: [The people you recorded at Ner Tamid are] ba'al teshuva . . . you know. And they never studied at a um—. So I don't know how much you can go by the way they learned. You know? *They might learn like women. . . . I don't know how advanced they are, you know. 'Cause they're um ba'al teshuva,* you know what I mean? . . .

SARAH: Well, [Avrum]'s not. He's FFB.

DEVORA: Oh, I don't know who he is.

SARAH: Oh, OK.

DEVORA: *So, then they were learning right.*

Devora suggests that men at Ner Tamid "might learn like women" based on her knowledge that new BTs tend to have less experience studying Gemora and that frum women tend not to study Gemora. Certainly many longtime BT men are highly skilled learners and teachers of Gemora, just as many longtime BT women are highly skilled learners and teachers of Tanach. But within frum circles the ideological connection between the categories of BTs and women persists, especially when it comes to learning. Devora's comments also point to the common notion that FFBs ("the real people") are more authentic Orthodox Jews than BTs. It is only after she realizes that one of the learning partners is FFB that she concludes they must be "learning right."

In short, among both BTs and FFBs, there is an ideological association between BTs and other categories on the left side of table 1.1: non-Orthodox, Modern Orthodox, non-New Yorkers, and, to a lesser extent, women (see more below and in chapter 8 on BTs' divergent experiences with gender norms). This association stems from a perception not of lower levels of observance but rather of lesser skill in text study and of cultural self-presentation that is less distinct.

BTs' Self-Representation

As BTs integrate into Orthodox communities, they have several options for self-representation. In addition to the Modern–Black Hat continuum, they can use symbolic practices to position themselves along the other axes. They can choose to identify with New Yorkers by living or visiting there, associating with ex–New Yorkers, or using New York–influenced language; or they can orient themselves primarily to local social networks and linguistic variants (such as elements of a Philadelphia regional accent). Both men and women can choose—to some extent—how to position themselves with respect to gender. Orthodox masculinity involves regular text study and a self-presentation that is more distinct from non-Orthodox Jews than that of women. In Black Hat communities, FFB men tend to cut their hair short, wear dark suits and black hats, and commit themselves to Gemora study and public prayer, while FFB women tend to wear modest dresses and sheitels and devote themselves to household responsibilities, as well as sometimes a breadwinning job.

In contrast, a BT man who keeps his ponytail, does not excel in Gemora study, and does not take a public role in synagogue rituals may be seen as less masculine (and more BT, closer to the Modern pole, etc.). And a BT woman who keeps a tightly cropped hairstyle, studies advanced texts, and does not concern herself with domestic affairs may be seen as less feminine (and more BT, closer to the Modern pole, etc.).[9] While the terms "feminine" and "masculine" may not be applied to cases like these, community members see them as flouting Orthodox gender norms. One woman reports being counseled to grow out her very short hair when she was unmarried and in the process of becoming frum. And an Orthodox rabbi in Israel takes action in support of gender normativity by cutting off the ponytails of newly Orthodox men in televised revival-like gatherings.[10]

Language is also important in the construction of gender. The use of linguistic features associated with text study (such as Aramaic loanwords, chanting intonation, phrasal verbs, and the authoritative-sounding [t] release) is considered more learned and, therefore, more masculine.[11] BT men who use features like these in everyday conversation are seen as more learned and, perhaps, more masculine. And BT women who use them would likely be seen as more learned and, perhaps, less feminine.

Just as BTs' masculinity and femininity are perceived partly based on linguistic choices, language also plays an important role in the extent they are seen as BT-like or FFB-like. Some BTs wish to pass as FFB and consider it the ultimate success when people assume they are. Others relish their identities as BTs and use social networks and unique combinations of symbolic practices to indicate their BT-ness.[12] As Michelle, a BT who has attended seminary and lived in a few Orthodox communities, says, "I think there are two different kinds [of BTs]. There are the kind that really try to fit in and to sort of just become immersed in the community so that they don't look like ba'alei teshuva anymore, and then there are the kind that are like, 'We're ba'alei teshuva, we're proud of it, and we'll refer to our past sometimes and we'll laugh at the stuff we don't know or be upset at the stuff we don't know, whatever it is, but we'll acknowledge there's a difference.'" Rabbi Nussbaum, an FFB man, also refers to these two types of BTs: "I've seen the whole gamut. I've seen them basically maintain pretty much everything from before. In other words, they hold on to the dog, they hold on to the English first name. They hold on to the way of dress. They just put on tzitzis and a yarmulke, but they basically dress the same. They'll use expletives—mild ones, but expletives—in their speech. They haven't really cleaned up their act in that sense. To the other extreme where they go overboard and wild, radical, extremists, fanatical. That's the other extreme." Most BTs in Milldale, he says, are somewhere in the middle.

That was my understanding, as well. Throughout my fieldwork in Ner Tamid and Milldale, I met very few BTs who wanted to pass as FFB. Those who do usually move to Orthodox communities where they can more easily hide their backgrounds. Many of the BTs in Milldale are proud of the fact that they are BTs. They are happy with the transition they have made, and they want others—FFBs, other BTs, non-Orthodox Jews, and even non-Jews—to know about it. When I met new people and mentioned my research topic, it was common for people to tell me immediately that they were BTs. Devora enthusiastically proclaimed—several times and with several audiences—that she is "very BT," by which she meant fervent in her newly found observance. Levi has the word "teshuva" as part of his e-mail address, and Samuel was thinking of starting a magazine for BTs. Even those who are not as enthusiastic about their BT status tend not to keep it secret. One BT man said, "Some people try to hide their backgrounds. I want to fit in, but I'm not going to hide who I am. You are who you are. You can learn [study Jewish texts] for many years, but you didn't grow up going to yeshiva, so you'll always have that difference. Everyone has their own *tafkid* [role]."

The experience of attending Orthodox schools in childhood plays a major role in the ability to pass as FFB. Mrs. Gitlin grew up in a non-observant family but attended Orthodox schools. As a teenager she decided to become observant and has identified as frum ever since. Now in her fifties, she says she sometimes feels uncomfortable when people assume she is FFB: "I've gone to places where everybody was frum from birth and I looked frum from birth and I could talk frum from birth and my family looked frum from birth. And then you sit around with a group of frum-from-birth women and they're talking about ba'alei teshuva. Little would they know that [they're talking to a ba'al teshuva]. If I'm not close to them, so they wouldn't necessarily know that." (Note her use of the extra connective "so.") She told me she was once in a vacation area frequented by New York Orthodox Jews and "almost felt like an imposter" the entire month she was there. Feeling inauthentic is an issue not only for very recent BTs, as this longtime BT reminds us.

Although many BTs may not wish to pass as FFB, some express discontent when people immediately recognize them as BTs based on their language. One woman who has had trouble learning Hebrew laments this situation. The opposite is also true. Tova, a BT whose father is a Conservative rabbi, smiled when she told me about an FFB friend who thought she was FFB. She mentioned that her father was a rabbi, and the friend thought she meant an Orthodox rabbi. Even if passing is not a goal, it can be a thrill on the rare occasions when it happens.

Cultural practices like language are important in how BTs are perceived with respect to BT-ness or FFB-ness. By becoming completely comfortable with Orthodox law and custom, by associating with FFBs, and by successfully incorporating many frum practices into their repertoires, BTs are seen as more FFB-like, sometimes even as FFB. By maintaining some of their pre-Orthodox practices, by not fully taking on some of the Orthodox ones, or by being overly zealous in their observance of law or custom, BTs are seen as more BT-like.

Alignment and Distinction

As BTs position themselves along the various axes of Orthodox life, they are engaged in both alignment and distinction. They are aligning themselves with frum Jews and distinguishing themselves from their non-Orthodox family and friends. They are aligning themselves with Modern or Black Hat Jews (or somewhere in the middle) and distinguishing themselves from those to the left and/or right of the spectrum. And they are doing the same along the other axes.

Any time individuals join a new community, whether it is based on religion, vocation, region, ethnicity, or some other dimension, they necessarily engage in both alignment and distinction. Even if there are few social distinctions within their new community, newcomers are necessarily aligning themselves with their new community and distinguishing themselves from others. In addition, even in situations of adult language socialization in which all community veterans were once adult novices, such as professional training programs, there is bound to be a period of transition, when the novices both align themselves with and distinguish themselves from the veterans. Such distinguishing may be inadvertent, and the newcomer might not even know that others perceive her as different. Or it may be intentional, stemming from the newcomer's feelings of inauthenticity or hesitance to become a full community member.

These dual trends of alignment and distinction are important not just in life transitions but also in sociolinguistic variation more generally.[13] A speaker can align herself with one group while distinguishing herself from another. And she can align herself with one group or role one minute and with another group or role soon after, even within the same conversation. To illustrate the interplay between alignment and distinction among BTs, I offer a discussion of obscenity and slang, two features of American English that many Orthodox Jews—especially those toward the Black Hat end of the spectrum—try to avoid. The creative ways that BTs make use of obscenity and slang enable them to align and distinguish themselves simultaneously.

Obscenity

Curse words are considered unacceptable in the Orthodox community. One FFB rabbi made this clear during a Ner Tamid class when he mentioned his recent flight across the country. He said he used the free headphones to watch reruns of *I Love Lucy*, but he stopped watching the feature film—which was surely edited for airplane use—after realizing that it included offensive language. The stigma against obscenity is nicely illustrated in the following description of Rabbi Avrohom Yaakov Hakohein Pam in the *Jewish Observer* (translations are mine):

A favorite topic [for his lectures] was *nekiyus hadibur* [verbal hygiene], encouraging his *talmidim* [students] to speak in a fine way. He would express himself in a style I've never heard from other *gedolim* [important men] of his stature. [He said,] "Words like 'crazy' or 'stupid' should never pass your lips." . . .

Bachurim [boys] in the *Beis Hamidrash* [study hall] had a discussion regarding the English word for *Gehinnom* [hell]. Is it proper to use the word?

They resolved to ask Rabbi Pam. The following conversation ensued.

"*Rebbe* [rabbi], there are some words that are not really 'dirty' words, but they are sometimes used as curse words . . ."

"What do you mean?"

"Well, um, you know, there are some words that have an innocent meaning, but some people consider them '*nivul peh*' [obscenity]."

"Like what?"

". . . words that crude people use . . . but they don't really mean anything bad . . ."

"Oh, I see; you mean words like *fress*! [gorge oneself, eat like a pig]"

The *bachur* [boy] had his answer.[14]

As the author implies, Rabbi Pam's is an extreme approach to obscenity; he may not have even been familiar with the word "hell." But the fact that the author uses the Hebrew *Gehinnom* to avoid writing "hell" highlights the stigma surrounding obscenity.

During my fieldwork in Milldale, I never heard "hell," "bullsh**," or "f*** up," but I did hear stand-ins: "heck" (FFB man: "What the heck does that mean?"), "boloney" (FFB woman: "That's boloney"), and "fudge up" (BT woman: "It would fudge up my answer"). I also heard some "crude" words only from BTs—words like "screw up" and "sucks." I heard two BT men use "screw" ("Someone screwed with [the air conditioning]"; "They screwed up"); one of them told me that his wife corrects him when he uses this word.

The two times I heard the word "sh**" were from BTs. One was from a recent BT who—clearly unintentionally—let it slip when she realized she was late for a class; only one other BT and I were present. The other was in the context of a joke. I was at Ner Tamid chatting with a few other non-Orthodox Jews, recent BTs, and Yakov Tzvi, a longtime BT who works in Jewish outreach in another city. One of the recent BTs said he was about to go on a *shiduch* date (in which a couple is setup by a mutual contact), and Yakov Tzvi responded with a joke: "Why do they call it a *shidach*? Because you get there and say 'Sh**! *Ach*!'"

Yakov Tzvi is quite comfortable being Orthodox and considers himself an "FFT"—Frum from Teshuva, a BT who has been Orthodox so long that he has relaxed his strict observance of some community norms (see chapter 8; the term "FFT" may have been coined by Rabbi Moshe Shur). By telling a joke with the word "sh**," Yakov Tzvi was performing this FFT identity, in contrast to a recent Black Hat BT who might feel less comfortable using profanity in this way. But even Yakov Tzvi would not use the phrase "f***ed up" in his imitation of Deadheads at a concert: "'Yeah, man, we didn't get tickets, but we were standing right outside. You could hear a lot of the music from out there, because it was real loud. We got so f-ed ["eft"] up, man.'" A Black Hat FFB would be unlikely to perform this imitation in the first place and even less likely to say "f***-ed up."

The same is true for a less-seasoned BT who might worry about the reaction to his treading near the boundary between decency and obscenity.

Because of the prohibition against saying God's name in vain (one of the Ten Commandments), Orthodox Jews are expected not to say things such as "Oh my God" or "What in God's name is going on?" However, for some BTs, these phrases are so ingrained in their verbal repertoire that they have trouble avoiding them. "Gosh" is sometimes used as a substitute for "God" in phrases like these, and one FFB girl told me that when she hears people say "Oh gosh" she assumes they are BT.

Slang

Related to the issue of obscenity is slang. American slang words are not as commonly heard among Orthodox Jews as among their non-Orthodox and non-Jewish neighbors. There is no prohibition against saying "dude" or "oh man." But the norm in communities to the right of Modern Orthodox is that these words are rarely used—except among BTs. For example, Stephanie Levine describes a BT man who blends into the Hasidic community socially and visually, but when he uses slang like "cool" and "a real trip" he betrays his secular upbringing.[15] Similarly, when Marissa, a recent BT woman, gave a dvar torah at Ner Tamid, she used some slang phrases: "kick 'em in the butt" and "Potiphar's wife had the hots for Yosef." The audience laughed at these phrases for several seconds, because of the incongruity of this colloquial language embedded in a religious speech act. Later that Shabbos, when FFB Rabbi Hollander was giving a dvar torah, he made joking references to Marissa's slang phrases but did not actually say them.

Using slang from time to time—whether or not it is intentional—allows BTs to hold on to part of their former identity. I observed several BTs who use many additive linguistic features, like loanwords, Yiddish grammatical constructions, and distinctive intonation, but do not subtract some of the slang words and borderline foul language that are rare among FFBs. They might not be as likely to use words like "dude" and "screw up" in front of FFBs, but they do not avoid them all together. Like the hybrid practices in dress, home decoration, and food described in chapter 3, the combination of slang with Orthodox linguistic features allows these BTs to present themselves not only as Orthodox Jews but also as BTs. As one BT pointed out, "If someone said 'Just keepin' it real, mamish,' I would know they're definitely BT." By tapping into the power of language, BTs can align themselves with some people and distinguish themselves from others—in short, position themselves along the social axes of frum life.

7

"I Finally Got the Lingo"

Progression in Newcomers' Acquisition
of Orthodox Language

It is clear from the previous chapter that BTs do eventually acquire many of
the Yiddish and Hebrew influences in Orthodox Jewish English. But, unlike students learning a foreign language, this acquisition does not happen in a formal language classroom. As I show in this chapter, BTs go through a long and
multifaceted process of language socialization as they integrate into Orthodox
communities.

Peripheral, Community, and Yeshiva/Seminary BTs

An important part of the language socialization process is the three stages of
religious and social integration that BTs tend to go through (introduced in
chapter 1): Peripheral (marginally affiliated with Orthodoxy), Community (following halacha and living in an Orthodox community), and Yeshiva/Seminary
(having studied intensively in an Orthodox institution of higher learning). A
quantitative analysis of overall use of distinctive Orthodox features shows that
these stages correlate with language use: Peripheral BTs had the lowest indices,
Community BTs were in the middle, and Yeshiva/Seminary BTs had the highest
indices (figure 7.1).

In every category except Yeshiva/Seminary BTs, men used more distinctive
linguistic features than women. I found a similar pattern of gender difference in
my research in a Chabad school in California. Among both students and teachers, males used more Hebrew, Aramaic, and Yiddish loanwords than females,
and they released their [t]s about twice as frequently. These differences are in
line with the distinct activities and expectations for men and women regarding
traditional learning and learnedness.[1]

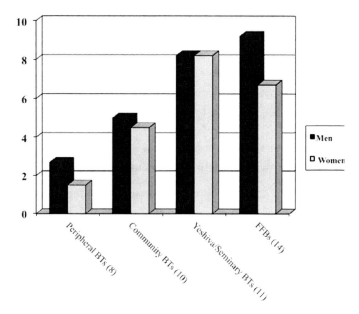

FIGURE 7.1. Average index of BTs' and FFBs' use of Orthodox linguistic features, according to gender

Note: The number of people in each category follows in parentheses. See chapter 6 for details about the index.

The one surprising finding is that Seminary BT women score just as high as Yeshiva BT men and even higher than FFB women. This can be attributed to two Seminary BT women who, at the time of the study, had been Orthodox for less than two years. The scores recorded for Devora and Rivka Bracha were well above average, eleven and fourteen, respectively. Both young women embraced Orthodoxy with great fervor at Ner Tamid and in Milldale, and, after spending time in BT seminaries in Israel, they have integrated religiously, socially, and culturally into the community. For both, using Orthodox language has been such an important part of their integration process that they hyperaccommodate to Orthodox linguistic norms. We also find outliers on the other end of the spectrum. For example, Samuel, the Community BT profiled along with Rivka Bracha in chapter 6, has a score of two, which is lower than even the average for Peripheral BT men. His low score is balanced out in the Community BT men's category by Levi's high score of nine. As the previous chapter explains, these individuals' disparate scores stem from their different ideologies about language and Orthodoxy, among other factors.[2]

As BTs integrate, they change not only their speech but also their comprehension. Shelley, a Community BT, said that soon after moving to an Orthodox community someone gave her an audio tape of a lecture that was intended for

FFBs and knowledgeable BTs: "I had no idea what he was talking about, because there was so much lingo thrown in." She put the tape aside for over a year, and then, "about a month or two ago I took the tape out just for the heck of it, and it was totally different. I really enjoyed listening to the tape, because I understood what he was talking about—because I got the lingo." It is clear that some BTs are able to increase their use and comprehension of Orthodox language significantly within just a few years. Let us examine how this transition happens.

Progression of Exposure to Linguistic Styles

The Orthodox socialization process can be illuminated by anthropologist Jean Lave and social learning theorist Etienne Wenger's model of learning as "legitimate peripheral participation."[3] The learners, or "apprentices," observe the "masters" and other apprentices, and they gradually gain increased access to roles and responsibilities within their new "community of practice." As linguists Penelope Eckert and Sally McConnell-Ginet define it, "a community of practice is an aggregate of people who come together around mutual engagement in an endeavor. Ways of doing things, ways of talking, beliefs, values, power relations—in short, practices—emerge in the course of this mutual endeavor."[4] Through their participation in communities of practice and through their increasing access, apprentices are able to try out the new practices and sometimes get feedback from the masters and other apprentices. Eventually they become so skilled at the practices expected of them that they are considered experts or masters.

In the two communities of practice in my research—Jews mutually engaged in Orthodox religious observance and education at the Ner Tamid Center downtown and in the Milldale neighborhood—the "apprentices" are the BTs, and the "masters" are the FFBs and longtime BTs. As BTs progress from Peripheral to Community and sometimes to Yeshiva/Seminary, they gain increasing access to roles, responsibilities, and practices, especially in language and other areas of culture.

I experienced this progression of access during my fieldwork. I started by attending classes and events at the Ner Tamid Center. At first, my main role (aside from ethnographer) was new student, and I interacted with the other students (Prospective BTs and Peripheral BTs), as well as the few Yeshiva BT and FFB rabbis who taught the classes. Within a few weeks, the rabbis began to give me new roles and responsibilities: collect tickets at the entrance to a Ner Tamid event, help the rebbetzin prepare salads for Shabbos dinner, and stuff envelopes for the annual gala. These tasks were a way for me to give back to the people who were helping me with my research, but they were also important in my learning about Orthodox life. When I sold tickets, I observed people's dress and greetings closely as they entered the room, and I familiarized myself with the

Hebrew and Yiddish names on the list of event attendees. When I stuffed envelopes, I chatted with the rabbi and another student as we listened to the Hebrew and Jewish English songs of Mordechai Ben-David on CD. And when I prepared salads, the rebbetzin showed me how to squeeze a lemon without violating the laws of Shabbos. Through these interactions, I heard more and more distinctive Orthodox language.

My access shifted dramatically the first time I spent Shabbos with a rabbi and his family in Milldale. There, I met a whole new crowd, including many Community and Yeshiva/Seminary BTs who had begun their Orthodox journeys at Ner Tamid and similar outreach centers. I gained access to frum language and life over Shabbos dinner, "midnight cholent," synagogue services, lunch, *shalosh seudos* (the late afternoon Saturday meal), and all the in-between moments hanging out with the rabbi, his wife, and their thirteen children. On that first visit to Milldale, I met several families and accepted invitations for future overnight visits. In the months that followed, I helped community members prepare Shabbos and holiday meals, learned how to make challah and potato kugel, visited the mikveh, attended lectures and classes, and participated in several life-cycle events. All these interactions enabled me to not only hear but also try out Hebrew and Yiddish words and other distinctive linguistic features.

I gained access to the most distinctive Orthodox English when I spent a week studying at a BT women's seminary in Israel. Like the other young women there, I took notes on what I heard, looked up words or asked questions about things I did not understand, and tried out frum speech with my peers and teachers. Although I did not move to Milldale or study in seminary for a long period, I learned from my simulated BT journey that BTs tend to experience this same kind of progression. For some it takes months and for others, years. But they all gain increasing access to frum culture as they become closer with community members and take on new roles.

When Seminary BT Devora spent Shabbos dinner with the Hollanders in Milldale, along with several Peripheral and Prospective BTs, she heard Mrs. Hollander use only a few loanwords. But a month later when Devora spent a Thursday evening with Mrs. Hollander in a more intimate setting, preparing for Shabbos dinner, she heard her use many loans and even a few Yiddish phrases: "*Ikh hob fargesn*" (I forgot), "*Zay gezunt*" (be well, goodbye), and "*Zorg zikh nisht*" (don't worry).

Similarly, when Peripheral BT Will met with Rabbi Hollander at Ner Tamid, he heard English with some loanwords, mostly translated. But when he went to Rabbi Hollander's house to attend the sheva brachos for the rabbi's son and new daughter-in-law, he heard him use many more untranslated loans, including several periphrastic verbs (such as "we should *be mesameach* the chossen and kallah" [we should entertain (literally, "gladden") the groom and bride]). Will experienced an important moment in his integration into Orthodox life when Rabbi Fischer asked him to give a dvar torah at Shabbos dinner. Will told me that he studied the Torah portion and rabbinic commentaries (in translation, as he was not yet proficient in Hebrew) and consulted with Rabbi Fischer and a BT friend. Although he did not mention language to me, it was clear that preparing for and delivering the dvar torah provided an opportunity for Will to read, hear, and try out distinctive linguistic features. In his dvar torah, he used a few Hebrew words (some tentatively), and he ended it with a hope for the coming of the Moshiach (Messiah) "speedily in our days," a common way for ending a dvar torah, but here without the Hebrew words that veteran teachers use. The transition to frum language does not happen overnight, but changing roles and responsibilities allow BTs increased access and opportunities to try it out.

Levi, a Community BT, told me that for him, a major turning point in his integration into the Milldale community was when he was asked to serve on the board of Shomrei Emunah. It is not uncommon for the synagogue board to invite newcomers to take on leadership roles, as they often have more administrative experience and financial means; in fact, Levi and his friends call it the "BT board." When they serve on the board, BTs necessarily interact with community veterans, gaining more and more opportunities to observe and try out Orthodox cultural practices.

While women tend not to serve on this synagogue's board, they do take on many responsibilities within the Milldale community. Levi's wife, Shira, has organized events and coordinated fundraisers at her children's school. Parents contact her to order scrip for the local grocery store (pre-paid credit that benefits the school). Through her leadership activities, she necessarily interacts with many women—BTs and FFBs—and she has become close with several parents of her children's classmates. Even BT women who do not take on leadership roles begin to interact more intensely with other frum women when they become mothers—at the park, in the shul lobby, in the school parking lot. In the conversations they have while holding babies and trying to stop their children from running into the street, BTs have ample opportunity to observe and try out frum speech. Especially when having five or more children is the norm, the mutual endeavor of parenting is an important component of frum communities of practice.

Community Veterans' Role in the Progression of Access

Veteran Orthodox Jews tend to be aware of the language learning involved in the progression from Peripheral to Community BT. When they first encounter someone who they think might be a non-Orthodox Jew or a Peripheral BT, they tend to use few loanwords. I once called an FFB man and introduced myself as a researcher, asking if he could do a survey at 10 P.M., to which he replied, "I have a study session." "You have a chavrusa at 10?" I asked. "Yes," he said, "a chavrusa by phone." Before he knew my knowledge level or religious background, he used the English phrase, but once he realized that I knew the word chavrusa, he used it as well. Similarly, near the beginning of my fieldwork in Milldale, I called Shomrei Emunah and left a message saying I was interested in "classes." When Rabbi Passo returned my call, he said he was calling about "classes at the synagogue." In my subsequent conversations with him, after he had a better sense of my knowledge of Orthodox Jewish English, he often used loanwords like *shiurim* (classes) and *shul* (synagogue).

It may seem obvious that Jews would avoid or translate Hebrew and Yiddish loanwords when they are not yet sure if their audience will understand them. But we also see a similar phenomenon with other salient features of Orthodox language, like English words used with their Yiddish meanings and Yiddish grammatical constructions. When speakers are aware of them, they often avoid them or use them in conjunction with their non-Orthodox equivalents. I heard several community veterans using Yiddish-influenced English words like "hold" and "learn" and then offering translations like "believe" and "study" for the benefit of newcomers.

Another common practice is for community veterans, who normally use mostly Ashkenazi Hebrew pronunciation, to use Israeli Hebrew pronunciation when speaking with new BTs and other non-Orthodox Jews, recognizing that they tend to be more familiar with Israeli Hebrew from their childhood Jewish education. I heard several FFBs and longtime BTs using "Shabbat" in conversations with newcomers, while they would normally say "Shabbos." One FFB introduces himself to non-Orthodox Jews and new BTs with his English name, Michael, rather than the name he normally goes by, Moyshe (pronounced with an Ashkenazi vowel). His main reason? He does not like it when BTs "mispronounce" his name as "Moshe."

The most dramatic examples I encountered of an FFB changing his speech for different audiences came from FFB Rabbi Nussbaum. I recorded him in two of his regular chavrusa study sessions: one with Mr. Weisman, an FFB, and one with Jacob, a Yeshiva BT. While Nussbaum used distinctly Orthodox language with both partners, his speech with Weisman was closer to the Black Hat pole (see chapter 5): he used more Yiddish-influenced syntax, chanting intonation, and Hebrew, Aramaic, and Yiddish loanwords. Even though Jacob fashions himself as closer to the Black Hat pole than Weisman does (for example, Weisman is clean shaven and Jacob has a long beard), Nussbaum considers it appropriate to use more Yeshivish language when speaking to Weisman, the FFB.

We can see evidence of Nussbaum's style-shifting according to audience when we look at his Hebrew pronunciation with his two chavrusas. First, I analyzed all the Hebrew and Aramaic words that have a schwa vowel after the first consonant, words like *təshuva* (repentance), *shəma* (listen), and *səfira* (counting). According to the prescriptive rules of Hebrew grammar, the schwa in these words should be pronounced. But Ashkenazi Hebrew and Israeli Hebrew (on the influence of Ashkenazi Hebrew) delete the schwa, rendering these words as *tshuva, shma,* and *sfira.* Among American Orthodox Jews (as well as non-Orthodox Jews) there is a good deal of variation in this vowel, based on the conflicting norms of prescriptive Hebrew grammar and spoken Ashkenazi and Israeli Hebrew, in conjunction with the pronunciation system of English, which does not have consonant clusters like [gz], [dv], and [xs]. FFBs sometimes pronounce the schwa, but they often delete it, as in *gzera* (decree) and *dveykus* (adhering). BTs also exhibit variation in their use of this schwa. But many of them are careful to pronounce it in an effort to speak the "correct" Hebrew they were taught, either as children or in their BT Hebrew classes. Nussbaum seems to recognize, at least subconsciously, that BTs are more likely than FFBs to pronounce the schwa. In his study session with Weisman, Nussbaum deletes his schwa much more than in his study session with Jacob. This pattern parallels Weisman and Jacob's actual usage (figure 7.2).

We see a similar pattern when we look at the [o] vowel, which can be pronounced [o] or [oy] (as in Torah or Toyrah). The [o] variant, used in Israeli Hebrew, is more common among non-Orthodox and Modern Orthodox Jews, and the [oy] variant, used in Ashkenazi Hebrew, is more common among Black Hat Jews. Nussbaum uses a much higher frequency of [oy] with FFB Weisman

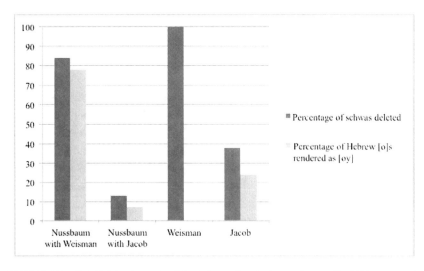

FIGURE 7.2. Rabbi Nussbaum's style-shifting in study sessions with Weisman and Jacob, compared to Weisman's and Jacob's speech

Note: N ranges from 8 to 37.

than with BT Jacob. But in this case, Nussbaum is not shifting to the actual speech of his study partners. Weisman uses only [o], and Jacob uses [oy] some of the time. Nussbaum has had ample opportunity to observe his friends' speech, as he has been studying with Jacob for four years and with Weisman for over twenty. He might even be aware that Weisman rarely if ever uses [oy] and that Jacob often does. But he also knows that [oy] is associated with FFBs and that Weisman is FFB and Jacob is not. Nussbaum is accommodating not to the actual speech patterns of his interlocutors, but to his classifications of them, probably based on his understanding of what speech to FFBs and to BTs should be. This type of style-shifting according to the perceived social categories of one's audience has also been found in studies of African Americans and other groups.[5]

As these examples show, community veterans are aware that newcomers speak differently, and they alter their speech depending on their perceptions of the people they are speaking to. They not only use fewer loanwords or translate the ones they use, but they also temper their use of other linguistic features associated with Orthodoxy and with FFBs. Even so, BTs are gradually exposed to more Orthodox language as they progress through the stages of social integration. This exposure is crucial to their acquisition of frum speech.

Classes

While BTs experience a progression of access in their informal interactions, they also encounter different linguistic styles in the lectures and events they attend in different venues: Peripheral BTs mostly at Ner Tamid and Community BTs mostly in Milldale. In the classes at Ner Tamid, the teachers—both FFBs and longtime BTs—use some Orthodox linguistic features. I heard a number of distinct intonation patterns and frequent [t] release (such as right[h] rather than righ'). I heard a few phrasal verbs (such as *tell over* and *learn out*) and a few other Yiddish grammatical influences. And I heard hundreds of loanwords. At the same time, the teachers at Ner Tamid often used English words where loans are common, and they often translated the loanwords and Hebrew quotes they used.

Once BTs start attending services and classes in Milldale, they encounter language that is even more distinctly frum. In his divrei torah (sermons) at Shomrei Emunah, FFB Rabbi Passo uses many Orthodox features and translates very few of his hundreds of loanwords. For recent Community BTs and Peripheral BTs just visiting Milldale, this frum speech can be frustrating. At services one day, when the rabbi used a relatively obscure loanword, I overheard a man on the other side of the mechitzah say, "What does that mean?" Someone translated in a whisper. Afterward, I asked the Peripheral BT next to me if she understood the rabbi's sermon. She responded, "Hardly at all." Similarly, after one of Rabbi Passo's classes, a recent Community BT asked me, not yet knowing the linguistic focus of my research, "Did you understand what he said tonight? He used a lot of Yeshivish."

Rabbi Passo recognizes that recent BTs have less knowledge of Hebrew, Aramaic, and Yiddish than others in his community. Although his lectures include many untranslated loanwords, some of which are relatively obscure, he sometimes uses English words when discussing an issue of special interest to BTs. For example, in his discussion of plates that may be used for Passover, he said some people "become *religious,* they become *frum*" and receive an expensive set of china from their *"alte bubbe"* (great-grandmother). In cases like these, he said, "we are *lenient* sometimes to allow them to go ahead and . . . use it." Although he does use one untranslated loan phrase in this discussion, *alte bubbe,* he translates *frum,* which is one of the most common loanwords, and he uses English "lenient" rather than its common Hebrew equivalent *meykil.* Despite moments like these, much of Rabbi Passo's class would have been unintelligible to most Peripheral BTs.

Videos

The best way to analyze the linguistic differences a BT encounters between Ner Tamid and Milldale is to examine the same speaker in both settings. While most of the rabbis who teach at Ner Tamid live in Milldale, the only classes they offer in Milldale are on Shabbos, when writing and recording are prohibited. However, in August of my year of fieldwork, I happened upon a useful way to compare speech in these two settings, which is generalizable to BTs around the country.

A New York–based Orthodox organization produces videos of lectures about loshon hora to be shown around the mournful holiday of Tisha B'Av, which commemorates the destruction of the Temple. During the year of my research, the organization videotaped and distributed two versions of a lecture by the respected Rabbi Pinchas Stern (a pseudonym): one for people with advanced knowledge and linguistic ability (FFBs and longtime BTs) and one for relative newcomers (new BTs and non-Orthodox Jews). The former was shown at a home in Milldale, and the latter was shown at Ner Tamid. I had a unique opportunity to attend both showings and compare the two lectures. The differences are staggering (table 7.1).

Comparing Rabbi Stern's two lectures, which were almost identical in content, we see that for the FFB audience he used over three times as many loanwords, less than a quarter as many English words that have common loanword correlates, and less than half as many translations. He also used more periphrastic verbs (such as "to be *zoche*" [to merit]) and Yiddish grammatical influences (such as "I want that you should know"). The FFB lecture also included many direct citations of rabbinic quotes, while the BT lecture included only a few. The FFB lecture included a number of "if . . . so . . ." sentences and several instances of "over there" (a discourse marker commonly used in yeshiva settings), while the BT lecture included none of these common Orthodox linguistic features. The BT lecture also included a hypercorrection in English grammar, which

TABLE 7.1
Linguistic differences between Rabbi Stern's two videotaped lectures

Linguistic features (types)	Lecture A: for knowledgeable Orthodox Jews, shown in Milldale	Lecture B: for non-Orthodox Jews and BTs, shown at Ner Tamid
Words used just in Hebrew/Yiddish	42	13
Words used just in English that have common Hebrew/Yiddish loanword correlates	7	32
Translated loanwords	14	37
Yiddish-origin periphrastic verbs	5	1
Yiddish grammatical features	5	3

Examples of loanwords and their (rough) English correlates as used in the two videos

	"We lost the *bayis*"	"The Temple was destroyed"
	"*Tzadikim, gedolim*"	"Great man"
	"Dovid Hamelech"	"King David"
	"*Darshen*"	"Expound or sermonize"
	"Acts of *chesed* and *rachmones*"	"Acts of kindness and mercy"
	"*Maysim tovim*"	"Good deeds"
	"*Soton* is *mekatreg*" (periphrastic)	"Prosecuted by the *Soton*" (passive)
	"The *kapora* process"	"Expiation of our suffering"
	"*Shchina*"	"Divine presence"
	"*Chazal*" (an acronym for "our sages, of blessed memory": *chochmeynu zichronam livracha*)	"Famous sages"

is very common in America: "between you and I" (compare to Standard English "between you and me"). It is interesting that Rabbi Stern uses this hyperstandard construction only in his lecture to BTs, who may have significant secular education. Both lectures include the Jewish abbreviation "B.C.E." (Before the Common Era), used by many Jews in place of "B.C." (Before Christ). However, in the second lecture he uses this phrase with a break in intonation contours, as if he were considering saying only B.C. for this not necessarily Orthodox audience but decided to say B.C.E. instead.

During the year of my fieldwork, I was the only person who attended both video showings. But a number of people have attended Ner Tamid showings in the past and now attend the annual showings in Milldale. As BTs progressively become more involved in the Milldale community, perhaps eventually moving there, they are exposed to more and more frum speech.

Schedules

The language differences between Ner Tamid and Milldale are evident even in writing. I compared two schedules for the month of June, one prepared by Ner Tamid and one by Shomrei Emunah. The Ner Tamid schedule is mailed to anyone who has signed up for past events there, and the Shomrei Emunah schedule is made available on a table in the synagogue lobby. Table 7.2 shows the differences between the two schedules. As with the two lectures, the Milldale schedule has many more loanwords, and the Ner Tamid schedule has more words in English that might have been in Hebrew or Yiddish. Like written Orthodox materials in general, both schedules have few Yiddish grammatical features.

There are several referents used in both publications, most of which appear in Hebrew or Yiddish on the Shomrei Emunah schedule and in English on the Ner Tamid schedule. In addition, the Shomrei Emunah schedule uses the Ashkenazi form "Shabbos," while the Ner Tamid one uses the Israeli or Sephardi "Shabbat." The creators of the Ner Tamid schedule—even though they tend to say "Shabbos"—recognize that non-Orthodox Jews and recent BTs are more likely to use the Israeli [t] than the Ashkenazi [s].

Both schedules have some Hebrew letters, but they use them in quite different ways. The Shomrei Emunah schedule presents over a dozen words and phrases in Hebrew characters, including the date, the announcement of the new month, the names of the services and other events, and "mazel tov." On the Ner Tamid schedule, there are only four Hebrew letters—ד, ג, ב, א (the first four letters of the alphabet)—in a large colorful font. These Hebrew letters seem to be used only as Jewishly marked eye-catchers and perhaps to remind the reader that study at Ner Tamid involves Hebrew texts. Finally, only the Shomrei Emunah schedule has the Hebrew letters בס"ד (b'siyata d'shamaya, "with heaven's help") in the top right corner, an Aramaic abbreviation that many Orthodox Jews include on printed or

TABLE 7.2

**Comparison of language in printed schedules
from synagogue and outreach center**

	Shomrei Emunah synagogue (Milldale)	*Ner Tamid outreach center*
Hebrew words (or abbreviations) in Hebrew characters	13	0
Hebrew/Yiddish loanwords in Latin characters	24	5
Words used in English that have common Hebrew/Yiddish loanword correlates	7	12
Yiddish grammatical influences	1	1

Examples of loanwords and their (rough) English correlates as used in the two schedules

	"*shiur*"	"class"
	"*parsha*"	"portion"
	"*Chumash*"	"Bible"
	"*davening*"	"prayer," "services"

handwritten documents, acknowledging the role of God even in mundane activities like writing notes and schedules. Clearly, in both speech and writing, BTs gain increasing access to Orthodox language as they transition from outreach centers like Ner Tamid to frum communities like Milldale.

Interactions of Language Socialization

When I asked BTs how they learned Orthodox language features, several respondents focused on length of exposure. Andrew said, "I just hear them a thousand times, and they finally sink in." Cecelia emphasized the unconscious nature of acquiring grammatical features through exposure: "People do not consciously start saying 'by.' What you hear often you just repeat." Time of exposure and unintentional repetition are certainly central to the language acquisition process. But newcomers do make a conscious effort to acquire certain features, and they are assisted in this process by interactions of socialization with FFBs and other BTs.

In some of these interactions, the more experienced community member initiates overt or covert language teaching, including explanation of words, translation, and correction. And in others, the BT takes the lead, asking questions and repeating the speech of FFBs and other BTs. These interactions of socialization have much in common with the interactions that facilitate young children learning their first language and, especially, older children and adults learning a second language or speech style. Much of the research on language acquisition and socialization discusses the importance of "language-related episodes," in which learners discuss fine points of language—words, pronunciations, and grammatical forms—with other learners or more competent speakers.[6] Interactions like these are seen as providing the "scaffolding" that helps novices "develop skills . . . as they move from guided or collaborative to independent action."[7] It is language-related episodes like repetition and correction that make adult language socialization similar to child language socialization. At the same time, these episodes point to the heightened consciousness and infantilization that characterize adult language socialization.

Another important finding of the current study is that different BTs have different strategies for learning: some are quite willing to ask questions, and others prefer to look words up on their own. Some request that their friends correct their mistakes, and others prefer not to use a word until they are sure they can say it perfectly. No matter which strategies they prefer, BTs are generally aware that language socialization is an essential part of their integration into the Orthodox community. And FFBs are generally happy to help in this process.

Language Instruction and Translation

I observed several instances of FFBs or BTs teaching words and other linguistic features to BTs. These *metalinguistic* (talking about language) interactions were sometimes triggered by the newcomer's question and sometimes initiated by the veteran. This happened frequently in chavrusa study sessions. For example, in BT Andrew and FFB Avrum's chavrusa, Avrum taught Andrew several words, going well beyond the goal of explicating the text at hand. In the following excerpt, Avrum is teaching Andrew the Hebrew verb *l'hakel* (to be lenient) by using the present-tense masculine singular form it usually takes in Orthodox Jewish English, *meykil*. He contrasts that to a word even more commonly heard among Black Hat Jews, *machmir* (stringent):

AVRUM: *Heykilu* means—it means easy. Oh, he's *meykil,* he's easy on that. *Machmir,* much stricter. So that—Because you hear that all the time and they never tell you what it means. You go hundreds of years, you never know what it means; now you do. You know what I mean? So—

ANDREW: Because of you.

AVRUM: No, because eventually, you get annoyed and you ask somebody.

. . .

AVRUM: . . . meykil and machmir, you know what I mean? I'm sure you've heard
   those terms before, like "Oh, he's meykil—"
ANDREW: Yeah, yeah, sure. I just never knew what it meant.
AVRUM: Exactly, cause no one—
ANDREW: Machmir I knew, but—
AVRUM: Yeah, but they always say that, and you never know what it means, and
   you're always too embarrassed to ask, and you're always expected like you
   know, you know. It's kind of rough.

Avrum articulates the experiences he imagines Andrew has had: hearing the
word many times, being expected to know it, and being too embarrassed to
ask about it. Although empathizing to this extent about the travails of frum
language learning seems to be rare, the explicit teaching of words is common.
Avrum spends so much time on *meykil* and *machmir* (about ninety seconds) not
because they are crucial for comprehension of the text but because they are
crucial for integration into the frum community.

   We see a similar teaching exchange for *shver*, a Yiddish word meaning "difficult" that never appears in the ancient Hebrew and Aramaic rabbinic texts they
are studying. After reading a difficult Aramaic passage, Avrum says:

AVRUM: As they say in the yeshiva, it's *shver*. It's difficult. It's hard for me.
ANDREW: (little laugh)
AVRUM: No, I'm serious. I hear that all the time.
ANDREW: Shver (starts to write it down).

Later in the same study session, they come across the Aramaic word *pshita* (simple). Andrew realizes that this is the opposite of shver, which he points out, but
with a mistake in pronunciation:

ANDREW: *Pshita* . . . (looking at his notes). It's *not sháver*.
AVRUM: It's not shver. (Higher pitch, humorous tone:) It's not shver! Good call.
   You know how to use that word. You see how well you're using these words?
   I want you to use shver whenever you speak to anyone now. You're just
   walking on the street—
ANDREW: (smiling) That's going to be very *shver* to do.

Avrum clearly thinks it is important for Andrew to become competent in the language style of the yeshiva. He even tutors him in pronunciation, as when he suggests that Andrew say *hasam* ([Aramaic] there) rather than *hatam* because that is
the norm in yeshiva. Avrum knows that Andrew will soon spend a year or more in
yeshiva, and he uses metalinguistic instruction to prepare him for that experience.

   Another common technique used to teach Orthodox language is translation.
In most situations where recent BTs or non-Orthodox Jews are present, especially

at Ner Tamid, FFBs and BTs translate many of their Hebrew and Yiddish loanwords. Usually, speakers translate loanwords by restating all or part of the phrase
in which it occurred, as in these examples from lectures at Ner Tamid:

> "This comes <u>from the *medresh*, from the commentaries</u>."

> "And one source tells us for instance that before the flood all the conti-
> nents were joined together and it was <u>the *mabul*, the *flood*</u> that disjoined the
> continents."

> "So <u>before the *mabul*, before the *flood*</u>, the negativity that the people had
> steeped themselves in had become so deeply ingrained and inculcated
> within their psyche that that became their essence and God had to start
> over again."

> "<u>*Nebech*, how sad it is</u>, that most human beings and even sadder that most
> Jews spend their whole lives as walking, talking vegetables because they
> spend their whole life searching for what better to eat and what better way
> to at least engage or indulge in the procreative function."

> "The next level is the level <u>of *ruach*, of *spirit*</u>, of intrinsic humanity."

Sometimes people translate in the reverse direction, from English to Hebrew or
Yiddish, as in, "a series of tests, a series of *nisyonos*." I even observed a number
of instances when teachers translated one loanword with another loanword they
thought newcomers were more likely to understand, such as "the *heychal*, the
beys hamikdash [Temple]," "all *chanúkias*, all *menorahs* [candelabras]," and "the
amud, the *bima*, the *shtender* [lectern/platform from which services are led]."

If teachers did not consider it important for the students to learn the loanwords, they would just use the English equivalents. But some teachers translate
the same loanword dozens of times throughout the same lecture. They want
to make sure that the students understand the content, but they also think it
is important to use—and teach—certain loanwords. Translation also serves an
additional purpose: emphasis. By using both a loan and its translation in the
same sentence, speakers highlight the importance of the concept they are discussing. No matter what the intention, an important effect of frequent translation is the socialization of newcomers to the Orthodox practice of using many
Hebrew, Aramaic, and Yiddish words within English speech.

Written material geared toward BTs also includes a good deal of translation.
For example, Akiva Tatz's book *Anatomy of a Search*, which describes the author's
journey to Orthodoxy and offers arguments in favor of observance and advice
to BTs, defines all loanwords in footnotes.[8] And Richard Greenberg's book of
interviews with dozens of BTs has a large glossary in the back.[9] Even mainstream
Orthodox English books and periodicals include some translations, because the
authors recognize that their readership includes many BTs.

Correction

Veteran community members expect new BTs to make mistakes. When they notice a BT's repeated mistake, they have a tough decision to make: correct them, which could cause immediate embarrassment but avoid it in the future, or not correct them, which could avoid immediate embarrassment but lead to it in the future. This issue is exacerbated by the strong Jewish prohibition against causing shame, an infraction equated with murder.[10]

I did observe some corrections, and a number of FFBs and longtime BTs told me that they correct BTs' incorrect plurals, mispronunciations, and misuses of loanwords. One longtime BT rabbi explained why he sometimes corrects people when they make a mistake in a Hebrew word: "I'm helping them they should know how to use the word" (note the Yiddish-influenced "should" construction). However, I also observed several mistakes that went uncorrected in the presence of FFBs and longtime BTs who surely noticed them.

Based on my observations, it seems that overt corrections are considered more appropriate in a classroom setting than in everyday interactions. Especially when the newcomer is reading Hebrew or Aramaic texts, the teacher or more advanced study partner often corrects mistakes. Outside the classroom, I heard only a few overt corrections. When a new BT addressed Rachmiel as "Rachimel," Rachmiel, himself a BT, responded bluntly, "You didn't pronounce my name right." When I used the English plural of the loanword for "matchmaker," *shadchans*, an FFB corrected me with the Hebrew/Yiddish plural, *shadchonim*. And when a BT used [h] for [ch] in the word *chumash*, an eleven-year-old boy corrected him in a disrespectful way.

The other corrections I heard outside the classroom were more covert, a type of feedback known as "corrective recast" or "embedded" correction. These less obvious corrections send the intended message while avoiding overt discussion of the mistake, which would not only interrupt the flow of conversation but also potentially shame the speaker.[11] As research on language acquisition and socialization has found, this type of feedback is common and is useful for child and adult learners, especially in the acquisition of lexicon. An example of corrective recast is from a conversation between Will (a Peripheral BT) and Rivka Bracha (a Seminary BT) a few weeks after the eight-day holiday of Sukkos. Will asked Rivka Bracha what she did for "kol hamoed" (should be *chol hamoed*). She asked, "For *chol* hamoed?" and then answered his question. The fact that Rivka Bracha couched her correction in a rephrasing of Will's question may have mitigated the embarrassment Will likely felt at receiving negative feedback.

I observed another instance of embedded correction in an exchange between Shelley, a Community BT, and Mrs. Kotler, an FFB. Shelly said, "I always forget what you say before *Yom Kippur* [Day of Atonement]. *Gmar chatimá tová?*" (May you finish with a good seal [in the Book of Life]). Mrs. Kotler answered kindly, "Right, *gmar chasíma tóva*." Mrs. Kotler affirmed Shelley's use of the phrase and then proceeded to correct her pronunciation. Mrs. Kotler's rendering of the phrase changed the [t] to [s] and the ultimate stress to penultimate, in accordance with the Ashkenazi norms common in Milldale. Shelley's pronunciation—common among non-Orthodox and Modern Orthodox Jews—was not a mistake, but it was a breach of local norms. And Mrs. Kotler felt obliged to correct this breach, probably in an effort to socialize Shelley to conform to the norms of her chosen community.

The literature on child language socialization includes many examples of correction in settings around the world, from Lesotho to the Ukraine.[12] Research on adult language socialization in classroom settings has found that both instructors and peers often offer corrections, both embedded and overt. Examples include citizenship classes for adult immigrants in Southern California, Japanese language classes in American universities, and law school.[13] However, in other analyses of adult language socialization I have not found examples of corrections outside the classroom (aside from students preparing for class). The simple reason for this is the dearth of research on adult language socialization in non-classroom settings. It is likely that adults transitioning to new religious, professional, or other identities are occasionally corrected by their peers and by more veteran community members, especially in less overt ways. And it is likely that these interactions result in the adults feeling embarrassed and infantilized.

Questioning

It is clear that veteran community members play a role in the language socialization of new BTs. But sometimes the newcomers themselves take the lead. My fieldnotes are filled with examples of BTs—mostly Peripheral but even some Community and Yeshiva/Seminary BTs—asking questions. They ask questions about religious practice, philosophy, culture, and language. They direct their questions to FFBs and other BTs, especially to the Ner Tamid rabbis and their wives and children. They ask teachers for immediate clarifications during class ("What does that mean?"), they whisper, "What did he say?" to their neighbor during a sermon, and in the course of everyday conversation they ask a friend, "What's the word for ___?"

To give just one example of the many questions I observed: Brandon, a recent Peripheral BT, and Erez, a longtime Yeshiva BT, got to know each other at a Saturday night event at Ner Tamid. As Brandon was leaving, Erez said, "*Shavua tov*" (good week), a parting phrase commonly used on Saturday night, which is the beginning of the Jewish week. Brandon said, "What's that—take care?" Erez said, "*Shavua* is week, so—" And Brandon cut in, "Oh, have a good week." Brandon could have just nodded and looked up the phrase when he got home. But he considered it important enough to ask about, even if doing so may have caused him some discomfort.

Longtime community members expect BTs to ask questions as part of their learning process. One FFB said that you know you can trust a BT's kashrus (observance of dietary laws) when "they ask the right questions." However, this expectation does not eliminate the vulnerability some BTs feel when they ask questions. I heard BTs preface questions with "This is going to sound silly, but . . ." A few BTs mentioned that they sometimes feel more comfortable directing questions about practices (such as dress, rituals, and language) to children rather than their parents. I did hear BTs asking questions to FFBs as young as six, children they have come to know well during Shabbos and holiday visits to their homes in Milldale.

Imitation/Repetition

At a concert sponsored by Ner Tamid, Reuven, a BT musician, told a story: There was once a king who had an empty palace. He found two architects and asked them each to decorate half of it in a year. One architect put much effort into it, including time-consuming construction and intricate ornamentation. The other architect waited until the last minute, and when he noticed how soon the deadline was, he started to worry. But then he had a brilliant idea: he covered his side of the palace with mirrors, so it reflected everything the other architect did. The king loved both sides of the palace.

Reuven told the audience that this story used to bother him, because the king approves of the architect who did not do much work. But then he realized that the moral is this: "Even if you don't have much learning or much time to learn, you can still please God. Just mimic what the *tzadik* (righteous man) does, and God will love you."

This allegory must have really hit home with many of the BTs in the audience. By imitating someone with more experience and skill (BT or FFB), they can please God. Most of them probably thought of the story in terms of religious practice, but it can also apply to language. Even if BTs do not have time to study Hebrew, Aramaic, or Yiddish, they can still learn the distinctive features of Orthodox Jewish English by imitating others. Throughout my fieldwork I observed many instances of new BTs imitating FFBs or more experienced BTs by repeating their words, grammar, and intonation.

As many studies have indicated, repetition is an important component of child language socialization.[14] Children try out words and other elements of language, often right after they hear them. In many cases, children's immediate repetitions of an adult's term "connote acceptance or ratification of the adult term" and allow the child to practice using it.[15] In the Orthodox community, new BTs also sometimes use immediate repetition for these dual purposes: uptake and practice.

One example of immediate repetition is from Mark, a recent BT, in conversation with FFB Rabbi Tovin, who was visiting from Israel:

(1) MARK: Anyone who can live in Israel but doesn't, that's not *kiddush Hashem* [sanctifying God's name].

(2) TOVIN: It's *chillul Hashem* [profaning God's name].

(3) MARK: It's chillul Hashem.

In line 1, Mark conveys the message he intended, but the loanword he uses is not what a more experienced Orthodox Jew would use. Rabbi Tovin expresses agreement with Mark, using the more appropriate loanword. Mark immediately mimics what Rabbi Tovin says, both ratifying his statement and practicing this phrase that he may have never used before. A few minutes later, in conversation with someone else, Mark uses the same phrase again: "The only way it wouldn't be chillul Hashem would be if you thought it was kiddush Hashem." His imitation in line 3 helped him to incorporate this phrase into his active vocabulary.

Another example of repetition involved three people. Olivia, a longtime BT, and Marissa, a recent BT, were talking with FFB Rabbi Hollander. Olivia mentioned that Elinor, a non-Orthodox woman, was interested in learning more about traditional Judaism:

OLIVIA: She really wants to get into the whole thing.

R. HOLLANDER: Good, *baruch Hashem* [blessed be God].

OLIVIA (smiling): *Baruch Hashem.*

MARISSA (smiling): *Baruch Hashem!*

OLIVIA (smiling): *Baruch Hashem!*

Marissa and Olivia's repetitions of Rabbi Hollander's phrase are somewhat tongue-in-cheek, but they represent both uptake and legitimate peripheral participation. By saying *baruch Hashem,* Olivia and Marissa are ratifying Rabbi Hollander's happiness that Elinor is expressing interest in Orthodoxy, starting on the path they took to becoming BTs. They are demonstrating that they too are thankful to God. And they are showing that they too use Hebrew phrases like this FFB rabbi. Although this is certainly not the first time Olivia and Marissa have used *baruch Hashem,* they are using repetition to indicate their frum identity—in both content and form.

The domain where I observed the most repetition was chavrusa study sessions.[16] When the learning partners had different levels of knowledge and experience, the newcomer often imitated the veteran. In BT Andrew and FFB Avrum's study sessions, I often heard Avrum read a passage and Andrew repeat it word for word. Avrum would translate, and Andrew would repeat his translation.

Once I even heard Andrew repeat a Yiddish-influenced construction that Avrum used in a translation:

ANDREW: (reading Aramaic phrase): *D'iy salka daytach*
AVRUM: *D'iy salka daytach*. And if I would have thought—
ANDREW: And if I would have thought—

I never heard Andrew use the if-clause "would" in his everyday speech, and I often heard him say things like "If I had thought . . ." It is likely that the if-clause "would" sounded strange to Andrew.[17] But he used it without comment in his study session, because he was imitating a more experienced learner.

In study sessions, I often heard BTs imitating their partners' intonation. When he was learning with Rabbi Nussbaum, Jacob sometimes read and translated the text at hand in spoken intonation. But often when Nussbaum chanted a phrase or used a rise-fall intonation contour, Jacob would imitate this intonation. Once when Nussbaum read a Hebrew phrase in a chant, Jacob used the same chanting contour in his translation of the phrase. But he had trouble with some words and never reached the end of the phrase, so his chant never reached the low tone like Nussbaum's did. Even so, he was using the FFB's speech as a model to imitate as he attempted to become a more proficient learner and a culturally competent member of the frum community.

In child language socialization, repetition sometimes reaches the point of routinization. For example, anthropologists Karen Watson-Gegeo and David Gegeo describe repeating routines among the Kwara'ae of the Solomon Islands. The caregiver uses an "eliciting imperative"—the word *uri*—or a special "invitational intonation contour" with a word or phrase. The young child is then expected to repeat the word or phrase.[18] In middle-class American communities, parents engage in similar routines with young children just beginning to speak and with older children surrounding politeness conventions ("Say thank you").[19]

In situations of adult language socialization, this type of prompting for repetition is rare. Adult apprentices would find it demeaning if a master/veteran told them to "say x," with the possible exception of second-language classrooms.[20] In legal anthropologist Elizabeth Mertz's study of language socialization in law school, she describes Socratic exchanges, in which professors sometimes put words in their students' mouths. But even in these belittling episodes, she only rarely found prompting for repetition (as in "Say yes" after the student answered "No").[21] In the informal and classroom discourse I observed among Orthodox Jews, BTs were never explicitly instructed to repeat after community veterans. This is an important contrast between child and adult language socialization, stemming from the heightened consciousness and the reluctance to shame adults.

Self-Teaching

Another unique aspect of adult language socialization is that adults are able to take the initiative to teach themselves outside of social interactions. While children learning language are also learning how to learn, adult novices already have years of experience with learning and self-teaching. Many BTs spend hours reading Orthodox books and periodicals, surfing Orthodox websites, and listening to recorded lectures about the philosophy, laws, and customs of Orthodox Judaism. The primary goal of this self-teaching is to absorb the content, but an additional outcome is that BTs also increase their repertoire of loanwords and other features of Orthodox language.

Mark, a Community BT, says he has learned a lot of his "Yeshivish" from listening to recorded lectures by rabbis, including "whatever I can get my hands on." I once heard him tell other BTs over dinner about a rabbi he had recently heard on cassette: "You should hear [Rabbi Goldenberg]—he sounds so Yeshivish!" Rhoda, a BT who recently transitioned from Peripheral to Community, said she uses Orthodox books and newspapers to learn Hebrew and Yiddish words. She owns the *Frumspeak* dictionary, and she often adds her own entries to it.[22] She says she underlines words she does not understand, often "every fifth or tenth word!" and asks friends for their translations. Self-teaching plays a critical role in BTs' linguistic socialization to Orthodoxy.

BTs Learning from Other BTs

Research on learning in and out of the classroom has highlighted the "importance of near-peers in the circulation of knowledgeable skill."[23] Novices learn to be competent members of their new community in part through their observations of and interactions with other novices. This is certainly the case for BTs. At Shabbos and holiday celebrations, BTs of various stages of integration take part in the rituals together, helping each other along the way. During classes, events, and informal interactions, BTs observe other BTs using religious and cultural practices, including frum speech. And they discuss these practices, asking questions and correcting each others' mistakes.

This learning from near-peers has a consequence: BTs sometimes acquire "mistakes," that is, practices that FFBs associate with BTs and sometimes criticize. Some community members are aware of the possibility of learning "flawed" language from other novices. One BT said he does not use Orthodox language as much as he used to, because "I live in a mixed [BT–FFB] community. . . . You hear things from ba'alei teshuva and FFBs, so you don't know if you're making mistakes." The acquisition of distinctly BT language might be a temporary stage, and the BT might eventually acquire the forms more common among FFBs. Alternatively, BTs might retain these features as part of their linguistic repertoire.

The centrality of peer-to-peer learning in the socialization process has the potential to change Orthodox language, especially in communities with a large percentage of BTs. I have noticed a few "mistakes" becoming crystallized, such that even FFBs use them. For example, many BTs and several FFBs, especially FFB women, analyzed *ba'alei teshuva* (plural) as a singular word, pluralizing it as *ba'alei teshuvas*. And I heard several BTs and a few FFBs use the Yiddish-influenced "by" in a motion phrase, as in "we're going by them," while Yiddish allows it only in stative phrases, such as "staying by them" or "eating by them."

One very learned FFB man, who generally uses Hebrew and Yiddish loan-words in ways associated with FFBs, used the words *Hashem* (God) and *daven* (pray) with influences from English, in ways I more often heard from BTs. He said, "There is one Hashem," and "It's hard to send the message of a loving Hashem." *Hashem* is a Hebrew and Yiddish name for God that literally means "the name." In both of those source languages, it would be ungrammatical to use an additional article—definite or indefinite—with *Hashem*. This is clearly an influence from English, where "God" can take an article. This FFB also said, "Have you ever davened for something really hard?" In Yiddish, *daven* indicates the act of saying prayers, and a different word, *bet*, is used for the "request" meaning of pray. Even though one can supplicate during a prayer service, Yiddish does not include phrases like "daven for something" or "daven that something will happen." This usage is influenced by the English word "pray," which has both meanings.

I have heard a number of BTs use *daven* and *Hashem* with English influences like this, and it seems that these uses (especially daven) are in the process of spreading to FFBs as well.[24] While it is possible that these English influences would have become part of FFBs' language without input from BTs, it seems that BT "mistakes" are having an impact on the evolution of Orthodox Jewish English.

Stages in Loanword Acquisition

In the process of transitioning from apprentice to veteran of Orthodox life, BTs pick up Orthodox practices at different paces. Just as there is no set timetable for transitioning from Peripheral to Community (to Yeshiva/Seminary) BT, people begin to call Passover *Pesach* and synagogue *shul* at different points in their socialization process. Even so, my observations and interviews suggest six stages that BTs tend to go through as they acquire Hebrew and Yiddish words and incorporate them into their English speech. The learner

1. hears the word without noticing it or without understanding it
2. hears it in a context that facilitates understanding or remembering it
3. asks about it or looks it up

4. uses it with a mistake
5. uses it in a marked way, often playfully
6. uses it seriously, correctly, and unselfconsciously

From the interactions I observed, it seems that speakers tend to go through stages 1 and/or 2, 4 and/or 5, and that stage 3 is optional. The order of stages 3, 4, and 5 is flexible. Some BTs never reach stage 6 for some words. These stages might apply to any linguistic feature of which the speaker is aware, such as chanting intonation contours and Yiddish influences in grammar. But for less salient features like [t] release or schwa deletion, these stages likely do not apply.

Throughout my fieldwork, I witnessed all these stages, but I rarely observed all stages for any particular BT learning a particular word, except in the study domain. My regular recordings of Peripheral BT Andrew and FFB Avrum's study sessions allowed me to observe all six stages for Andrew's acquisition of the Yiddish/Hebrew word *chazer* (review, go through [a text] with the goal of completely understanding it; not to be confused with its homonym, meaning "pig"):

Stage 1:   11/26: Andrew hears the word a few times, likely without understanding (he may have also heard it in the past).

Stage 2:   11/26: Avrum explains the word (without a question from Andrew,
Avrum assumes he does not know it) by telling a story about his study partner in yeshiva who thought that "learning Gemora and not chazering it is like [planting] a field and not cultivating it."

Stages 3, 4:   12/3: As Andrew is about to chazer the text, he asks about the word and makes a mistake in pronouncing it: "Now what's the—what's this called when we uh sort of summarize what we did? It's *kaaaa*—" Avrum tells him.

Stage 5:   12/3: When Avrum asks Andrew to go through what they just learned, Andrew uses the word in a marked way: "You want me to (pause, smile, rise in tone) *chazer* it, huh?"

Stage 5:   2/18: Avrum uses the word, and Andrew repeats it with a slight smile. Avrum: "Wanna chazer?" Andrew: "Let's chazer." His smile, as well as the fact that he repeats it rather than responding "sure" or "OK," indicates that he still feels self-conscious using this loanword.

Stage 6:   3/18: Andrew uses *chazer* regularly without a smile or other marking.

Outside of the study domain, I observed stages 1 through 4 for Norman learning the word *shadchan* (matchmaker). Norman is a middle-aged divorced Peripheral BT who is starting to search for a marriage partner. Because he knows he wants to become more involved with Orthodoxy, he is dating only women with similar religious interests, and he is meeting them through a matchmaker—a common practice in frum circles. He was talking to Charlotte, a veteran community member, about his dating experiences, and he used the word "matchmaker." When Charlotte responded, she used the loanword *shad-chan* (stages 1 and 2). Norman said, "Excuse me?" (stage 3). Charlotte said the word again. Norman tried to repeat it but got it wrong. They went back and forth several times: she said it, and he tried to repeat it. I also tried to help, saying the word slowly and spelling it in English. Norman, a bit frustrated, said, "I need a guide to pronunciation. Is there a tape on that?" The conversation about dating continued, and the next time he mentioned the matchmaker, he used the loanword, but with a mistake in pronunciation: *shabcham* (stage 4). Eventually Norman found his match, and, although I did not hear him use the word again, he was likely able to credit his shadchan unselfconsciously—without mistakes and without marking the word as foreign.

Despite their feelings of frustration and infantilization, BTs continue to try out new words and other Orthodox linguistic features. Although inviting a friend to "Come *to* us for Shabbos" and answering "How are you?" with "baruch Hashem" are not religiously mandated, they are part of Orthodox culture. BTs and FFBs alike recognize the importance of distinctive Orthodox language, and they work together to accomplish the work of language socialization.

8

"A *Ba'al Teshuva* Freak"

Distinguishing Practices of Newly Orthodox Jews

One Shabbos afternoon, I was lounging around at the Cohen home after a delicious lunch. My belly was still heavy from the cholent, so I preferred to stay in the living room with nine-year-old Avrumy and fourteen-year-old Shmuly rather than join their brothers and sisters who were running around in the yard. As Shmuly read *The Jewish Press*, I chatted with Avrumy. The subject turned to my research, and I mentioned that I was interested in how people can tell if others are BTs. He said, "Their voice sounds weird, like not a Jewish voice." This kind of comment, which I heard from many BTs and FFBs, holds some degree of truth, especially among recent BTs. As might be expected based on previous chapters, BTs take diverse approaches to frum language and culture. Some embrace their distinctness, some do what they can to blend in, and some do both at various times or in progression. This chapter explains these strategies, focusing on hyperaccommodation, deliberate distinctiveness, and the bungee effect. It ends with analysis of a song called "B.T. Blues," a creative response to the in-between status of newcomers, which illustrates these trends.

How BTs Distinguish Themselves

During my fieldwork, dozens of people of all ages—BTs and FFBs—told me that they can often tell who is a BT by the way they talk. A number said that recent BTs are especially conspicuous linguistically. When I asked for elaboration, they mentioned their mistakes, overuse of certain words and expressions, Hebrew pronunciation, and an awkward or unnatural sound. Comments like these were sometimes accompanied by similar observations about awkwardness in clothing and head coverings.[1]

While some BTs do acquire Orthodox styles quite well and can even pass as FFB, others do not. Especially in the early phases of becoming Orthodox, BTs make inadvertent mistakes, some of which are examples of hyperaccommodation. On the other hand, some perceived mistakes are actually BTs' deliberate attempts to distinguish themselves from FFBs. Mistakes (including hyperaccommodation and deliberate distinctiveness) are important components in both how BTs indicate their identity and how others perceive them.[2]

Mistakes

When speakers of one dialect attempt to speak another dialect, they often exhibit imperfections.[3] Among BTs learning Orthodox Jewish English, I observed many mistakes in the pronunciation, grammar, and use of Hebrew or Yiddish loanwords and Yiddish constructions. Examples include:

PRONUNCIATION

1. [k] instead of [ch]: *kol hamoed* for *chol hamoed*
2. [uh] (as in "bus") instead of [a]: *chusuna* for *chasuna* (wedding) (probably on analogy with *chussen*, a common pronunciation of *chossen* [groom], but also more general confusion regarding two similar Hebrew vowels)
3. [uh] (as in "bus") instead of [u] (as in "push"): *from* for *frum*

GRAMMAR

1. Plural as singular: "That *nigunim* [melodies] . . . was so beautiful" (should be "*nigun*")
2. Singular as plural: "I'm not one of the *chacham* [learned one] like [Rabbi Goldman] and [Rabbi Passo]" (should be "*chachamim*")
3. Yiddish adjective suffix "e" used when the adjective does not precede a noun: "somebody who's more *Yeshivishe*" (should be "*Yeshivish*" or "a *Yeshivishe* guy")

USE

1. Overusing *kaynahora*, *baruch Hashem*, and *chas v'sholom* and using them in inappropriate situations
2. Using the greeting *sholom aleichem* when parting, rather than greeting
3. Response to "I'm pregnant": "*Mazel tov!* Oh, not yet. I mean, *b'sha'a tova!*" (*mazel tov* is "congratulations," and *b'sha'a tova*, the appropriate response, is "at a good time")

WORD CHOICE

1. "Being cut off from the Children of Israel for . . . eating *matzah* [unleavened bread] on Pesach" (should be *chametz* [leavened food])

2. "I fried *sheitel* [wig] with the rebbetzin" (should be *schnitzel* [chicken patty])
3. "We had a squad of six *shiduchim* [matched couples] come in" (should be *shadchonim* [matchmakers])

LOAN USAGES FROM YIDDISH

1. "Does Rabbi *hold to* the Dragon Inn?" (should be "hold of" or "hold by" [approve of])
2. "Where *do you hold with your kosherness?* (should be "Where are you holding in your *kashrus?*")
3. "I'm staying *by [Laura's] brother's*" (should be "brother")

New BTs are certainly aware that they are liable to make mistakes. They sometimes avoid saying words with which they do not yet feel comfortable, for fear of making a mistake. For example, Jenny was taking a Hebrew class and was very excited to learn the future tense of the verb *rotse* (want). The future masculine singular form, *yirtse*, is used in the Hebrew/Yiddish/Jewish English expression *im yirtse Hashem* (if God wills it), which is often pronounced *mirtseshem* or *mertseshem*. A few hours after that Hebrew lesson, Jenny told me, "I never said *im yirtse Hashem* before, because I knew I was saying it wrong. But today I've said it many times."

Hyperaccommodation

Many of the mistakes BTs make are what sociolinguists call "hypercorrections."[4] Sociolinguist Peter Trudgill defines hypercorrections as "attempts to adopt a more prestigious variety of speech which, through overgeneralization, leads to the production of forms which do not occur in the target prestige variety."[5] As sociolinguist Malcah Yaeger-Dror argues, "correction" may not be the most appropriate term, since the phenomenon at hand may not be conscious and often does not involve accommodation to a "prestigious" variety or to what the accommodators view as correct. Instead, Yaeger-Dror proposes the term "hyperaccommodation," defined as "the shift toward or away from a given speech variety (for social reasons which need to be determined), creating linguistic patterns which overshoot the speech in that target variety."[6]

A number of sociolinguistic studies have found that speakers hyperaccommodate when they are not proficient speakers of their target speech style. Sociolinguist William Labov found that, in the more formal and careful speech characteristic of reading passages and word lists, New Yorkers who may have aspired to a higher socioeconomic class used [r] after a vowel even more frequently than people in the class above them.[7] This is referred to as *quantitative hyperaccommodation*, when speakers use a higher frequency of a variant than the speakers to whom they are accommodating.[8] Sociolinguist John Baugh describes instances of *qualitative hyperaccommodation*, when speakers generate innovative forms as they try to approximate a target: African American Vernacular English speakers saying "loveded" (loved) and "two-faceded" (two faced) in formal situations when they are approximating Standard English.[9] In my observations of newly Orthodox Jews, I have observed many instances of both quantitative and qualitative hyperaccommodation.

QUANTITATIVE HYPERACCOMMODATION. I met Shoshana, a Seminary BT, at Shabbos dinner at the Cohens'. She agreed to be interviewed the next Tuesday evening. In those two evenings that I spent with her, I heard the phrases *baruch Hashem* and *bli ayin hara* (without the evil eye) more than I hear most Orthodox Jews use them in several weeks. Usually these phrases are appended to expressions of important things, like having good health or many children. To give a few examples, Shoshana said: "He met a guy, and he was frum, baruch Hashem." "Baruch Hashem, [they're] helping people find jobs." "Rabbi [Passo] knows so much, bli ayin hara." "Rabbi [Marks] is very nice, bli ayin hara. He has nine children, bli ayin hara." And when her daughter said she could only count to 100, Shoshana responded, "You could count to 200, bli ayin hara." These instances represent qualitative hypercorrection, in that the speaker has a different understanding of how these Hebrew phrases should be used. They also represent quantitative hypercorrection, in that the speaker is using the words more frequently than many of the people she is trying to emulate. Shoshana and others like her may be aware that they overuse these phrases compared to their FFB friends, and they might attribute this to their heightened desire to acknowledge God's presence and keep the "evil eye" away. But more likely (or perhaps in addition), they are unintentionally going too far in their attempt to sound frum.

Quantitative hyperaccommodation is also evident when we look at the overall use of distinctive Orthodox features. Take, for example, the speech of Rivka Bracha and Devora, two Seminary BT women who have been Orthodox for only a few years (discussed in chapter 7). Their linguistic indices are much higher than other BT and FFB women; Rivka Bracha even uses Yiddish grammatical constructions that most FFBs do not use. In their attempt to speak like Orthodox Jews, they go beyond the community norms.

QUALITATIVE HYPERACCOMMODATION. I heard many examples of qualitative hyperaccommodation from BTs, including:

PRONUNCIATION
1. [h] => [ch]: *chalacha* for *halacha* (Jewish law)
2. [k] => [ch]: *medayech* for *medayek* (deduce)
3. [t] => [s]: *amarsa* for *amarta* (you said) (in Whole Hebrew)

GRAMMAR

1. double adjective suffix: *heymishdik* for *heymish*: *heym* (home) + *-ish* (adjective suffix) + *-dik* (adjective suffix)
2. *-e* suffix when adjective is not before a noun: "He's so *Yeshivishe* looking"

These speakers are aware of the linguistic transformations involved in switching from the English and Hebrew spoken by non-Jews and non-Orthodox Jews to the English and Hebrew spoken by Orthodox Jews, such as selectively replacing [t] with [s] and adding the *-e* suffix to Yiddish adjectives. But they do not understand all the intricacies of the transformations and they overextend them. Once I heard a BT originally from New York produce two hyperaccommodations in one word: she pronounced *muktza* as *muchser*, using [ch] for [k], as well as the extra [r] that many New Yorkers add after a vowel in an attempt to avoid the stigmatized dropping of [r].

OVEREXTENSION BY AUDIENCE. Another way that BTs hyperaccommodate is to use Hebrew or Yiddish loanwords in conversations with non-Jews, while FFBs generally mitigate the distinctness of their outsider speech. For example, Community BT Levi says he often uses Hebrew or Yiddish words at work, even though he is one of the only Jews in his office. He has a "No Loshon Hora" sign on his desk, and he often silences gossiping colleagues by saying, "Shhh. Loshon hora." He says that one of his "*goyishe*" (non-Jewish) co-workers now says *mamish* (really) and *takeh* (truly). For a co-worker to pick up these words, Levi must have used them many times. In contrast, FFB Rabbi Hollander apparently tries not to use phrases like this at his non-Jewish workplace. When he was talking to his Torah class about the phrase "God willing," he said that if you "let it slip out of your mouth, they say, 'What's God doing in the workplace? Keep him in church.'" As unlikely as this reaction is, this quote shows that Rabbi Hollander, like other FFBs, attempts to de-Judaize his speech to non-Jews. Levi and some other BTs use not only religious phrases but even Hebrew and Yiddish words. This allows them to highlight their Orthodox Jewish identity, so new and salient to them, in the presence of outsiders.

I observed another example of this phenomenon when I was driving Joanne to the bus station after an event at Ner Tamid. We were waiting in the car for her bus to come, and an African American man approached the car and asked us for some change. Joanne gave him a dollar, and he said something like, "May God be with you." Joanne, a new BT, responded enthusiastically, "*Baruch Hashem, amen*" (blessed be God, amen). This may have been a performance for my sake, as we had just been speaking about Orthodox language. But it was also a chance for Joanne to connect with the stranger over their shared belief, as well as to indicate to me her zeal for Orthodoxy. An FFB in the same situation would likely not have used these Hebrew words.

Of course, not all BTs overextend their language according to audience. During most of the times I observed BTs with non-Orthodox Jews or non-Jews, they did not use Hebrew or Yiddish words. I asked one Peripheral BT if she says *baruch Hashem* around non-Orthodox Jews, and she said, "No, because they'd look at me like I'm nuts." Indeed, when I observed another BT, Miriam, using several loans with non-Jews, she got a reaction of confusion. Two non-Jewish customers came in to the Judaica shop where Miriam worked in Milldale, and in helping them she used the words *Pesach*, *seder* plate, and *kiddush* cup. When they asked for clarification, she explained the words, using them a few times in the explanations. It seems that her intent was to teach these non-Jews about Jewish culture and language, in addition to performing her new identity as an observant Jew, both common acts among BTs.

OVEREXTENSION OF LEXICAL REPLACEMENT. Sometimes BTs' unintentional overuse of Hebrew and Yiddish words seems to be a result of having replaced an English word in their mental lexicon. Chaya, who grew up Catholic and converted to Orthodox Judaism, was talking to a non-Jewish girl in the neighborhood. She asked, "Are you here to visit your *bubby*? Your grandmother?" She immediately corrected herself with the English equivalent. Devora also corrected herself when she was at the home of a Polish Catholic seamstress, getting her borrowed wedding dress altered. She said, "I'm not allowed to get more than an inch removed, because it has to be OK for another *kallah*. For another bride."

Although it is possible that Chaya and Devora were performing their Jewish/Orthodox identity for the benefit of the non-Jews or the ethnographer, their self-corrections suggest that their use of the loanwords was accidental. It seems that they replaced their mental entries "grandmother" and "bride" with *bubby* and *kallah* and that when they tried to access the lexical items for those referents they accessed the new words instead. This is a process I refer to as *overextension of lexical replacement*: speakers who use Word X learn Word Y, which has a similar meaning but differs in use, and then they use Word Y even when Word X would be appropriate.

Overextensions of lexical replacement are made not only by people who acquire a new way of speaking but also by people who learn a new lexical item, such as when a store or restaurant changes its name. To give examples of my own overextensions of lexical replacement: My college, Columbia, was on the semester system, and my graduate school, Stanford, was on the quarter system. When I started graduate school, I learned to replace the lexical item "semester" with "quarter." But I often found myself referring to academic terms at schools on the semester system as quarters. The same holds true for my use of "woman" as a lexical replacement for some uses of "girl." In college, I learned to refer to myself and my female peers as "women," and many years later I still sometimes find myself using "woman" in reference to teenage or preteen girls. Usually, I notice my overextension mistakes and correct myself, as these BTs did.

DISCOURSE ABOUT HYPERACCOMMODATION. Many FFBs, BTs, and even non-Orthodox Jews talk about BTs' hyperaccommodation, without, of course, using that word. One BT man said, "In their attempt to make sure that they're saying things properly, they end up making more of a botch of it. . . . There are people who try too hard. . . . Every other word is some kind of [Hebrew or Yiddish] expression." Similarly, an FFB woman commented: "Sometimes a BT wants to sound frum, so they throw in frum expressions. BTs do it more because they're trying to make up for lost time and because they're trying to fit in. That's a mark of being frum. They don't want to be looked down upon. They pepper their [language] with *baruch Hashem* more. I use them too, but not every third word."

There are even jokes about BTs' overextension of linguistic rules. In addition to the "ginger kale" joke reported in chapter 1, I also heard: "What do BTs name their children? *Kel*isheva and *Kel*iyahu" (instead of Elisheva and Eliyahu). In line with the prohibition against saying God's name outside a liturgical context, Orthodox Jews often say *Kel* instead of *El* (one of God's names). The notion of BTs applying this rule to names and English words is an example of the discourse of hyperaccommodation.

NONLINGUISTIC HYPERACCOMMODATION: BT ZEAL. The sense that BTs hyperaccommodate to Orthodox norms extends beyond language. Both BTs and FFBs talk about BTs shuckling (swaying back and forth) harder when they pray, dressing in a hyper-modest way, and following every stringency they know in Jewish law. I heard several jokes about this, some from FFBs but mostly from BTs. "Have you heard the one about the ba'al teshuva whose wife accidentally uses a fleishik [used for meat] spoon for ice cream? He tells her solemnly, 'Pack our things, we're moving.'" Another common one goes: "How many BTs does it take to screw in a light bulb?" "You mean you can do that?"[10] These jokes highlight BTs' overly rigid observance, partly due to their fear of transgressing.

My fieldnotes include several examples of BTs hyperaccommodating in religious observance and cultural practice, based on my observations and people's reports of themselves and others. BTs avoid certain acceptable activities, and they go overboard in the observance of positive commandments. Many stay away from music, movies, books, and games from their pre-Orthodox days. Some men wear their tzitzis hanging out more conspicuously than is customary, and some women wear sleeves and skirts longer than required and necklines higher than their FFB counterparts.

BTs do this in part because they want to make sure that they are observing laws and customs correctly, but also, as the FFB woman suggested, "to make up for lost time." One BT told me that when she gets married she plans to wear both a sheitel and a hat, a practice common among some women in more Black Hat communities, especially in the New York area. She said, "I had days when I was not tznius [modest]. So for me, I feel like the way to do teshuva on that is I'm going to double cover." Similarly, in a *New York Times* article, the rapper and BT Shyne is quoted: "I want to know the laws. I don't want to know the leniencies. I never look for the leniencies because of all of the terrible things I've done in my life, all of the mistakes I've made." Shyne took on the strictures of Orthodox Judaism when serving a prison sentence and subsequently moved to Jerusalem, underwent a pro forma conversion, and changed his legal name from Jamaal Barrow to Moses Levi.[11] These examples illustrate the culture of penitence common among BTs, a culture that sometimes manifests in hyperaccommodation.

Another reason that some BTs are overzealous in their observance of Orthodox law and custom is to show off the knowledge and culture that is so new and exciting to them. A number of times I heard BT students insert a loanword when the teacher had used English, such as a newcomer's "The *akeyda!*" when the teacher had said, "The binding of Isaac." An example from home decoration is the placement of bookshelves. Some Orthodox Jews, such as the learned FFB Rabbi Passo, keep most of their books in a dedicated office in the basement. But others display their books prominently in the living room or other areas where guests can see them. In most BT homes I visited in Milldale, the books were in the living room. Shoshana, the Community BT who says *baruch Hashem* frequently, has two bookcases in her living room with some Hebrew *seforim* (holy books) and many English books about Orthodox observance. As I was waiting to interview her while she put her children to bed, she said, "You're welcome to look at our library." During my many visits to FFB homes with impressive collections of seforim, nobody explicitly called my attention to them.

Another way that BTs hyperaccommodate to Orthodox norms is to shed connections to their pre-BT days. As one FFB says, some BTs "throw the baby out with the bath water." BTs have told me that they threw away all their old clothing, music, art, or photographs, even those that were not offensive or immodest. As one frum blogger writes, "How many BTs have I met that the first thing they did was to throw out all their CDs and stop listening to goyishe music."[12] Some BTs even cut off contact with old friends, partly because of the complications that arise in maintaining such relationships, but also in an effort to make a clean break from their non-Orthodox past.

Other research mentions some BTs' desire to take on all elements of observance and every possible stringency.[13] Even so, outreach professionals warn new BTs against this. For example, a self-help book for newly Orthodox Jews, *The Baal*

Teshuva Survival Guide, advises BTs to take the process "slowly but surely," offering cautionary examples of people who burned out because they took on "too much too fast."[14]

HYPERACCOMMODATION AND THE HAREDIZATION OF ORTHODOX JEWS. BTs' hyperaccommodation to Orthodox norms is influenced by and contributes to the "Haredization" of the Orthodox community at large. As a number of historians have explained, Haredi (Black Hat) communities in the twentieth century took on stringencies in religious and social practice that their grandparents did not follow. An example is the Hazon Ish's ruling that the amount of wine required on Shabbos and holidays is actually more than had been practiced for centuries (the Hazon Ish—Rabbi Avraham Yeshaya Karelitz—was a twentieth-century talmudic scholar and halachic authority in Eastern Europe and Israel). In the last century, stringencies like this became widely accepted in the Haredi world as individuals began looking to texts for definitive advice on practice, rather than to one's family customs, which had always been the authoritative source of tradition. This turn toward stringency was possible due to the ruptures caused by early twentieth-century migration from Eastern Europe and by the Holocaust. These ruptures led to the increasing centrality of the yeshiva among Haredi Jews, and the students began to prefer the authority of texts and their teachers who analyze those texts over the authority of their family traditions.[15] This trend continues in the Orthodox world today: some FFB children of FFBs refuse to follow their parents' traditions, preferring to abide by the stringencies codified in recent rabbinic texts. Thus it is not only BTs who observe Judaism more strictly than their parents.

For many Jews, the twentieth-century ruptures of migration and genocide, as well as the earlier transitions of urbanization and the *Haskalah* (Jewish Enlightenment), led to a reduction or even the cessation of Jewish religious practice. Whether this change happened within individual families in Europe or America, in 1850 or 1950, the descendants of these Jews no longer looked to halacha as the guiding force in their lives. Some of these descendants, BTs, have recently looked back to the practices of their ancestors. And, like much of the Orthodox world, BTs look to texts and textual masters as authorities, rather than their families—who are much less observant than they are. Even more than some of their FFB peers, they tend to gravitate toward the stringencies of religious and cultural practice.

Since the 1960s, Orthodox communities toward the Modern end of the continuum have shifted toward Haredi / Black Hat "contra-acculturative" norms. Many have become less accepting of secular studies and stricter about gender separation.[16] As Heilman points out, this is due in part to changes in Modern Orthodox education: the influx of Haredi teachers in Modern Orthodox schools and the rise of the post–high school year in Israel. For socioeconomic reasons, Modern Orthodox Jews were choosing secular careers over teaching and the rabbinate, and schools and synagogues turned to Haredim to fill these gaps. With parental involvement in Jewish education decreasing (partly due to the increase in dual-career families), students gradually absorbed the values and ideologies of their teachers. In addition, spending a year studying in yeshiva or seminary in Israel after high school has become almost universal practice among Orthodox day school graduates. Influenced by Haredi teachers in these "total institutions" away from their families, many students take on stringencies and contra-acculturative ideologies, sometimes deciding to forego their plans for university and secular careers.[17]

Heilman also points to changes in American society as factors in Orthodoxy's shift to the right. Since the 1960s, as many ethnic groups have proudly embraced cultural differentiation, so too have Orthodox Jews gained confidence in their distinctiveness. And along with other non-liberal groups, many Orthodox Jews saw American society as shifting away from the "wholesomeness" of the 1950s. Their concern that college campuses, in particular, were sites of chaos and assimilation led to a devaluing of secular higher education.

In addition to these factors, I argue that the rise of the BT movement—from the 1960s to the present—has also contributed to the Haredization of Orthodox Jews. If BTs are overly zealous in their observance and hyperaccommodate to cultural norms, then FFBs may feel insecure and motivated to become more stringent themselves. When I told an FFB teenager that my research is about how ba'alei teshuva learn to speak and act like Orthodox Jews, she responded, "You mean they learn it and then they go way beyond other people and make us feel like we're not religious?" The two friends she was with agreed, pointing out that this issue comes up frequently because there are so many BTs in their shul. I heard the same idea from a few other FFBs.

Most FFBs I spoke to did not put it in such stark terms, but several talked about BTs having a spiritual freshness that FFBs should emulate. Although FFBs did not attribute their own changes in cultural practices to BT zeal, I suspect that this plays a role. Take the example of FFB Rabbi Citrin. As a young man he did not have a beard. As his shul "moved more to the right and almost everybody had a beard," he felt that his clean shave stood out. "When I was growing up, a rabbi without a beard was taken seriously. Now a rabbi without a beard is not taken seriously." Against the wishes of his wife, he did eventually grow a full beard: "not for religious reasons, just to conform." Although he did not specify the role of BTs in his transition, it should be noted that about half the members of his shul are BTs. In short, BTs' hyperaccommodation may have played a role in the past several decades of FFBs "sliding to the right" in some of their religious and cultural practices.[18]

Deliberate Distinctiveness: Highlighting Difference to Avoid Inauthenticity

While many BTs are overzealous in their accommodation to Orthodox cultural norms, some BTs intentionally go in the other direction, accommodating selectively in an effort to maintain aspects of their previous selves. One reason is the sense that BTs, especially in their early stages of integration, seem phony when they use Orthodox practices. New BTs observe the ways that veteran community members act, dress, and talk, and they may see those practices as an eventual goal. But they often feel that if they were to take on those practices right away they would be acting inauthentically. For example, Matt, a Conservative Jew who spent a few years in Orthodox communities, says that he never adopted the speech style because "it wasn't me." He and others agree with Joseph's sentiment, quoted in chapter 5, that some BTs who say "*Toyrah*" (rather than "*Torah*") are "trying hard to look really Yeshivish."

For many BTs, feeling or being called inauthentic does not stop them from participating in Orthodox practices. When Mark was a Peripheral BT, he told me that he felt he was not acting like himself when he used chanting intonation or wore a black hat. But he sometimes adopted these behaviors anyway, because, he said, "it's fun." So when he was planning his wedding, he told friends and family that it would be "black hat optional, and I'm opting in." Although putting on this "costume" did not seem authentic to him, it was an enjoyable way of connecting with the community. As Ira, an advisor at a BT yeshiva, says, "To a large part, everyone's putting on a costume in [a BT] yeshiva." This self-consciousness tends to be only temporary; BTs who continue to participate in a cultural practice eventually feel it is an authentic part of who they have become.

How do BTs deal with their feelings of inauthenticity and their discomfort with some frum practices? I observed two different strategies: avoiding practices and using them in a marked way. Some BTs avoid certain Yiddish grammatical influences, Hebrew pronunciations, loanwords (or their overuse), and chanting intonation. Some BTs resist wearing black hats or sheitels. And some BTs refuse to cook gefilte fish, chicken, and farfel for Shabbos dinner. These BTs tend to identify themselves closer to the Modern Orthodox end of the spectrum, even if they live in a more Black Hat community.

The other strategy is to participate in Orthodox practices in a way that emphasizes the individual's difference as a BT. Some BTs do this through unique semiotic combinations, as discussed in chapter 3, such as the BT who adds Indian spices to her gefilte fish and the BT who wears his black hat with trendy sunglasses. By combining practices like this, BTs are able to identify as Orthodox Jews without giving up their previous selves completely. This deliberate distinctiveness might, in some cases, be intended and/or interpreted as a critique of frum culture, as if the BT is telling her new community, "I can be fully religious without fully conforming to your cultural norms." At the same time, it can be seen as a way to present oneself as a hybrid, inhabiting the space between non-Orthodox and deeply embedded in frum culture: the BT borderland.

In the linguistic realm, BTs indicate their hybrid status by using non-Orthodox and Orthodox features together, such as slang and loanwords in the same sentence. For example, Isaac uses many loanwords, Yiddish grammatical influences, and other Orthodox features, but he continues to use phrases that are considered crude, like "screwed up." Another linguistic strategy, especially common among BTs trying out loanwords, is to mark new features as foreign.

Marking Non-Ownership

I noticed several instances of new BTs making a joke about a linguistic feature, pointing out that they just learned it, or attributing it to someone else. For example, Leah recognized that she might be making a mistake in forming the plural of *talmid chacham* (wise scholar), which should be *talmidei chachamim*. She said playfully, "*Talmid chachams, talmid chachamim*—Whatever, that's just me being pluralistic." And Dan ended a dvar torah in Milldale with "Speedily in our days, and all that." This indicated Dan's at least partial familiarity with the formulaic dvar torah ending "We should all be zoche to witness the coming of the Moshiach speedily in our days." It is possible that Dan knew the full sentence but did not feel he had the authority to say it.

Another way of marking new forms as foreign is through prosodic cues, such as interrupting the flow of the sentence or raising the pitch or volume. This type of marking is used when the speaker has recently learned the new form and the person he is speaking to is aware of that. Andrew did this in his first unprompted use of the word *chazer*, soon after a discussion about the word (chapter 7). When Avrum asked him to review part of the text, Andrew said with a smile, "You want me to [short pause, rise in pitch and volume] *chazer* it?" By marking *chazer* through playful prosodic cues, he pointed out that he had just learned it and perhaps did not feel comfortable using it normally. Linguistic crossers—people using elements of a language or dialect not their own—also tend to use marking, or "flagging." Like new BTs, white teenagers using African American Vernacular English or Anglos using Indian English recognize that they are not seen as "authentic" speakers of the language. They indicate this recognition of inauthenticity by marking their words as not their own.[19]

I observed an example of marking, as well as other distinctive BT language, at a Shabbos dinner at Ner Tamid. FFB Rabbi Hollander had asked Peripheral BT Marissa to prepare a dvar torah, an honor given to students who have been involved for a while. She used the word *cheyn* (grace) in her dvar torah and added, "as Rabbi [Hollander] would say." Although she felt it was appropriate to use this loanword, she did not feel full ownership over it, marking it as belonging to someone else. In the same dvar torah, as discussed in chapter 6, she also used a distinctly BT combination of loanwords and slang phrases, including "kick 'em in the butt" and "Potiphar's wife had the hots for Yosef."

Later that Shabbos, when Rabbi Hollander was giving a dvar torah, he made a few allusions to Marissa's use of slang, but he avoided the actual slang words. He said things like, "It'll come back to bite you in the—" and "She thinks he's—whatever [Menucha] said" (Menucha is Marissa's Hebrew name). Then he went on to point out how he has trouble keeping up with slang: "When I was young, it was cool. Now it's hot. Then, fat was an insult. Now it's a compliment." By almost using slang words and attributing them to a BT, Rabbi Hollander marked slang as foreign to him, just as Marissa marked loanwords as foreign to her by attributing them to an FFB. His marking and self-deprecation may make BTs feel more comfortable with their language, but they also may be intended to reinforce the differences between FFBs and new BTs.

Leah, Dan, Andrew, and Marissa—along with many of their BT peers—used linguistic marking to highlight their discomfort with and ambivalence about new words and other linguistic features (stage 5, discussed in chapter 7). Eventually, they grew accustomed to these new features and used them in an unmarked way (stage 6). This happened through their long-term participation in the community. As Jean Lave and Etienne Wenger write, "An extended period of legitimate peripherality provides learners with opportunities to make the culture of practice theirs."[20] However, even after many years in the community, some BTs still do not feel complete ownership of these practices. For example, a well-respected longtime Yeshiva BT says that even though he is pretty comfortable with the way he speaks, he sometimes still feels insecure about his language when he talks to very learned FFBs.

The Bungee Effect

It is clear that both hyperaccommodation and deliberate distinctiveness are strategies BTs use in the process of becoming frum. Some BTs use only one or the other, but more often individuals use both at different times. Some use them in a progression, which I call *the bungee effect*: a deep jump and then a bounce back.[21] Newcomers, eager to integrate into the community, go overboard in their use of Orthodox practices at first. As "Friedman the Tutor" writes in an unpublished guide for BTs, they go "off the deep end."[22] But eventually they bounce back to a happy medium, moderating their use of these practices.

Although I am, to my knowledge, the first to name this phenomenon, it has been a topic of discussion in frum circles. For example, a blogger describes the early phase of the bungee jump: "You can always spot a BT in shull [by] merely measuring who bows the farthest during shmona esray [the prayer also known as the Amidah] and who clops their chest like a hungry caveman during silach lanu [part of the Amidah that includes tapping the fist on the chest]." The blogger also offers a number of indicators that a BT has bounced back to a less extreme phase: "they start to talk in shull," "they begin to listen to secular music again," "they start visiting their parents again," and so on. Several BTs who posted comments agree with the writer. One writes: "I totally and painfully regret throwing out all my music, films, books, and magazines." Another comment highlights BTs' self-consciousness and awareness of language: "I knew I went from BT to frummie when I stopped saying taka and mamash."[23]

I found several examples of the bungee effect among BTs in Milldale and elsewhere. Levi, a Community BT who has been Orthodox for several years, says that he used to try too hard to fit in. Now, he no longer wants to pass as FFB, he does not wear his black hat and dark suit all the time, and he has consciously toned down his use of frum language:

> Initially you're constantly trying to prove yourself, and then eventually you get to a point where, you know, I'm comfortable with my knowledge and . . . what I know how to do and I'm not fooling anybody but myself. . . . And you come to grips with who you are. . . . There's a lot of sort of going out and finding where you feel comfortable. So you really have to *go beyond it and then slip back to it.* So that's . . . the difficult part of the transition.

When Levi talks about "finding where you feel comfortable," he refers to the various social axes in the Orthodox community, especially Modern to Black Hat and BT to FFB. Levi and other BTs try out different locations on these axes by following stringencies or leniencies in Jewish law and by using various practices in language, dress, and other areas of culture. While many stick with what they initially chose, or even move farther toward the Black Hat and FFB poles, others "slip back" to a location where they feel more comfortable religiously and culturally, toning down their use of these practices.

Another example of the bungee effect is Mark, who made the transition from Peripheral to Community BT during my year of fieldwork. In December, when he was still a Peripheral BT, he told me he enjoyed using chanting intonation for fun. The following October, he told me he avoids chanting intonation and uses less Yeshivish speech in general. When I e-mailed him to ask why, he wrote, "Maybe it was a bit too forced? And, it's not really me. I mean, I may be observant, but that doesn't make me 'Yeshivish.'" Mark has changed his preference for where he wants to locate himself along the Modern to Black Hat axis, partly because of the inauthenticity he experienced. He now feels more comfortable identifying himself as a BT—by using some distinctive Orthodox language, but not all the features he hears from his FFB friends and mentors. After his initial plunge into Orthodoxy, he has bounced back to somewhere in the middle.

Sociologist Minny Mock-Degen reports a similar trajectory among some of the Dutch BTs she interviewed. For example, one woman began her Orthodox journey identifying as "*haredi*-leaning" and subsequently identified as Modern Orthodox. After becoming less strict in her observance of certain dietary restrictions and deciding to take off her wig at home, she reported, "Instead of superfrum and a nervous wreck, now I'm less frum, but happier."[24]

An instance of the bungee effect recently made news within and beyond Jewish circles. Matisyahu, the Orthodox reggae singer profiled at the beginning of this book, became famous as a bearded Hasidic Jew, singing and dancing in a dark suit and black hat. He gradually began to perform in more casual clothing, and in December 2011 he made waves throughout the blogosphere when he shaved off his beard. At first he jumped into Black Hat Orthodoxy, and then he bungeed back, tempering his symbolic practices to identify closer to the Modern Orthodox pole.

The notion of a bungee jump implies that BTs' journeys are linear—more and then less. Of course the reality is more complex: they might shed some elements of Orthodoxy while taking on others, based on meeting new role models or encountering new texts. But Orthodox Jews do often use linear terms to discuss the continuum between Modern and Black Hat Orthodoxy, especially when individuals shift their self-presentation along that continuum.

"B.T. Blues"

Although the terminology used in this chapter may be new, BTs have long discussed the phenomena of hyperaccommodation, deliberate distinctiveness, and the bungee effect. One talented man, Rabbi Moshe Shur, highlighted them in a song called "B.T. Blues." True to its contents, this song is culturally hybrid: Orthodox Jewish English lyrics performed in a bluegrass style, complete with fiddle and banjo solos:

> Now this is a story about a man named Joe.
> He did some tshuva, or at least he thought so.
> But after fifteen years, eight whole months, and just about a week,
> They still called him a ba'al tshuva freak.
>
> *Refrain*:
> L-rd, don't make me into a *benoni* [in-between].[25]
> All my friends are tzadikim [righteous people]; it's so hard on me.

'Cause I work on myself, but I'm still a bit confused.
Guess I got me a case of them ba'al tshuva blues.

Joe went off to a simcha and took a glance
They were all dancing the loshon hora [pun on gossip and Jewish dance]
    and we didn't have a chance
They were 100% authentic, super glatt [high-level kosher] F.F.B.'s,
A different kind of breed than a real live B.T. (*Refrain*)

Joe went down to shul to learn how to davin
He shuckled so hard, his head was a-bobbin'.
They all stared at him, not knowing what to say.
"You're much too quiet for us."
"You're not talking or making a fuss."
"You can't do just what you wanna."
"You got way too much kavanna [fervor]."

Joe went out on a shiduch [set-up date] to find a ba'alas tshuva [female
    BT] freakess.
He even ironed his tzitsis, he knew he had a weakness.
But when he saw her standing there, her chumash and birkenstocks,
He knew she was his zivug [match], another one of the flock. (*Refrain*)

Now Joe has a family, a mortgage and a car.
He's come a long way, though he hasn't gone too far.
But when his kids show him the pictures of "them good old days,"
He says, "It really doesn't look like me.
It must be my old friend Tzvi.
I could have never ever looked like that.
I'm not wearing my Stetson hat."

Now they call our Joe Yossil [Yiddish diminutive] Frumovitz.
He even talks during davening and hangs out at the shvitz [steam bath].
He's trimmed his beard and payus, and he only learns once a week.
He's become one of them, a real chevra [society] man.
He's now an F.F.T., Frum from Tshuva, you see, about his past he will not
    speak.
'Cause he never lets on that he ever once was a ba'al tshuva freak.
    (*Refrain*.)[26]

"B.T. Blues" nicely illustrates some of the points I have made in this book, such
as the prominence of loanwords in Orthodox Jewish English, the importance
of cultural practices in the construction of Orthodox identity (names, clothing, hair, and dancing), and the fact that FFBs are seen as more "authentic"

Orthodox Jews. Joe hyperaccommodates by shuckling too hard and having too much fervor, and the woman uses distinctive combinations that highlight her BT-ness: carrying a Jewish book while wearing Birkenstock sandals (rare among FFBs but common among BTs). And it demonstrates the bungee effect: after his initial plunge into Orthodoxy, Joe bounces back and tempers his use of symbolic practices. He trims his beard and sidelocks, he cuts down on the time he spends learning, and he allows himself to talk during prayer services. He becomes an "FFT," a BT who has been Orthodox so long that he is well integrated into FFB social circles and can sometimes even pass as FFB.

These lyrics also bring up the concept of in-betweenness or liminality: "L-rd, don't make me into a *benoni.*" *Benoni* (an intermediate or in-between person) is the only loanword italicized in the liner notes of the album in which the song appears, probably because it is not commonly heard in Orthodox Jewish English. In the Talmud, it is a category between *rasha* (wicked man) and *tzadtik* (righteous man).[27] It has also been defined as "an individual whose spiritual labors have brought him to a level of perfection in thought, word and deed, despite his still-active evil inclination."[28] While the songwriter likely has these rabbinic concepts in mind, he also highlights the liminality that BTs feel, the sense of being caught in a borderland between their former non-Orthodox self and the FFB status they can never fully attain.

As the discussion above has shown, BTs address this liminality in various ways. Some become "FFT"—at times even passing as FFB—and others highlight their BT identity. To the extent that they have control over their self-representation, they choose where to position themselves along the axes of Orthodoxy. To do this, they tap into the wide array of linguistic and cultural practices associated with being frum.

9

Matisyahu and *My Fair Lady*

Reflections on Adult Language Socialization

The Matisyahu Phenomenon

During a guitar solo, Matisyahu dances in the middle of the stage. His white tzitzis hang out from under his collar shirt, halfway down to his sneakers. The colorful lights illuminate his contagious smile, just days after he shaved off his iconic beard. He removes his kipah and takes a running leap off the stage and into the audience. He surfs the crowd, rolling, sitting, and standing on the hands of fans—men and women, Orthodox and not. He makes his way back up to the stage, puts his kipah back on, and sings the rest of the song.

After eight chapters explaining the intricacies of language and culture among ba'alei teshuva, Matisyahu's self-presentation—and the many changes he has made—should not seem implausible. The secular Phish-head turned bearded Hasidic reggae star turned clean-shaven tzitzis-wearing crowd surfer offers a highly publicized example of the processes many BTs go through. Through selective accommodation, he distinguishes himself both from his secular past and from most of his BT and FFB peers. He dives headfirst into frum culture and then bungees back to reclaim elements of his pre-Orthodox self.

Matisyahu may not be a typical BT but, as this study indicates, there is no single BT prototype. We might categorize some BTs as accommodators and others as distinguishers, but most seem to fall somewhere in between. Some BTs maintain their in-between status for the rest of their lives, and others gradually shed practices that distinguish them from FFBs until they (mostly) blend in. Matisyahu, along with Rivka Bracha, Samuel, Shoshana, Levi, Devora, Andrew, and the other BTs profiled in this book, highlights the diversity of approaches that various individuals take to becoming frum.

Language Socialization in Comparative Context

Many of the findings in this book are also applicable to other situations of adult transitions. Other ethnographic studies of adult language socialization, including research on American college students learning Japanese and engineering students, have pointed to a process of legitimate peripheral participation, in which novices gradually gain access to new ways of speaking as they acquire new roles within their community.[1] Research outside the language socialization paradigm has also found that learning a new competency involves legitimate peripheral participation. In fact, Lave and Wenger articulated the concept using data on the socialization of midwives, butchers, and others.[2]

Before the term "peripheral participation" was coined, research on adult socialization came to similar conclusions. For example, a study of marijuana users found that individuals began to enjoy the effects of the drug through interactions with more experienced users, involving questioning, correction, and narratives of prior experiences.[3] And a study of Alcoholics Anonymous found that newcomers gradually adopted the group's ideology through interactions with veteran group members, including their personal sponsors.[4] The personal sobriety narrative was an important part of the process, and the twelfth step involved spreading the message and helping newcomers.[5]

While the language socialization of BTs has similarities to that of other adult novices, there are also two important differences. First, in contrast to situations of professional training, BTs will always be categorized as distinct from some of the community veterans they look to as mentors: even master BTs do not become FFBs (see below). This is a primary factor in the selective accommodation we find among some BTs, a phenomenon we might observe only in the early stages of vocational transitions. If medical students, cosmetologists-in-training, and apprentice butchers feel uncomfortable at first with the professional jargon they encounter, they eventually pick it up, just as their mentors and trainers once did. Some BTs do come to feel comfortable with frum language, but others continue to distinguish themselves as BTs throughout their lives.

Second, many other situations of adult language socialization take place in communities of practice populated primarily by adults. While adult-only yeshivas and seminaries feature prominently in the socialization of many BTs, BTs are joining a community that also includes children. This fact likely leads to more intense feelings of infantilization and inauthenticity among BTs than among professional trainees, alcoholics in recovery, or adults coming out as gay, for example. In these ways, becoming frum is more similar to regional and international migrations, as well as ethnic and social class transitions.[6] Let us explore these differences.

Once a BT, Always a BT?

Kimmy Caplan, an Israeli scholar of Orthodoxy, asks this question and points out that research on BTs has not sufficiently dealt with it.[7] Of course there is always the possibility of opting out—of shedding one's Orthodox identity. But among those who remain Orthodox, will they always be seen as BTs? Are they stuck in the BT borderland for life? Yes and no. Most BTs experience some long-term liminality in that others know they are BTs. But eventually many become skilled enough in Orthodox practices and feel comfortable enough with their Orthodox selves that their liminality may not manifest on a regular basis. Some BTs have integrated so much that new people they meet have no idea of their non-Orthodox past unless they or others refer to it. Other BTs continue to highlight their BT status—consciously and unconsciously. Cultural practices, including language, are crucial in these performances and perceptions. But as Caplan found in his analysis of Haredi writings in Israel, even BTs who blend in well are still seen as BTs (assuming they do not hide their past)—by both FFBs and BTs.[8]

The quasi-permanent status of BTs is similar to that of migrants and immigrants and distinguishes theirs from other situations of adult socialization.[9] Trainees become full tailors when they receive the blessing of their mentors, and apprentices in Alcoholics Anonymous become masters when they reach the twelfth step (although they are forever seen as recovering alcoholics).[10] It is possible for a BT to attain high status in the Orthodox community, becoming a synagogue president, teacher, rebbetzin, rabbi, or director of a school or outreach organization. At least in the Milldale community BTs tend to be integrated socially with FFBs. And, assuming they became Orthodox before having children, they necessarily raise FFB children, a fact that many BTs told me about proudly. However, no matter how integrated BTs are and how much they have mastered frum culture, they cannot become FFB. This may have little impact on everyday life, but it leaves BTs with a small degree of outsider status.

While many Orthodox communities, including Milldale, are extremely welcoming of BTs and do much to help them integrate, a number of BTs in various locales told me they have also encountered prejudice or discrimination. For example, they are aware of instances in which FFBs have gossiped about BTs' backgrounds, and they know they have less chance of being matched with an FFB by a shadchan (see chapter 3). Some BTs say that they worry about their (FFB) children's chances of being accepted into elite yeshivas or landing choice shiduchim from prestigious families, partly because of community ideologies surrounding lineage.[11] Sociologist Debra Kaufman reports that even the descendants of BTs are sometimes not considered FFBs: she recalls the principal of an Orthodox school, in an attempt to inform a visitor that many of the students come from BT families, saying something like, "We have many BTs; some have been BT for a few generations."[12] The question of whether BTs are treated as second-class citizens is the topic of much discussion in frum circles. A blog posting on the topic received over one hundred impassioned responses, some narrating their authors' experiences with discrimination and some describing their complete integration and acceptance.[13]

Even if BTs do not experience discrimination, they tend to be reminded of their non-Orthodox past every now and then. When an FFB reminisces about her frum childhood, a BT might feel left out. A BT mother showed me a cookbook published by her children's elementary school, complete with quotes from the students about the holidays in their homes. The introduction, written by an FFB teacher, says, "Think back to the kitchen of your childhood. . . . Your mother is making the gefilte fish and braiding the round challah. . . ." This may remind a BT parent that she is different from some of the other parents in the school. As several BTs told me, reminders such as these make them all the more passionate about ensuring that their FFB children grow up surrounded by frum Jews and immersed in frum life.

BT Adults and FFB Children: Similarities and Differences in Language Socialization

Unlike some other situations of adult language socialization, the communities of practice into which BTs are socialized are likely to include masters who were born into the community and began their apprenticeships in infancy. Except for those in adult-only institutions, BTs tend to have some interaction with FFB children, Orthodox Jews who are decades younger than they are.

In some respects, FFB children are similar to the masters or veterans in professional training programs and apprenticeships. BTs see them as models to emulate, and they learn a good deal by observing and interacting with them. Some BTs told me they feel more comfortable asking certain questions to the children of a rabbi and rebbetzin than to the rabbi or rebbetzin themselves. To a recent BT, even a preschool child may come across as being quite knowledgeable and competent with regard to language and other practices of Orthodoxy.

On the other hand, FFB children are also in the process of being socialized into the Orthodox community and its cultural practices. Throughout my fieldwork, I noticed a number of similarities between the socialization of FFB children and the socialization of BT adults. Both processes involve mistakes, hyperaccommodation, interactions of language socialization, and a gradual progression of access to the styles of Orthodoxy.

Children make mistakes in analyzing the morphology and phonology of Hebrew words, just as they do with English words. Three-year-old Mendy was showing off his knowledge of the Hebrew word for fish—*dag*—which he recently learned in preschool, and he said *dagims*, whereas the correct plural is *dagim*. Two five-year-old girls gleefully chanted, "*Chas alila, chas alila,*" inaccurately imitating the Hebrew phrase *chas v'chalila* (God forbid). They did not know what it meant, but they said it over and over, clearly entertained by its sound. The adults present laughed about the girls' "cute" pronunciation—an unlikely reaction to a BT mistake.

I observed an FFB child hyperaccommodating to adult Orthodox norms on a road trip with the Kramers. Thirteen-year-old Shimon Kramer did not want to sit on the van bench next to Sara, a BT friend whom the Kramers consider part of the family. Shimon explained, "It's not tznius." His sisters made fun of him and pointed out to me that Shimon, who had just become a bar mitzvah—an adult according to Jewish law—the previous week, was still getting used to the laws of tznius, which apply more fully to adults. It is possible that Shimon interpreted the laws differently than his sisters, but it is also likely that he used this encounter as an opportunity to highlight his new adult status. In either case, Shimon's overextension of rules is similar to the hyperaccommodation I observed among BTs.

Orthodox children experience interactions of linguistic socialization similar to those described in chapter 7. They ask questions and repeat words they hear—both English and loanwords, and adults and other children teach and correct them overtly and covertly. Like BTs, they gradually gain access to and participate in more specialized styles. For example, boys regularly hear the rabbi give a dvar torah in shul and are expected to do the same when they turn thirteen (at their bar mitzvah *vort* [sermon, literally "word"]), and they learn how to interact in the full-blown "Yeshivish" style when they study in a yeshiva as teenagers. Girls progress in their access to levels of Torah study as they advance from grade to grade. In addition, girls gradually gain access to child-rearing duties by helping their mothers and eventually babysitting, especially when they are among the older children in a large family. As they assume more responsibilities, they are able to try out the Yiddish diminutives characteristic of child-directed speech.

One major difference between the socialization of BTs and FFBs is the timing of the stages. For FFB children, access and responsibility increase when they reach a new age, a new grade, or a new level of maturity. Their process of legitimate peripheral participation is, to some extent, institutionalized. BTs, on the other hand, must take the initiative and seek out new stages themselves. In addition, young children do not have access to some of the self-teaching practices that adult BTs do, like web searches, dictionaries, and recorded lectures.

Another difference is the level of self-consciousness. As adults, BTs might feel that they should exhibit a certain skill level. When they recognize their mistakes, they are likely more self-conscious and embarrassed than FFB children. The five-year-old girls who said "*chas alila*" would probably not flinch if someone told them they left out a few letters. But BTs report feeling ashamed when they are corrected or otherwise learn they have been using loanwords incorrectly. Accordingly, some BTs avoid certain words until they are sure they can say them perfectly. Also, adults experience more stigma than children when they ask a language question, at least outside a classroom setting. This difference in self-consciousness and shame is a crucial characteristic of adult language socialization.

Another distinctive trait of the BT trajectory and some other situations of adult language socialization is that the learning may remain incomplete. Due to cognitive constraints, newcomers may never be able to fully acquire the distinctive linguistic features of the communities they have joined. This is especially likely when the repertoire they encounter includes system-level phonological features, as in regional moves or transitions in ethnic or social class identities. Also, adults may not wish to fully integrate linguistically into their new community. While young children around the world certainly reject some of their parents' linguistic practices in favor of those of their peers, this process seems to be less self-conscious than among adult BTs (teenagers are a different story). Despite these important differences, it is clear that the processes of child and adult language socialization have several similarities.

Infantilization

As adults, BTs are generally competent in many domains: they are proficient speakers of their native language, and they have learned the norms of participation in their society. In addition, many have achieved high levels of success and prestige in their careers and personal lives. But in their attempts to integrate into Orthodox communities, they often feel like children. The first time a prospective BT spends Shabbos in Milldale, he likely notices that the seven-year-old child knows more than he does about Judaism and can effortlessly partake in practices such as washing the hands ritually, singing Hebrew songs, and incorporating Hebrew and Yiddish words into English. Some BTs report feeling "like that child that's lost in a classroom" when they cannot follow the Hebrew or find the page in the prayerbook.[14] Although BTs have accrued a great deal of cultural capital in the secular world, they are only beginning to access the frum cultural capital that FFB children have accrued since birth.

BTs are especially liable to feel infantilized when they are unable to help their own children with the assignments they bring home from elementary school. One rabbi organized a weekly class to teach BTs what their children were learning in third grade. Levi, a longtime BT, reports feeling like a child during classes and study sessions: "I'm a forty-year-old guy here; I am learning on a fourth-grade level." One of his teachers consoled him by pointing out that he has a higher understanding of the concepts and a more sophisticated interest in learning than a child. An FFB woman addresses this issue by telling young BTs, "You have a head start on Rabbi Akiva," an ancient Jewish sage who reportedly began studying Torah only at age forty.

I mentioned my thoughts about infantilization to Jacob, a longtime BT in Milldale. He responded with a smile, "I *absolutely* feel like a child." Jacob, who has close ties to a Hasidic community in Brooklyn, told me about a Passover seder he went to there. At some point during the evening, the children recited a Yiddish script about the story of Passover, and Jacob was asked to translate line-by-line into English. Although he was in his twenties, the family grouped him with the children in this activity. However, he said it did not bother him to feel and be treated like a child; that is part of the process of becoming frum.

The infantilization of BTs pales in comparison to that of immigrants who must learn a whole new language and way of life. Anthropologist Deborah Poole analyzed the exchanges between teachers and students in an American ESL (English as a Second Language) classroom and found that they are similar to the exchanges between parents and children in white middle class American communities, in that they highlight the power differential between expert and novice. For example, teachers used fill-in-the-blank sentences and "known information questions" intended for the student to display knowledge. They also used the "parental we," and they gave the students credit for accomplishing language tasks on their own when they had actually accomplished them with help from the teacher.[15]

Similarly, anthropologist Deborah Golden's research in an *ulpan* (intensive Hebrew course) for Russian immigrants in Israel found some of the teacher's interactions with her adult students to be infantilizing. In an interview, the teacher described her students: "They were older than me but completely helpless and incapable of doing anything. . . . I felt that I'm here [to help them] start walking, like a little baby, to walk again, to get by, like a little child."[16] One day the teacher brought in her seven-year-old daughter to demonstrate a holiday ritual and instructed the students to imitate her, an act that may have been infantilizing for these accomplished adults. The teacher was generally respectful and open to classroom debates, but she sometimes cut off conversation on controversial topics with statements like this: "Maybe in another five years when you know Israeli society better, then we'll be able to talk about it."[17]Although the BTs I studied sometimes felt like children, they never experienced infantilization to the same degree as many immigrants learning new languages and societal norms.

I was thinking about infantilization one afternoon at Shomrei Emunah when I was reminded of its connection to gender. During the celebration of the synagogue's new Torah scroll, I watched a mother pass a girl, about two years old, to her father over the *mechitzah*, the barrier that separates the men's and women's sections. Gender separation, as well as several other Orthodox gender norms, do not apply to young children.[18] While adults are forbidden to touch members of the opposite sex, boys and girls can be seen holding hands as they play together in preschool, and mothers hold their friends' sons or pat them on the head. Infant and toddler girls may wear pants, although dresses are also common. Boys generally do not wear ritual garments—kipahs and tzitzis—until three, the age when many have their first haircut. One mother told me that her two-year-old son was bothered by his long hair, and people outside the community often assumed he was a girl. To rectify the situation, she sometimes put a barrette in his hair that said, "I'm a boy."

In the non-Orthodox world, it is acceptable for a grown man to have long hair, to sit with women in synagogue, and to walk around without a kipah or tzitzis, just like a two-year-old Orthodox boy. A grown woman is expected to shake hands with men and can wear pants and keep her hair uncovered. New BTs are used to expressing their gender identities in the secular world, where the "mechitzahs," or gender boundaries, are more subtle and fluid. When they are Peripheral BTs, they may have a good deal in common with the two-year-old who can cross the mechitzah, only later taking on the practices that allow them to perform the masculine or feminine identities common in their new community. A young man coming from the secular world into the frum world learns how to speak, study, dance, and shave like an Orthodox man. A woman entering the community exchanges her pants for long feminine skirts, learns not to yearn for the masculine leadership roles of synagogue life, and grows into her role as the mother of Jewish children. Like FFB children, BTs eventually learn to express their gender Orthodox style, staying on the appropriate side of the mechitzah— literally and figuratively.

These feelings of infantilization, especially with regard to gender, may serve as an impetus for BTs to expedite their learning process. The more successful they are at learning and adopting frum religious and cultural practices, the less likely they will feel like children. FFBs and longtime BTs know this, and they use the methods described in chapter 7 to facilitate newcomers' socialization, to help them increase their frum cultural capital.

Reflections on Adult Language Socialization

While scholars have begun to research adult language socialization, much work remains to be done. As this book indicates, a combination of ethnographic observation, interviews, sociolinguistic analysis, and experimental methods can yield useful data on how adults in transition are socialized to use language. An additional method that would increase our understanding is a longitudinal analysis of several individuals as they integrate into a new community. By following novices over several years from non-member to peripheral member to full member, we can gain a fuller picture of the process of adult language socialization.

The findings in this book can also be tested in other situations involving shifting identities. When American Christians convert to Islam, do they hyper-accommodate in their use of Arabic loanwords, including God-centered phrases like "insha'Allah" (God willing)? When gay men "come out," do they learn gay stylistic practices through a similar process of legitimate peripheral participation in a gay friendship group? When urban northerners move to the rural South, what role does ideology play in their variable use of vowels? When working-class African Americans join a middle-class white-dominated workplace, to what extent do they see themselves as existing in a cultural borderland, and how do they express that liminality linguistically?

Although I have not conducted research on other adult transitions, I have informally observed several friends training to join professional communities, especially in academics, law, medicine, and Jewish nonprofit management. Throughout the two to ten years of training we go through to become profession-als in our fields (and well into our careers), we learn many of the skills necessary to do our jobs. But we also learn the distinctive ways of speaking that go along with being academics, lawyers, doctors, and Jewish communal professionals.

Just as BTs sometimes use new words in unusual contexts (overextension of lexical replacement), new professionals do too. For example, new doctors might replace the term "heart attack" in their mind with "myocardial infarction" or "MI," and when they are speaking to a patient or a friend, they might acciden-tally use the new term. Or they might transfer medical jargon to everyday life, as my husband sometimes did during medical school: "That's contraindicated" or "The differential [diagnosis] is . . ." Issues of authority also arise. When do we feel we have the authority to take part in certain practices? While some social science graduate students might feel uncomfortable using words like "prob-lematize" and "reification" or might avoid referring to their work as a "theory" or "model," others go overboard and use such terms even when a veteran aca-demic would not. A new Jewish nonprofit professional told me he has to find the perfect balance of jargon (phrases like "value added," "due diligence," and "link-ing the silos"): just enough to demonstrate his competence, but not too much (hyperaccommodation) to highlight his newcomer status. In all these situations of socialization, ideology is fundamental—views about how certain people act and speak and how they should act and speak, as well as individuals' desire to position themselves along various axes within their new community.

During their schooling, trainees go through a process of legitimate periph-eral participation, whether or not it is officially called an apprenticeship or internship. They gradually increase their roles and responsibilities, as well as their access to individuals and their cultural practices, and they eventually learn to speak and act like a full member of the professional community. The learning in all these situations happens in multiple communities of practice. Just as a BT has the outreach center, the synagogue, a chavrusa, and various groups that gather around certain activities, a law student might have her classroom, her study group, her internet chat group, her summer law firm, her courtroom team, and her bar review course.[19] In those settings, masters (professors and professionals) and other novices teach and correct novices overtly and covertly, and novices ask questions and attempt to teach themselves.

In addition to these situations of professional socialization, I have also noticed similar phenomena in my transition to motherhood. After I gave birth to my first child, I felt strange talking to my baby, as if I were acting. I also felt uncomfortable using some of the language my friends who are parents use with each other, like "get a good latch" (in breastfeeding), "put the baby down for a nap," and "Ferberize" (a term for sleep training based on books by Dr. Richard Ferber). Based on interactions with more experienced parents, however, I learned that this language of parenthood was common and expected in my middle-class American community. At first I used these terms in a marked way, sometimes with air quotes. And I did speak to my newborn a bit, with an ironic tone. Gradually I became accustomed to the language of parenting, and within a few months it became second nature. Now (with all three children out of diapers) I am a veteran parent, and I sometimes find myself involved with the socialization of friends who are themselves new parents, helping them to acquire not only the primary skills of parenting but also the language that is part of the process.

I could write a similar paragraph about playing in a jazz band, starting college, participating in a leadership training program, being pregnant, purchasing a house, adopting new technologies or environmental values, and so on. I marvel at how the process of researching and writing this book (combined with my graduate training) has changed the way I understand learning, language, and social interactions. Now I cannot get away from language socialization—I observe elements of it at the gym, during klezmer jam sessions, and on National Public Radio.

Even if the phenomena in this book are not as ubiquitous in the minds of readers as they are for me, one cannot help but think about adult language socialization when watching *My Fair Lady*, Alan Jay Lerner and Frederick Loewe's musical based on George Bernard Shaw's play *Pygmalion*. The main character, Eliza Doolittle, transforms from a working-class "guttersnipe" to an upper-class lady after just a few months of locution lessons. Eliza's transformation has much in common with the BT process. She makes many mistakes and breaches of community norms, like her use of slang and obscenity at an upper-class horse race. She makes qualitative hyperaccommodations, such as adding an extra [h]: "urricanes ardly *h*ever appen." And, in what might be considered an example of quantitative hyperaccommodation, a phonetician assumes she is not a native English speaker because her English is too good.

Ideology plays an important role in *My Fair Lady*. Throughout the story, language is connected with other practices, like dress, cleanliness, and decorum. And characters, especially Professor Henry Higgins, frequently articulate their ideologies about the relationships between these practices and social class. Eliza does not change her phonology until she decides she really wants to be part of the upper-class community. Once her transformation is complete, she finds herself in a borderland: she does not quite feel comfortable in her new role as upper-class lady, but, when she goes back to visit her old community, her friends do not recognize her because her appearance and speech are so different.

There are many similarities between Eliza's story and becoming frum. But in this case, art is not a completely accurate representation of life. Based on my research, it should be obvious that a newcomer cannot pass as a community veteran after a few weeks of formal lessons, even from a world-renowned phonetician. Adults learn new ways of speaking, dressing, and acting through a process of peripheral participation in a community of practice. This process may involve some formal instruction and overt interactions of linguistic socialization. But the lion's share of learning happens informally, as the learner gains increasing access to roles and practices within the new community. If only linguists could have such an impact on the transformation and socialization of newcomers as Henry Higgins did, Orthodox outreach centers around the world would have linguists on staff. As Eliza put it, "Wouldn't it be loverly?" Or, as the Hebrew/Aramaic/Yiddish/Jewish English expression goes, "*Halevay!*" (if only).

NOTES

I. INTRODUCTION

1. Clifford Geertz, "Religion as a Cultural System," in *The Interpretation of Cultures* (1966; repr. New York: Basic Books, 1973), 87–125; Haym Soloveitchik, "Rupture and Reconstruction: Transformation of Contemporary Orthodoxy," *Tradition* 28/4 (1994): 64–131; Lewis Rambo, *Understanding Religious Conversion* (New Haven, Conn.: Yale University Press, 1995); Andrew Buckser and Stephen D. Glazier, eds., *The Anthropology of Religious Conversion* (Lanham, Md.: Rowman and Littlefield, 2003); Andrew Buckser, "Social Conversion and Group Definition in Jewish Copenhagen," in *The Anthropology of Religious Conversion*, ed. Andrew Buckser and Stephen D. Glazier (Lanham, Md.: Rowman and Littlefield, 2003), 69–84; Joel Robbins, *Becoming Sinners: Christianity and Moral Torment in a Papua New Guinea Society* (Berkeley: University of California Press, 2004); Ayala Fader, *Mitzvah Girls: Bringing Up the Next Generation of Hasidic Jews in Brooklyn* (Princeton, N.J.: Princeton University Press, 2009).
2. Ayala Fader, "Learning Faith: Language Socialization in a Hasidic Community," *Language in Society* 35/2 (2006): 207–229; Ayala Fader, "Reclaiming Sacred Sparks: Linguistic Syncretism and Gendered Language Shift among Hasidic Jews in New York," *Journal of Linguistic Anthropology* 17/1 (2007): 1–22; Fader, *Mitzvah Girls*.
3. Janet Aviad, *Return to Judaism: Religious Renewal in Israel* (Chicago: University of Chicago Press, 1983); William Shaffir, "The Recruitment of *Baalei Tshuvah* in a Jerusalem Yeshiva," *Jewish Journal of Sociology* 25/1 (1983): 33–46.
4. Malcah Yaeger-Dror, "Introduction," *Language and Communication* 12/3–4 (1992): 181–193. See details in chapter 8.
5. Arthur Greil and David Rudy, "Conversion to the Worldview of Alcoholics Anonymous: A Refinement of Conversion Theory," *Qualitative Sociology* 6 (1983): 5–28; Lynn Davidman, *Tradition in a Rootless World: Women Turn to Orthodox Judaism* (Berkeley: University of California Press, 1991); William Shaffir, "Becoming Observant and Falling from the Faith: Variations of Jewish Conversion Experiences," in *Symbolic Interaction: An Introduction to Social Psychology*, ed. Nancy J. Herman and Larry T. Reynolds (Lanham, Md.: Alta Mira, 1994), 326–341; Louise E. Tallen, "Jewish Identity Writ Small: The Everyday Experience of *Baalot Teshuva*," in *Diasporas and Exiles: Varieties of Jewish Identity*, ed. Howard Wettstein (Berkeley: University of California Press, 2002), 234–252; Susan Harding, *The Book of Jerry Falwell: Fundamentalist Language and Politics* (Princeton, N.J.: Princeton University Press, 2000).
6. Exodus 24:7.
7. On dense, multiplex networks enforcing linguistic norms, see Lesley Milroy, *Language and Social Networks* (Oxford: Blackwell, 1980).

8. The term "ideology" has been used by scholars and the general public in many ways. I define "ideology" in a neutral sense as "a body of ideas characteristic of a particular social group or class" (Terry Eagleton, *Ideology: An Introduction* [London: Verso, 1991], 1), rather than associating it with "false ideas" (1), "rigid preconceptions" (4), or hegemonic institutions.

9. E.g., Solomon Poll, *The Hasidic Community of Williamsburg: A Study in the Sociology of Religion* (New York: Schocken, 1962); Charles Liebman, "Orthodoxy in American Jewish Life," *American Jewish Year Book* 66 (1965): 21–97; Samuel Heilman, *Synagogue Life: A Study in Symbolic Interaction* (Chicago: University of Chicago Press, 1972); Samuel Heilman, *Defenders of the Faith: Inside Ultra-Orthodox Jewry* (New York: Schocken, 1992); Samuel Heilman, *Sliding to the Right: The Contest for the Future of American Jewish Orthodoxy* (Berkeley: University of California Press, 2006); William Helmreich, *The World of the Yeshiva: An Intimate Portrait of Orthodox Jewry* (1982; Hoboken, N.J.: Ktav, 2000); Samuel Heilman and Steven M. Cohen, *Cosmopolitans and Parochials: Modern Orthodox Jews in America* (Chicago: University of Chicago Press, 1989); Davidman, *Tradition*; Debra Renee Kaufman, *Rachel's Daughters: Newly Orthodox Jewish Women* (New Brunswick, N.J.: Rutgers University Press, 1991); Menachem Friedman, "The Lost Kiddush Cup: Changes in Ashkenazi Haredi Culture—A Tradition in Crisis," in *The Uses of Tradition: Jewish Continuity in the Modern Era*, ed. Jack Wertheimer (New York: Jewish Theological Seminary of America Press, 1992), 175–186; Michael K. Silber, "The Emergence of Ultra-Orthodoxy: The Invention of a Tradition," in *The Uses of Tradition: Jewish Continuity in the Modern Era*, ed. Jack Wertheimer (New York: Jewish Theological Seminary of America Press, 1992), 23–84; Soloveitchik, "Rupture"; Tamar El-Or, *Educated and Ignorant: Ultraorthodox Jewish Women and Their World* (Boulder, Colo.: Rienner, 1994); Janet Belcove-Shalin, ed., *New World Hasidim: Ethnographic Studies of Hasidic Jews in America* (Albany: State University of New York Press, 1995); Stephanie Wellen Levine, *Mystics, Mavericks, and Merrymakers: An Intimate Journey among Hasidic Girls* (New York: New York University Press, 2003); Kimmy Caplan, *Internal Popular Discourse in Israeli Haredi Society* [in Hebrew] (Jerusalem: Zalman Shazar Center, 2007); Jeffrey Gurock, *Orthodox Jews in America* (Bloomington: Indiana University Press, 2009); Fader, *Mitzvah Girls*; Nurit Shtadler, *Yeshiva Fundamentalism: Piety, Gender, and Resistance* (New York: New York University Press, 2009); Jeremy Stolow, *Orthodox by Design: Judaism, Print Politics, and the Art Scroll Revolution* (Berkeley: University of California Press, 2010); Yoel Finkelman, *Strictly Kosher Reading: Popular Literature and the Condition of Contemporary Orthodoxy* (Boston: Academic Studies Press, 2011).

10. El-Or, *Educated*; Davidman, *Tradition*; Kaufman, *Rachel's Daughters*; Fader, "Learning"; Fader, *Mitzvah Girls*; Shtadler, *Yeshiva*.

11. Laurence Kotler-Berkowitz, Steven M. Cohen, Jonathon Ament, Vivian Klaff, Frank Mott, and Danyelle Peckerman-Neuman, *The National Jewish Population Survey 2000–01: Strength, Challenge and Diversity in the American Jewish Population* (New York: United Jewish Communities, 2003); Heilman, *Sliding*.

12. Kotler-Berkowitz et al., *National*.

13. Faranak Margolese, *Off the Derech: Why Observant Jews Leave Judaism* (New York: Devora Publishing, 2005); Lynn Davidman and Arthur Greil, "Characters in Search of a Script: The Exit Narratives of Formerly Ultra-Orthodox Jews," *Journal for the Scientific Study of Religion* 46/2 (2007): 201–216.

14. On the ironic history of the word "Orthodox," see Jeffrey C. Blutinger, "So-Called Orthodoxy: The History of an Unwanted Label," *Modern Judaism* 27/3 (2007): 310–328.

"Orthodox" originally referred to traditionalist German Lutherans and in the nineteenth century came to refer to German Jews who opposed liberal Jewish reforms.

15. But see discussion of recent changes in Adam Ferziger, "Church/Sect Theory and American Orthodoxy Reconsidered," in *Ambivalent Jew: Charles Liebman in Memoriam*, ed. Stuart Cohen and Bernard Susser (New York: Jewish Theological Seminary of America Press, 2007), 107–124.

16. "Together," by Uncle Moishy and the Mitzvah Men, volume 9, used with permission from Suki and Ding Productions. Transcribed from cassette; translations are mine.

17. Fader, *Mitzvah Girls*.

18. Roberta G. Sands, "The Social Integration of *Baalei Teshuvah*," *Journal for the Scientific Study of Religion* 48/1 (2009): 86–102.

19. William Shaffir, "Conversion Experiences: Newcomers to and Defectors from Orthodox Judaism (*hozrim betshuvah* and *hozrim beshe'elah*)," in *Tradition, Innovation, Conflict: Jewishness and Judaism in Contemporary Israel*, ed. Zvi Sobel and Benjamin Beit-Hallahmi (Albany: State University of New York Press, 1991), 173–202; Shaffir, "Becoming"; William Shaffir, "Movements In and Out of Orthodox Judaism: The Cases of Penitents and the Disaffected," in *Joining and Leaving Religion: Research Perspectives*, ed. Leslie J. Francis and Yaacov J. Katz (Trowbridge, Waltshire: Gracewing, 2000), 269–285; Margolese, *Off the Derech*; Hella Winston, *Unchosen: The Hidden Lives of Hasidic Rebels* (Boston: Beacon, 2006); Davidman and Greil, "Characters"; Gurock, "Orthodox."

20. E.g., Shaffir, "Becoming."

21. Davidman and Greil, "Characters," 202.

22. Levine, *Mystics*.

23. E.g., Liebman, "Orthodoxy"; Heilman, *Synagogue*; Heilman and Cohen, *Cosmopolitans*; Davidman, *Tradition*; Kaufman, *Rachel's Daughters*; Helmreich, *World*; Ferziger, "Church/Sect"; Fader, *Mitzvah Girls*; Gurock, *Orthodox*.

24. Heilman, *Sliding*. Shalom Berger, Daniel Jacobson, and Chaim Waxman, *Flipping Out? Myth or Fact: The Impact of the "Year in Israel"* (New York: Yashar Books, 2007); Shani Bechhofer, "Day Schools in the Orthodox Sector—A Shifting Landscape," in *International Handbook of Jewish Education*, ed. Helena Miller, Lisa Grant, and Alex Pomson (Dordrecht: Springer, 2011), 729–747; Adam Ferziger, "Holocaust, Hurban, and Haredization: Pilgrimages to Eastern Europe and the Realignment of American Orthodoxy," *Contemporary Jewry* 31 (2011): 25–54.

25. Heilman, *Sliding*, 192.

26. Liebman, "Orthodoxy"; Heilman, *Defenders*, chap. 2.

27. Fader, *Mitzvah Girls*; Miriam Isaacs, "Haredi, Haymish and Frim: Yiddish Vitality and Language Choice in a Transnational, Multilingual Community," *International Journal of the Sociology of Language* 138 (1999): 9–30.

28. El-Or, *Educated*; Davidman, *Tradition*; Kaufman, *Rachel's Daughters*; Fader, "Learning"; Fader, *Mitzvah Girls*; Shtadler, *Yeshiva*.

29. A Modern Orthodox rabbi, quoted in Davidman, *Tradition*, 159. Note that many Modern Orthodox Jews have changed their approach to gender since the 1980s, when this quote was recorded. Two examples of this shift in New York are Drisha, a Modern Orthodox institute for Jewish women's learning, and Yeshivat Maharat, "the first institution in Jewish history to train women to be fully integrated into the Orthodox community as spiritual leaders and halakhic authorities" (http://yeshivatmaharat.org/).

30. Orna Blumen, "Criss-Crossing Boundaries: Ultraorthodox Jewish Women Go to Work," *Gender, Place and Culture* 9/2 (2002): 133–151; Fader, *Mitzvah Girls*; Shtadler, *Yeshiva*.

31. E.g., Davidman, *Tradition*; Kaufman, *Rachel's Daughters*.

32. Steven M. Lowenstein, *The Jewish Cultural Tapestry: International Jewish Folk Traditions* (New York: Oxford University Press, 2000).

33. My analysis of data from United Jewish Communities, "National Jewish Population Survey, 2000–01" (New York: United Jewish Communities [producer]; Storrs, Conn.: North American Jewish Data Bank [distributor], 2003).

34. See discussion at http://www.frumsatire.net/2011/05/29/what-does-out-of-town-mean -to-you/.

35. Roberta G. Sands and Dorit Roer-Strier, "*Ba'alot Teshuvah* Daughters and Their Mothers: A View from South Africa," *Contemporary Jewry* 21 (2000): 55–77; Buckser, "Social"; Shari Jacobson, "Modernity, Conservative Religious Movements, and the Female Subject: Newly Ultraorthodox Sephardi Women in Buenos Aires," *American Anthropologist* 108/2 (2006): 336–346; Fader, *Mitzvah Girls*. See Isaacs, "Haredi," on the linguistic implications of Orthodox transnationalism.

36. Judith Irvine and Susan Gal, "Language Ideology and Linguistic Differentiation," in *Regimes of Language: Ideologies, Polities, and Identities*, ed. Paul Kroskrity (Santa Fe: SAR Press, 2000), 35–83.

37. Herbert M. Danzger, *Returning to Tradition: The Contemporary Revival of Orthodox Judaism* (New Haven, Conn.: Yale University Press, 1989). Danzger locates the birth of the movement in the counterculture of the 1960s.

38. David Glanz and Michael I. Harrison, "Varieties of Identity Transformation: The Case of Newly Orthodox Jews," *Jewish Journal of Sociology* 20/2 (1978): 129–142; Aviad, *Return*; Shaffir, "Recruitment"; Shaffir, "Becoming"; Danzger, *Returning*; Davidman, *Tradition*; Kaufman, *Rachel's Daughters*; Sands and Roer-Strier, "Ba'alot"; Michael Robert Shurkin, "Decolonization and the Renewal of French Judaism: Reflections on the Contemporary French Jewish Scene," *Jewish Social Studies* 6/2 (2000): 156–177; Kimmy Caplan, "Israeli Haredi Society and the Repentance (*Hazarah Biteshuvah*) Phenomenon," *Jewish Studies Quarterly* 8/4 (2001): 369–398; Tallen, "Jewish"; Jacobson, "Modernity"; Marta F. Topel, "Brazilian *Ba'alot Teshuvah* and the Paradoxes of Their Religious Conversion," *Judaism* 51/3 (2002): 329–345; Marta F. Topel, *Jerusalem and São Paulo: The New Jewish Orthodoxy in Focus* (Lanham, Md.: University Press of America, 2008); Sands, "Social"; Minny E. Mock-Degen, *The Dynamics of Becoming Orthodox: Dutch Jewish Women Returning to Judaism and How Their Mothers Feel About It* (Amsterdam: Amphora Books, 2010).

39. Fader, *Mitzvah Girls*, uses the term "non-liberal," based on Saba Mahmood, *Politics of Piety: The Islamic Revival and the Feminist Subject* (Princeton, N.J.: Princeton University Press, 2005).

40. The community *kollel* has recently played an increasingly important role in *kiruv*, or Orthodox-initiated outreach (Ferziger, "Church/Sect"). Ferziger describes kollels as "institutions where married yeshiva graduates receive a living stipend in order to dedicate themselves to full-time Torah study" (Ferziger, "Church/Sect," 117); many also offer classes, study sessions, and other outreach activities directed toward non-Orthodox Jews.

41. E.g., Adin Steinsaltz, *Teshuva: A Guide for the Newly Observant Jew* (New York: Free Press, 1987); Akiva Tatz, *Anatomy of a Search: Personal Drama in the Teshuva Revolution* (New York: Mesorah Publications, 1987); Lisa Aiken, *To Be a Jewish Woman* (Northvale, N.J.: Jason Aronson, 1994); Lisa Aiken, *The Baal Teshuva Survival Guide* (Beverly Hills, Calif.: Rossi Publications, 2009); Mordechai Becher, Moshe Newman, and M. Nyuman, *After the Return: Maintaining Good Family Relations and Adjusting to Your New Lifestyle—A Practical Halachic Guide for the Newly Observant* (New York: Feldheim, 1995); Richard H. Greenberg, *Pathways: Jews Who Return* (Northvale, N.J.: Jason Aronson, 1997); Tzipora Heller, *More Precious Than Pearls: Selected Insights into the Qualities of the Ideal Woman*

(New York: Feldheim, 2011). Also, see Stolow, *Orthodox*, on the Hebrew-English books published by Art Scroll, some of which are geared toward BTs.

42. Jacobson, "Modernity."
43. Shurkin, "Decolonization."
44. Dalit Berman Assouline, "Linguistic Maintenance and Change in Israeli Haredi Yiddish" (Ph.D. diss., Hebrew University of Jerusalem, 2007).
45. E.g., Topel, "Brazilian"; Jacobson, "Modernity."
46. Jacobson, "Modernity"; Sands and Roer-Strier, "Ba'alot."
47. Danzger, *Returning*; Topel, "Brazilian"; Topel, *Jerusalem*; Mock-Degen, *Dynamics*.
48. Topel, *Jerusalem*.
49. Mock-Degen, *Dynamics*.
50. Davidman, *Tradition*; Kaufman, *Rachel's Daughters*.
51. Sands and Roer-Strier, "Ba'alot"; Mock-Degen, *Dynamics*.
52. Davidman, *Tradition*, 185.
53. For those who already live within walking distance of a synagogue, like the New Yorkers Davidman (*Tradition*) describes in a Modern Orthodox community, a physical relocation is not necessary. The correlate step for them might be attending services or meals on a regular basis.
54. Davidman, *Tradition*, based on Arthur Greil and David Rudy, "Social Cocoons: Encapsulation and Identity Transformation," *Sociological Inquiry* 54 (1984): 260–278.
55. Erving Goffman, *Asylums: Essays on the Social Situations of Mental Patients and Other Inmates* (New York: Anchor, 1961); Jeylan T. Mortimer and Roberta G. Simmons, "Adult Socialization," *Annual Review of Sociology* 4 (1978): 421–454; Susan Urmston Philips, "The Language Socialization of Lawyers: Acquiring the 'Cant,'" in *Doing the Ethnography of Schooling*, ed. George Spindler (New York: Holt, Rinehart, and Winston, 1982), 176–209; Greil and Rudy, "Social."
56. Shaffir, "Recruitment."
57. E.g., Aviad, *Return*; Shaffir, "Recruitment"; Shaffir, "Becoming."
58. Jack Wertheimer, *A People Divided: Judaism in Contemporary America* (1993; repr. Waltham, Mass.: Brandeis University Press, 1997); Chaim I. Waxman, "The Haredization of American Orthodox Jewry," *Jerusalem Letters* 376 (Jerusalem: Jerusalem Center for Public Affairs, 1998), http://www.policyarchive.org/handle/10207/bitstreams/18274 .pdf; Heilman, *Sliding*; Ferziger, "Holocaust."
59. Stolow, *Orthodox*. In addition, as Finkelman's (*Strictly*) analysis indicates, several Haredi authors are BTs.
60. Steven M. Cohen, *American Assimilation or Jewish Revival?* (Bloomington: Indiana University Press, 1988).
61. Isa Aron, Michael Zeldin, and Sara Lee, "Jewish Education," in *The Cambridge Companion to American Judaism*, ed. Dana Evan Kaplan (Cambridge: Cambridge University Press, 2005), 145–168.
62. Wertheimer, *People*; Steven M. Cohen and Ari Y. Kelman, "The Continuity of Discontinuity: How Young Jews Are Connecting, Creating, and Organizing their Jewish Lives" (New York: Andrea and Charles Bronfman Philanthropies, 2007), http://www.bjpa .org/Publications/details.cfm?PublicationID=327. Steven M. Cohen, J. Shawn Landres, Elie Kaunfer, and Michelle Shain, "Emergent Jewish Communities and their Participants: Preliminary Findings from the 2007 National Spiritual Communities Study" (New York: S3K Synagogue Studies Institute and Mechon Hadar, 2007), http://www .synagogue3000.0rg/files/NatSpirComStudyReport_S3K_Hadar.pdf; Paula Amann, *Journeys to a Jewish Life* (Woodstock, Vt.: Jewish Lights Publishing, 2007).

63. Wade Clark Roof, *A Generation of Seekers: The Spiritual Journeys of the Baby Boom Generation* (San Francisco: Harper, 1993); Wade Clark Roof, *Spiritual Marketplace: Baby Boomers and the Remaking of American Religion* (Princeton, N.J.: Princeton University Press, 1999); Robert Wuthnow, *After Heaven: Spirituality in America since the 1950s* (Cambridge, Mass.: Harvard University Press, 1998); Steven M. Cohen and Arnold M. Eisen, *The Jew Within: Self, Family, and Community in America* (Bloomington: Indiana University Press, 2000).

64. Amann, *Journeys.*

65. Vanessa Ochs, *Inventing Jewish Ritual* (Philadelphia: Jewish Publication Society, 2007).

66. Sarah Bunin Benor, "Towards a New Understanding of Jewish Language in the 21st Century," *Religion Compass* 2/6 (2008): 1062–1080.

67. Sarah Bunin Benor, "Do American Jews Speak a 'Jewish Language'? A Model of Jewish Linguistic Distinctiveness," *Jewish Quarterly Review* 99/2 (2009): 230–269.

68. Other work in social science has also highlighted individual agency, in contrast to an essentialist approach to Jewish identity. Examples include Bethamie Horowitz, "Connections and Journeys: Shifting Identities among American Jews," *Contemporary Jewry* 19 (1998): 63–94; Riv-Ellen Prell, "Developmental Judaism: Challenging the Study of American Jewish Identity in the Social Sciences," *Contemporary Jewry* 21 (2000): 33–54; Cohen and Eisen, *Within*; Laurence Silberstein, ed., *Mapping Jewish Identities* (New York: New York University Press, 2000).

69. Elinor Ochs and Bambi Schieffelin, "Language Acquisition and Socialization: Three Developmental Stories and Their Implications," in *Culture Theory: Essays on Mind, Self, and Emotion*, ed. Richard Shweder and Robert LeVine (Cambridge: Cambridge University Press, 1984), 276–320; Bambi Schieffelin and Elinor Ochs, eds., *Language Socialization across Cultures* (Cambridge: Cambridge University Press, 1986); Bambi Schieffelin and Elinor Ochs, "Language Socialization," *Annual Review of Anthropology* 15 (1986): 163–191; Elinor Ochs, *Culture and Language Development: Language Acquisition and Language Socialization in a Samoan Village* (Cambridge: Cambridge University Press, 1988); Bambi Schieffelin, *The Give and Take of Everyday Life: Language Socialization of Kaluli Children* (New York: Cambridge University Press, 1990); Don Kulick, *Language Shift and Cultural Reproduction: Socialization, Self, and Syncretism in a Papua New Guinea Village* (Cambridge: Cambridge University Press, 1992); Paul Garrett and Patricia Baquedano-López, "Language Socialization: Reproduction and Continuity, Transformation and Change," *Annual Review of Anthropology* 31 (2002): 339–361; Don Kulick and Bambi Schieffelin, "Language Socialization," in *A Companion to Linguistic Anthropology*, ed. Alessandro Duranti (Oxford: Blackwell, 2004), 349–368; Patricia A. Duff, "Second Language Socialization as Sociocultural Theory: Insights and Issues," *Language Teaching* 40 (2007): 309–319; Patricia Duff and Nancy Hornberger, eds., *Encyclopedia of Language and Education. Volume 8: Language Socialization* (New York: Springer, 2008); Patricia A. Duff, "Language Socialization, Higher Education, and Work," in *Encyclopedia of Language and Education. Volume 8: Language Socialization*, ed. Patricia Duff and Nancy Hornberger (New York: Springer, 2008), 257–270; Patricia Duff, "Language Socialization into Academic Discourse Communities," *Annual Review of Applied Linguistics* 30 (2010): 169–192.

70. Schieffelin and Ochs, *Language Socialization*, 163.

71. See Duff, "Second," "Higher Education," and "Academic," for reviews of work on second language socialization and socialization into academic and work communities. On academic discourse socialization in a second language, see Naoko Morita and Masaki Kobayashi, "Academic Discourse Socialization in a Second Language," in *Encyclopedia*

of Language and Education. Volume 8: Language Socialization, ed. Patricia Duff and Nancy Hornberger (New York: Springer, 2008), 243–255. On heritage language socialization see Agnes Weiyun He, "Heritage Language Learning and Socialization," in *Encyclopedia of Language and Education. Volume 8: Language Socialization*, ed. Patricia Duff and Nancy Hornberger (New York: Springer, 2008), 201–213.

72. Philips, "Language"; Elizabeth Mertz, "Linguistic Ideology and Praxis in U.S. Law School Classrooms," in *Language Ideologies: Practice and Theory*, ed. Bambi Schieffelin, Kathryn Woolard, and Paul Kroskrity (Oxford: Oxford University Press, 1998), 149–162; Elizabeth Mertz, *The Language of Law School: Learning to "Think Like a Lawyer"* (Oxford: Oxford University Press, 2007); Lanita Jacobs-Huey, *From the Kitchen to the Parlor: Language and Becoming in African American Women's Hair Care* (Oxford: Oxford University Press, 2006).

73. In addition, this book contributes to research on adult language socialization in several ways: by investigating not only socialization *through* language but also socialization *to use* language, by investigating language socialization in situations of individual religious transformation, and by incorporating analysis of lexicon, grammar, and phonology (in contrast to the main focus of research on adult language socialization, discourse and pragmatics). It also describes a case in which adults can become full masters but are still marked as non-native (in contrast to professional training). For more on this study's contributions to language socialization scholarship, see Sarah Bunin Benor, "Adult Language Socialization: How Newcomers Learn to Speak Like Orthodox Jews," unpublished manuscript.

74. For a beginner's introduction to sociolinguistics, see Ronald Wardhaugh, *An Introduction to Sociolinguistics*, 5th ed. (Oxford: Blackwell, 2005). For a more comprehensive account, see J. K. Chambers, Peter Trudgill, and Natalie Schilling-Estes, eds., *The Handbook of Language Variation and Change* (Oxford: Blackwell, 2002). Foundational research on sociolinguistic variation in the United States demonstrated correlations between linguistic structures and social categories like ethnicity, gender, age, and socioeconomic status, e.g., William Labov, "The Social Motivation of a Sound Change," *Word* 19 (1963): 273–309; William Labov, *The Social Stratification of English in New York City* (Washington, D.C.: Center for Applied Linguistics, 1966); Walt Wolfram, *A Sociolinguistic Description of Detroit Negro Speech* (Washington, D.C.: Center for Applied Linguistics, 1969); William Labov, *Sociolinguistic Patterns* (Philadelphia: University of Pennsylvania Press, 1972); Susan Ervin-Tripp, "On Sociolinguistic Rules: Alternation and Co-occurrence," in *Directions in Sociolinguistics: The Ethnography of Communication*, ed. John Gumperz and Dell Hymes (New York: Holt, Rinehart, and Winston, 1972), 213–250. Subsequent research has applied these principles to sociolinguistic situations around the world. More recent work on language variation and style has focused on individuals' identities and their relationship to local social structures, e.g., Penelope Eckert, *Jocks and Burnouts: Social Categories and Identity in the High School* (New York: Teachers College Press, 1989); Barbara Johnstone, *The Linguistic Individual: Self-Expression in Language and Linguistics* (Oxford: Oxford University Press, 1996); Penelope Eckert, *Linguistic Variation as Social Practice* (Oxford: Blackwell, 2000). Norma Mendoza-Denton, "Style," *Journal of Linguistic Anthropology* 9/1–2 (2000): 238–240; Mary Bucholtz and Kira Hall, "Language and Identity," in *Companion to Linguistic Anthropology*, ed. Alessandro Duranti (Oxford: Blackwell, 2003), 369–394; Nikolas Coupland, *Style: Language Variation and Identity* (Cambridge: Cambridge University Press, 2007); Norma Mendoza-Denton, *Homegirls: Language and Cultural Practice among Latina Youth Gangs* (Oxford: Blackwell, 2008).

75. Labov, *Stratification*.

76. On style-shifting according to topic, situation, and audience, see Labov, *Sociolinguistic Patterns*; Nikolas Coupland, "Style-Shifting in a Cardiff Work-Setting," *Language in Society* 9/1 (1980): 1–12; Allan Bell, "Language Style as Audience Design," *Language in Society* 13 (1984): 145–204.

77. Stella Bortoni-Ricardo, *The Urbanization of Rural Dialect Speakers: A Sociolinguistic Study in Brazil* (Cambridge: Cambridge University Press, 1985); Paul Kerswill, *Dialects Converging: Rural Speech in Urban Norway* (Oxford: Clarendon Press, 1994); J. K. Chambers, "Dialect Acquisition," *Language* 68/4 (1992): 673–705; Sali A. Tagliamonte and Sonja Molfenter, "How'd You Get That Accent? Acquiring a Second Dialect of the Same Language," *Language in Society* 36 (2007): 649–675; Annik Foreman, "A Longitudinal Study of Americans in Australia," in *Proceedings of ALS2k, the 2000 Conference of the Australian Linguistics Society* (2000), http://www.als.asn.au/proceedings/als2000/foreman.pdf; Peter Trudgill, *Dialects in Contact* (Oxford: Blackwell, 1986); Jeff Siegel, *Second Dialect Acquisition* (Cambridge: Cambridge University Press, 2010). Our understanding of second dialect acquisition would be enhanced significantly if future research combined the rigorous linguistic analysis of these studies with ethnographic methods, attention to style-shifting in everyday life, and a focus on language socialization.

78. Phillip Carter, "Phonetic Variation and Speaker Agency: Mexicana Identity in a North Carolina Middle School," *University of Pennsylvania Working Papers in Linguistics* 13/2 (2007), Article 1, p. 3.

79. Ibid., 13.

80. R. B. Le Page and Andrée Tabouret-Keller, *Acts of Identity: Creole-Based Approaches to Language and Ethnicity* (Cambridge: Cambridge University Press, 1985); Judith Irvine, "'Style' as Distinctiveness: The Culture and Ideology of Linguistic Differentiation," in *Style and Sociolinguistic Variation*, ed. Penelope Eckert and John Rickford (Cambridge: Cambridge University Press, 2001), 21–43; Bucholtz and Hall, "Language and Identity."

81. This constructivist approach has gained acceptance not only in sociolinguistics (e.g., Eckert, *Linguistic*; Coupland, *Style*) but in social science more broadly, e.g., Pierre Bourdieu, *Outline of a Theory of Practice* (Cambridge: Cambridge University Press, 1977); Ann Swidler, "Culture in Action: Symbols and Strategies," *American Sociological Review* 51 (1986): 273–286; Etienne Wenger, *Communities of Practice: Learning, Meaning, and Identity* (New York: Cambridge University Press, 1998).

82. Siegel, *Second*.

83. E.g., Wilder Penfield, "A Consideration of the Neurophysiological Mechanisms of Speech and Some Educational Consequences," *Proceedings of the American Academy of Arts and Sciences* 82/5 (1953): 201–214; Thomas Scovel, *A Time to Speak: A Psycholinguistic Inquiry into the Critical Period for Human Speech* (Cambridge, Mass.: Newbury House, 1988); Theo Bongaerts, Brigitte Planken, and Erik Schils, "Can Late Starters Attain a Native Accent in a Foreign Language? A Test of the Critical Period Hypothesis," in *The Age Factor in Second Language Acquisition: A Critical Look at the Critical Period Hypothesis*, ed. David Singleton and Zsolt Lengyel (Clevedon, UK: Multilingual Matters, 1997), 30–50; David Singleton and Zsolt Lengyel, eds., *The Age Factor in Second Language Acquisition: A Critical Look at the Critical Period Hypothesis* (Clevedon, UK: Multilingual Matters, 1997).

84. Arvilla C. Payne, "Factors Controlling the Acquisition of the Philadelphia Dialect by Out-of-State Children," in *Locating Language in Time and Space*, ed. William Labov (New York: Academic Press, 1980), 143–178.

85. Pierre Bourdieu, *Language and Symbolic Power* (Cambridge: Polity Press, 1991).

86. On mediated indexicality, see Michael Silverstein, "Shifters, Linguistic Categories, and Cultural Description," in *Meaning in Anthropology*, ed. Keith Basso and Henry Selby (Albuquerque: University of New Mexico Press, 1976), 11–55. Elinor Ochs, "Indexing Gender," in *Rethinking Context: Language as an Interactive Phenomenon*, ed. Alessandro Duranti and Charles Goodwin (Cambridge: Cambridge University Press, 1992), 335–358; Irvine, "Style"; Asif Agha, "The Social Life of a Cultural Value," *Language and Communication* 23 (2003): 231–273.

87. Jean Lave and Etienne Wenger, *Situated Learning: Legitimate Peripheral Participation* (Cambridge: Cambridge University Press, 1991); Wenger, *Communities*.

88. Research on adult language socialization has little if any contact with an older research tradition within sociology and social psychology: adult socialization; e.g., Orville Brim and Stanton Wheeler, *Socialization after Childhood: Two Essays* (New York: John Wiley, 1966); Mortimer and Simmons, "Adult"; Greil and Rudy, "Conversion"; Jack Haas and William Shaffir, *Becoming Doctors: The Adoption of a Cloak of Competence* (Greenwich, Conn.: JAI Press, 1987). This body of work, which focuses on life stage transitions, professional training, and organizational participation, offers insight into the phases individuals go through and the roles of mentors and community structures in the socialization process.

89. An exception is Michael Graubart Levin, *Journey to Tradition: The Odyssey of a Born-Again Jew* (Hoboken, N.J.: Ktav, 1986).

90. Some studies of adult socialization have mentioned feelings of infantilization or made comparisons to child language learning, e.g., Deborah Poole, "Language Socialization in the Second Language Classroom," *Language Learning* 42 (1992): 593–616; Deborah Golden, "'Now, Like Real Israelis, Let's Stand Up and Sing': Teaching the National Language to Russian Newcomers in Israel," *Anthropology and Education Quarterly* 32 (2001): 52–79.

91. Victor Turner, "Betwixt and Between: The Liminal Period in *Rites de Passage*," in *The Forest of Symbols: Aspects of Ndembu Ritual* (Ithaca, N.Y.: Cornell University Press, 1967), 93–111.

92. Gloria Anzaldúa, *Borderlands/La Frontera: The New Mestiza* (San Francisco: Aunt Lute Books, 1987); See also Homi Bhabha, *The Location of Culture* (New York: Routledge, 1994); Dennis Malone, *The In-Between People: Language and Culture Maintenance and Mother-Tongue Education in the Highlands of Papua New Guinea* (Dallas: SIL International, 2004); Robbins, *Becoming.*

93. Tallen, "Jewish"; Sands, "Social."

94. Bambi Schieffelin, Kathryn Woolard, and Paul Kroskrity, eds., *Language Ideologies: Practice and Theory* (Oxford: Oxford University Press, 1998); Kathryn A. Woolard, "Language Ideology as a Field of Inquiry," in *Language Ideologies: Practice and Theory*, ed. Bambi Schieffelin, Kathryn Woolard, and Paul Kroskrity (Oxford: Oxford University Press, 1998), 3–47; Irvine and Gal, "Language"; Irvine, "Style."

95. Bambi Schieffelin and Rachelle Charlier Doucet, "The 'Real' Haitian Creole: Ideology, Metalinguistics, and Orthographic Choice," in *Language Ideologies: Practice and Theory*, ed. Bambi Schieffelin, Kathryn Woolard, and Paul Kroskrity (Oxford: Oxford University Press, 1998), 285–316, 286.

96. Ochs, "Indexing."

97. Bambi Schieffelin, "Introducing Kaluli Literacy: A Chronology of Influences," in *Regimes of Language: Ideologies, Polities, and Identities*, ed. Paul Kroskrity (Santa Fe: School of American Research Press, 2000), 293–327; Susan Ervin-Tripp, "Variety, Style-Shifting, and Ideology," in *Style and Sociolinguistic Variation*, ed. Penelope Eckert

and John Rickford (Cambridge: Cambridge University Press, 2001), 44–56; Garrett and Baquedano-López, "Language"; Sarah Bunin Benor, "Second Style Acquisition: The Linguistic Socialization of Newly Orthodox Jews" (Ph.D. diss., Stanford University, 2004).

98. On second language learning, see Norman Segalowitz, "Individual Differences in Second Language Acquisition," in *Tutorials in Bilingualism*, ed. A.M.B. de Groot and Judith Kroll (Mahwah, N.J.: Erlbaum, 1997), 85–112.

2. "NOW YOU LOOK LIKE A LADY"

1. Greil and Rudy, "Conversion," found a similar practice in Alcoholics Anonymous. Giving newcomers an official role makes them feel needed and provides more opportunities for socialization.

2. Aviad, *Return*; Shaffir, "Recruitment"; Danzger, *Returning*; Davidman, *Tradition*; Greenberg, *Pathways*.

3. El-Or, *Educated*.

4. Fader, *Mitzvah Girls*.

5. Although Dunkin' Donuts are not made with nonkosher products, the shop where I bought my donut does not have *hashgacha*, the rabbinic certification that food is kosher.

6. Davidman, *Tradition*, 53.

7. James Clifford, *The Predicament of Culture: Twentieth-Century Ethnography, Literature, and Art* (Cambridge, Mass.: Harvard University Press, 1988), 47.

8. Heilman, *Synagogue*. See also reflections in Jonathan Boyarin, "Marginal Redemption at the Eighth Street Shul," in *Between Two Worlds: Ethnographic Essays on American Jewry*, ed. Jack Kugelmass (Ithaca, N.Y.: Cornell University Press, 1988), 52–76.

9. Bronislaw Malinowski, *A Diary in the Strict Sense of the Term* (London: Routledge and Kegan Paul, 1967); Jay Ruby, ed., *A Crack in the Mirror: Reflexive Perspectives in Anthropology* (Philadelphia: University of Pennsylvania Press, 1982); James Clifford, "Introduction: Partial Truths," in *Writing Culture: The Poetics and Politics of Ethnography* (Berkeley: University of California Press, 1986).

10. Reconstructionism is an offshoot of the Conservative movement that views religious tradition as folkways of the Jewish civilization rather than as binding commandments. The Conservative movement of Judaism does see *halacha* as binding, but its interpretation of laws is less stringent than that of Orthodox movements.

11. E.g., Davidman, *Tradition*; Kaufman, *Rachel's Daughters*; El-Or, *Educated*; Fader, *Mitzvah Girls*; Harding, *Book*, 40.

12. I did not make an audio recording of this conversation, but I took notes on it later that evening.

13. Since the 1970s, ritual celebrations for baby girls have become common in non-Orthodox communities (see Ochs, *Inventing*).

14. On egalitarian minyanim, see Riv-Ellen Prell, *Prayer and Community: The Havurah in American Judaism* (Detroit: Wayne State University Press, 1989), and Chava Weissler, *Making Judaism Meaningful: Ambivalence and Tradition in a Havurah Community* (New York: AMS Press, 1989).

15. Greenberg, *Pathways*.

16. E.g., Greil and Rudy, "Conversion"; Peter G. Stromberg, *Language and Self-Transformation: A Study of the Christian Conversion Narrative* (Cambridge: Cambridge University Press, 1993); A. C. Liang, "The Creation of Coherence in Coming-Out Stories," in *Queerly Phrased: Language, Gender, and Sexuality*, ed. Anna Livia and Kira Hall (Oxford: Oxford

University Press, 1997), 287–309; Kathleen M. Wood, "Narrative Iconicity in Electronic-Mail Lesbian Coming-Out Stories," in *Queerly Phrased: Language, Gender, and Sexuality*, ed. Anna Livia and Kira Hall (Oxford: Oxford University Press, 1997), 257–273; Harding, *Book*; Davidman and Greil, "Characters."

17. E.g., Davidman, *Tradition*; Kaufman, *Rachel's Daughters*.
18. Wallace E. Lambert, Richard C. Hodgson, Robert C. Gardner, and Stanley Fillenbaum, "Evaluational Reactions to Spoken Language," *Journal of Abnormal Social Psychology* 60 (1960): 44–51; Wallace E. Lambert, "A Social Psychology of Bilingualism," *Journal of Social Issues* 23 (1967): 91–109; Howard Giles and Nikolas Coupland, *Language: Contexts and Consequences* (Buckingham: Open University Press, 1991).
19. On the high rates of [t] release among Orthodox Jews see Sarah Bunin Benor, "*Talmid Chachams* and *Tsedeykeses*: Language, Learnedness, and Masculinity among Orthodox Jews," *Jewish Social Studies* 11/1 (2004): 147–170.
20. On loshon hora see Lewis Glinert, Kate Miriam Loewenthal, and Vivienne Goldblatt, "Guarding the Tongue: A Thematic Analysis of Gossip Control Strategies among Orthodox Jewish Women in London," *Journal of Multilingual and Multicultural Development* 24/6 (2003): 513–524.
21. Labov, *Sociolinguistic*.
22. Other researchers have reported similar experiences, e.g., Natalie Schilling-Estes, "Investigating 'Self-Conscious' Speech: The Performance Register in Ocracoke English," *Language in Society* 27 (1998): 53–83.
23. E.g., Kaufman, *Rachel's Daughters*; Davidman, *Tradition*; El-Or, *Educated*; Levine, *Mystics*.
24. Helmreich, *World*.
25. Heilman, *Defenders*.
26. Aviad, *Return*; Ellen Koskoff, "The Language of the Heart: Music in Lubavitcher Life," in *New World Hasidim: Ethnographic Studies of Hasidic Jews in America*, ed. Janet Belcove-Shalin (Albany: State University of New York Press, 1995), 87–106.
27. Heilman, *Defenders*.

3. "HE HAS *TZITZIS* HANGING OUT OF HIS PONYTAIL"

1. See scholarly works: Aviad, *Return*; Danzger, *Returning*; Davidman, *Tradition*; Kaufman, *Rachel's Daughters*; Tallen, "Jewish." And see works geared toward BTs: Steinsaltz, *Teshuva*; Tatz, *Anatomy*; Greenberg, *Pathways*; Aiken, *Survival*.
2. Aviad, *Return*, 2.
3. See Fader, *Mitzvah Girls*, for an in-depth discussion of the symbolic meanings of clothing in a Hasidic community and how they relate to language and gender.
4. Lynne Schreiber, ed., *Hide and Seek: Jewish Women and Hair Covering* (Jerusalem: Urim Publications, 2003), 12. See also discussion of hair covering in Topel, "Brazilian."
5. See discussion of ponytails in Michele Rosenthal, "'Désirez-vous vous couvrir la tête?' Les bénédictions de Rabbi Amnon Yitzhak," *Les Cahiers du Judaïsme* 31 (2011): 48–56.
6. Jacobson, "Modernity."
7. For an analysis of visual culture in the Chabad movement, including portraits of rebbes, see Maya Balakirsky Katz, *The Visual Culture of Chabad* (Cambridge: Cambridge University Press, 2011).
8. As Stolow, *Orthodox*, and Finkelman, *Strictly*, point out, the Orthodox publishing industry has expanded significantly over the past decade or two, successfully marketing English-language books to both BTs and FFBs.
9. Roberta Sands, personal communication, December 2010.

10. As elsewhere in the book, the names in this section are pseudonyms, similar to the ones used by the people described.

11. See discussion of a similar practice among Birthright Israel participants who had no Hebrew names before the trip: Shaul Kelner, *Tours That Bind: Diaspora, Pilgrimage, and Israel Birthright Tourism* (New York: New York University Press, 2010), 170. On the impact of Islam on Yoruba naming practices see Salami Oladipo, "Arabic and Sociocultural Change among the Yoruba," in *The Sociology of Language and Religion: Change, Conflict and Accommodation*, ed. Tope Omoniyi (London: Palgrave Macmillan, 2010), 45–57.

12. On Orthodox women's study groups see El-Or, *Educated*. On Orthodox men's study groups see Samuel Heilman, *The People of the Book: Drama, Fellowship, and Religion* (Chicago: University of Chicago Press, 1983).

13. We see similar trends with the internet. Nathaniel Deutsch, "The Forbidden Fork, the Cell Phone Holocaust, and Other Haredi Encounters with Technology," *Contemporary Jewry* 29 (2009): 3–19; Andrea Lieber, "A Virtual 'Veibershul': Blogging and the Blurring of Public and Private among Orthodox Jewish Women," *College English* 72/6 (2009): 621–637.

14. Sands, "Social."

15. Mark Kligman, "Contemporary Jewish Music in America," *American Jewish Yearbook* 101 (2001): 88–141. Also see Helmreich, *World*, 207–208, for an anecdote about a yeshiva *bochur* (male student) who listened to Simon and Garfunkel and his roommate who defended him to the yeshiva authority by saying, "He plays these former *yeshivaleit* [yeshiva students], Shimon and Garfinkel [Judaized versions of their names]. They made a couple of *Yiddishe zachen* [Jewish things/songs]."

16. See Heilman, *Sliding.*

17. See Ferziger, "Holocaust."

18. See more on this in Levine, *Mystics.*

19. Ibid.

20. Heilman, *Synagogue*, 56.

21. El-Or, *Educated*, also reports being accepted in a Hasidic community because she was married with children.

22. Certainly this is not an exhaustive list of practices that distinguish Orthodox Jews from non-Orthodox and non-Jews. Other practices include reading Orthodox literature, especially children's books (Finkelman, *Strictly*); childrearing techniques centered on morality (Fader, *Mitzvah Girls*); an emphasis on *hachnasas orchim* (hospitality); and the prominence of the Jewish calendar in conceptions of time. BTs do tend to take on these practices as well. One practice that BTs tend not to pick up is avoiding eye contact with members of the opposite sex (Shtadler, *Yeshiva*, 56). In my conversations with a number of FFB men, especially young yeshiva bochurs, I noticed that they often avoided looking me in the eye. However, I never noticed a BT man avoiding eye contact with me. This practice, and body habitus in general, are important and deserve further research.

23. While I have touched on some elements of variation, this chapter is by no means intended as an exhaustive description of Orthodox diversity in dress, music, etc.

24. Pierre Bourdieu, *Distinction: A Social Critique of the Judgement of Taste* (1979; repr. Cambridge, Mass.: Harvard University Press, 1984).

25. Pierre Bourdieu, "The Forms of Capital," in *Handbook for Theory and Research for the Sociology of Education*, ed. John G. Richardson (1983; repr. New York: Greenwood, 1986), 241–258, 244.

26. Rabbi Yaakov Asher Sinclair, "Parshat Ki Tetzei," *Ohr Somayach* (September 13, 2008), http://ohr.edu/yhiy/article.php/3639.

4. "THIS IS NOT WHAT TO RECORD"

1. Copyright Abie Rotenberg, 1994, *Journeys*, Volume 3, used with permission.
2. Charles Ferguson, "Diglossia," *Word* 15 (1959): 325–340. For a model of multiglossia in Jewish communities see Joshua Fishman, "The Sociology of Jewish Languages from a General Sociolinguistic Point of View," in *Readings in the Sociology of Jewish Languages*, ed. Joshua Fishman (Leiden: Brill, 1985), 3–21.
3. In the cases of Eastern Yiddish and Ottoman Judeo-Spanish, speakers maintained languages after a migration, and these were subsequently influenced by the Slavic and Balkan languages of their new non-Jewish neighbors. In addition, Jewish languages tend to have other distinctive features not influenced by contact languages. See details in Max Weinreich, *History of the Yiddish Language*, translated from Yiddish by S. Noble and J. Fishman (1973; repr. New Haven, Conn.: Yale University Press, 2008); Paul Wexler, "Jewish Inter-Linguistics: Facts and Conceptual Framework," *Language* 57/1 (1981): 99–149; Fishman, "Sociology"; Bernard Spolsky and Sarah Bunin Benor, "Jewish Languages," in *Encyclopedia of Language and Linguistics*, 2nd ed., ed. Keith Brown (Oxford: Elsevier, 2006), 6:120–124; Benor, "Towards."
4. David Gold, "Jewish English," in *Readings in the Sociology of Jewish Languages*, ed. Joshua Fishman (Leiden: Brill, 1985), 280–298; David Gold, "On Jewish English in the United States," *Jewish Language Review* 6 (1986): 121–135; Benor, "American."
5. Jeffrey Shandler, *Adventures in Yiddishland: Postvernacular Language and Culture* (Berkeley: University of California Press, 2005).
6. For a survey-based analysis of how American Jews use language to signal their religious knowledge and affiliations, see Sarah Bunin Benor, "*Mensch, Bentsh,* and *Balagan*: Variation in the American Jewish Linguistic Repertoire," *Language and Communication* 31/2 (2011): 141–154; Sarah Bunin Benor and Steven M. Cohen, "Talking Jewish: The 'Ethnic English' of American Jews," in *Ethnicity and Beyond: Theories and Dilemmas of Jewish Group Demarcation. Studies in Contemporary Jewry*, vol. 25, ed. Eli Lederhendler (Oxford: Oxford University Press, 2011), 62–78.
7. Benor, "American"; Stolow, *Orthodox*.
8. Jerusalem Talmud, Shekalim, quoted in Alvin Schiff, *The Mystique of Hebrew: An Ancient Language in the New World* (New York: Shengold, 1996), 145.
9. Lewis Glinert, "Language Choice in Halakhic Speech Acts," in *Language, Society, and Thought: Essays in Honor of Joshua A. Fishman's 65th Birthday*, ed. Robert L. Cooper and Bernard Spolsky (Berlin: Mouton de Gruyter, 1991), 161–186. Lewis Glinert and Yoseph Shilhav, "Holy Land, Holy Language: Language and Territory in an Ultraorthodox Jewish Ideology," *Language in Society* 20 (1991): 59–86.
10. There has been a good deal of work on the maintenance of Yiddish among Ultra-Orthodox Jews, especially Hasidim, e.g., Lewis Glinert, "We Never Changed Our Language: Attitudes to Yiddish Acquisition among Hasidic Educators in Britain," *International Journal of the Sociology of Language* 138 (1999): 31–52; Isaacs, "Haredi"; Bryna Bogoch, "Gender, Literacy, and Religiosity: Dimensions of Yiddish Education in Israeli Government-Supported Schools," *International Journal of the Sociology of Language* 138 (1999): 123–160; Fader, "Learning"; Fader, "Reclaiming"; Fader, *Mitzvah Girls*; Simeon Baumel, *Sacred Speakers: Language and Culture among the Haredim in Israel* (New York: Berghahn Books, 2005); Bruce Mitchell, *Language Politics and Language Survival: Yiddish among the Haredim in Post-War Britain* (Paris: Peeters, 2006); Shandler, *Adventures*; Isa Barrière, "The Vitality of Yiddish among Hasidic Infants and Toddlers in a Low SES Preschool in Brooklyn," in *Proceedings of Czernowitz Yiddish Language 2008 International*

Centenary Conference (*Jews and Slavs* 22), ed. Wolf Moskovich (Jerusalem: Hebrew University, 2010), 170–196; Michal Tannenbaum and Netta Abugov, "The Legacy of the Linguistic Fence: Linguistic Patterns among Ultra-Orthodox Jewish Girls," *Heritage Language Journal* 7/1 (2010): 74–90. On the sanctification of Yiddish among secular and Orthodox Jews, see Joshua A. Fishman, "The Holiness of Yiddish: Who Says Yiddish Is Holy and Why?" *Language Policy* 1/2 (2002): 123–141.

11. Bogoch, "Gender"; Fader "Reclaiming"; Fader, *Mitzvah Girls.*

12. These are pseudonyms, similar to the names she mentioned.

13. However, many non-Orthodox Jews who are highly engaged in Jewish life do have strong text skills, and some are fluent in Israeli Hebrew (Benor, "Mensch").

14. Benor, "Mensch." See diversity in work on Orthodox Jewish English: Sol Steinmetz, "Jewish English in the United States," *American Speech* 56/1 (1981): 3–16; Sol Steinmetz, *Yiddish and English: A Century of Yiddish in America* (Tuscaloosa: University of Alabama Press, 1986); Gold, "Jewish English"; Gold, "United States"; Chaim Weiser, *Frumspeak: The First Dictionary of Yeshivish* (Northvale, N.J.: Jason Aronson, 1995); Sarah Benor, "Yavnish: A Linguistic Study of the Orthodox Jewish Community at Columbia University," *'Iggrot ha'Ari: Columbia University Student Journal of Jewish Scholarship* 1/2 (New York: Columbia University Jewish Student Union, 1998), 8–50; Benor, *Second*; Benor, "Talmid Chachams." Aliza Sacknowitz, "Linguistic Means of Orthodox Jewish Identity Construction: Phonological Features, Lexical Features, and the Situated Discourse"(Ph.D. diss., Georgetown University, 2007); Fader, "Reclaiming."

15. Sarah Bunin Benor, "Ethnolinguistic Repertoire: Shifting the Analytic Focus in Language and Ethnicity," *Journal of Sociolinguistics* 14/2 (2010): 159–183.

16. Benor, "Mensch"; Benor and Cohen, "Talking." Respondents were allowed to choose from a long list of denominations. The analysis here considers Orthodox anyone who selected "Modern Orthodox," "Orthodox," or "Black Hat / Yeshivish or Chassidish."

17. Weinreich, *History,* 351–352.

18. Uriel Weinreich, *Languages in Contact: Findings and Problems* (1953; repr. The Hague: Mouton, 1974); Shana Poplack, David Sankoff, and Christopher Miller, "The Social Correlates and Linguistic Processes of Lexical Borrowing and Assimilation," *Linguistics* 26 (1988): 47–104; Sarah Thomason, *Language Contact: An Introduction* (Washington, D.C.: Georgetown University Press, 2001).

19. http://www.torah.org/advanced/jerusalemviews/5759/class14.html#, accessed January 2012; italics, underlining, and translations are mine. Note that it can be difficult to distinguish between a loanword/phrase and a code switch.

20. Sarah Benor, "Loan Words in the English of Modern Orthodox Jews: Hebrew or Yiddish?" in *Proceedings of the Berkeley Linguistic Society's 25th Annual Meeting, 1999,* ed. Steve Chang et al. (Berkeley: Berkeley Linguistic Society, 2000), 287–298.

21. Steinmetz, *Yiddish*; Sol Steinmetz, *Dictionary of Jewish Usage: A Popular Guide to the Use of Jewish Terms* (Lanham, Md.: Rowman and Littlefield, 2005); Lewis Glinert, *The Joys of Hebrew* (Oxford: Oxford University Press, 1992); Weiser, *Frumspeak*; Joyce Eisenberg and Ellen Scolnic, *The JPS Dictionary of Jewish Words* (Philadelphia: Jewish Publication Society, 2001).

22. James Matisoff, *Blessings, Curses, Hopes, and Fears: Psycho-Ostensive Expressions in Yiddish,* 2nd ed. (1979; repr. Stanford, Calif.: Stanford University Press, 2000). On similar phrases from Arabic used in Yoruba see Oladipo, "Arabic."

23. See Fader, "Reclaiming," *Mitzvah Girls.*

24. This form of "bubby" is probably not etymologically related to the homonym that means "grandma."

25. Note that in child-directed speech, kinship terms, and names, Orthodox Jewish English uses two types of diminutive suffixes: -ele/-elach, which is derived from Yiddish, and -i, which is influenced both by English (as in Jenny, Billy, doggie, and shoesies) and by Israeli Hebrew (as in Yossi [Yosef], Yoni [Yonatan], Dudi [David], and Dasi [Hadassah]). See Benor, "Yavnish," 37, for details about Orthodox Jewish English names ending in -i, as well as discussion of a debate between Steinmetz ("Jewish," 8) and Gold ("United States," 126) about whether word-final [i] represents a phonological or morphological phenomenon.

26. Regarding the dual influences on words like "Mommy," see Kathryn A. Woolard, "Simultaneity and Bivalency as Strategies in Bilingualism," *Journal of Linguistic Anthropology* 8/1 (1998): 3–29; Fader, *Mitzvah Girls*; Ghil'ad Zuckermann, "Cultural Hybridity: Multisourced Neologization in 'Reinvented' Languages and in Languages with 'Phono-Logographic' Script," *Languages in Contrast* 4/2 (2004): 281–318; Ghil'ad Zuckermann, "Hybridity versus Revivability: Multiple Causation, Forms and Patterns," *Journal of Language Contact* 2 (2009): 40–67.

27. Debby Friedman, "*Kiddush Hashem?* That's Easy!" *Jewish Observer*, December 2001, 44–46.

28. Benor, "Talmid Chachams."

29. Weiser, *Frumspeak*.

30. We see this phenomenon in other Jewish languages, such as Judeo-Spanish. Sarah Bunin Benor, "Lexical Othering in Judezmo: How Ottoman Sephardim Refer to Non-Jews," in *Languages and Literatures of Sephardic and Oriental Jews: Proceedings of the Sixth International Congress*, ed. David M. Bunis (Jerusalem: Bialik Institute and Misgav Yerushalayim, 2009), 65–85.

31. Steinmetz, *Yiddish*, 84.

32. Heilman, *Sliding*, 2006.

33. http://northofbrooklyn.blogspot.com/2008/10/whats-matzav-of-that-zach.html, accessed January 2009.

34. Max Weinreich, "The Reality of Jewishness versus the Ghetto Myth: The Sociolinguistic Roots of Yiddish," in *To Honor Roman Jakobson: Essays on the Occasion of his Seventieth Birthday*, vol. 3 (The Hague: Mouton, 1966), 2199–2211, 2205. As I describe in previous work (Benor, "Lexical"), Judeo-Spanish has a similar discerning phrase, as well as the practice of using different component languages to distinguish between Jewish and non-Jewish referents.

35. Max Weinreich, "Yiddishkayt and Yiddish: On the Impact of Religion on Language in Ashkenazi Jewry," in *Mordecai M. Kaplan: Jubilee Volume on the Occasion of His Seventieth Birthday*, ed. Moshe Davis (New York: Jewish Theological Seminary of America Press, 1953), 481–514, 508. See a different type of "*lehavdl loshen*" in Weinreich, *History*, 193–195.

36. However, "soul," "angel," and "saint" are sometimes heard from both BTs and FFBs.

37. Jewish languages around the world have secretive, humorous, and/or derisive names for non-Jewish religious concepts and leaders. See Benor, "Lexical," on this phenomenon in Judeo-Spanish.

38. Chani Aftergut Kurtz, "We Wish You a Merry . . . Chanuka?" *Jewish Observer*, November 2001, 38.

39. I assume that the phrasal verbs in table 4.3 are not used in the same way in general American English, as I have never heard them outside of the Orthodox community and they do not appear with the same meaning in the Random House *Dictionary of the English Language* (2nd ed., 1987, unabridged). The meanings presented here are

based on my fieldwork and Weiser, *Frumspeak*, and the Yiddish meanings are from Uriel Weinreich, *English-Yiddish Yiddish-English Dictionary* (New York: YIVO Institute for Jewish Research, 1968).

40. Weinreich, *Dictionary*.

41. The usage in this example is also common in general American English, especially in legal language.

42. Weiser, *Frumspeak*, 37.

43. Israeli Hebrew uses *kvar* (already) in a similar way, exhibiting strong influence from Yiddish.   .

44. See Benor, *Second*, for more in-depth discussion of Yiddish morphosyntactic influences and loan translations.

45. On word-final devoicing in Central Yiddish, German English, and New York (Jewish) English, see Marvin Herzog, Uriel Weinreich, Vera Baviskar et al., *The Language and Culture Atlas of Ashkenazi Jewry*, vol. 1 (Tübingen: M. Niemeyer, 1992), 38; Thomas Purnell, Joseph C. Salmons, Dilara Tepeli, and Jennifer Mercer, "Structured Heterogeneity and Change in Laryngeal Phonetics: Upper Midwestern Final Obstruents," *Journal of English Linguistics* 33/4 (2005): 307–338; Mary Rose, "Language, Place, and Identity in Later Life" (Ph.D. diss., Stanford University, 2006); C. K. Thomas, "Jewish Dialect and New York Dialect," *American Speech* 7/5 (1932): 321–326; David L. Gold, "The Pronunciation of ng as Taught in a New York City High School about 1962," *American Speech* 49/1–2 (1974): 159–160.

46. Mary Bucholtz, "Geek the Girl: Language, Femininity, and Female Nerds," in *Gender and Belief Systems*, ed. Natasha Warner et al. (Berkeley: Berkeley Women and Language Group, 1996), 119–131; Kathryn Campbell-Kibler, Robert Podesva, and Sarah Roberts, "Sharing Resources and Indexing Meaning in the Production of Gay Styles," in *Language and Sexuality: Contesting Meaning in Theory and Practice*, ed. Kathryn Campbell-Kibler et al. (Stanford, Calif.: CSLI Publications, 2001), 175–190; Robert J. Podesva, "Phonetic Detail in Sociolinguistic Variation: Its Linguistic Significance and Role in the Construction of Social Meaning" (Ph.D. diss., Stanford University, 2006); Erez Levon, "Mosaic Identity and Style: Phonological Variation among Reform American Jews," *Journal of Sociolinguistics* 10 (2006): 185–205; Penelope Eckert, "Variation and the Indexical Field," *Journal of Sociolinguistics* 12 (2008): 453–476; Jennifer Sclafani, "Martha Stewart Behaving Badly: Parody and the Symbolic Meaning of Style," *Journal of Sociolinguistics* 13/5 (2009): 613–633.

47. Sarah Bunin Benor, "Sounding Learned: The Gendered Use of [t] in Orthodox Jewish English," in *Penn Working Papers in Linguistics: Selected Papers from NWAV 29*, ed. Daniel Ezra Johnson and Tara Sanchez (Philadelphia: University of Pennsylvania, 2001), 1–16; Benor, "Talmid Chachams."

48. On this variable in a Lubavitch Orthodox community see George Jochnowitz, "Bilingualism and Dialect Mixture among Lubavitcher Hasidic Children," *American Speech* 43/3 (1968): 188–200. Many Latinos also use non-raised pre-nasal short [a] (Carter, "Mexicana"). On the regional patterning of this variable in the United States see William Labov, Sharon Ash, and Charles Boberg, *The Atlas of North American English: Phonetics, Phonology, and Sound Change* (Berlin: Mouton de Gruyter, 2006).

49. Uriel Weinreich, "Notes on the Yiddish Rise-Fall Intonation Contour," in *For Roman Jakobson: Essays on the Occasion of his Sixtieth Birthday*, ed. Morris Halle (The Hague: Mouton, 1956), 633–643; Samuel Heilman, "Sounds of Modern Orthodoxy: The Language of Talmud Study," in *Never Say Die! A Thousand Years of Yiddish in Jewish Life and Letters*, ed. Joshua Fishman (The Hague: Mouton, 1981), 227–253; Heilman, *People*; Lionel A. Wolberger, "The Music of Holy Argument: The Ethnomusicology of Talmudic

Debate" (Ph.D. diss., Wesleyan University, 1991); Zelda Kahan Newman, "The Jewish Sound of Speech: Talmudic Chant, Yiddish Intonation and the Origins of Early Ashkenaz," *Jewish Quarterly Review* 90 (2000): 293–336.

50. Recordings of several quotes in this section are available on the book website: http://becomingfrum.weebly.com.

51. Weinreich, "Notes," 640.

52. Ibid.

53. John R. Rickford and Angela E. Rickford, "Cut-Eye and Suck-Teeth: African Words and Gestures in New World Guise," *African American Vernacular English: Features, Evolution, Educational Implications* (1976; repr. Oxford: Blackwell, 1999), 157–173, originally published in *Journal of American Folklore* 89 (1976): 294–309; Cecilia Cutler, "'Keep-in' It Real': White Hip-Hoppers' Discourses of Language, Race, and Authenticity," *Journal of Linguistic Anthropology* 13/2 (2003): 211–233. Note that the hesitation click is different from the "no" click that is widespread in the Arab and Mediterranean world, including among Israeli Jews. While both the hesitation click and the "no" click are made by touching the tongue to the roof of the mouth and bringing air inward, the hesitation click is made without lip rounding and does not form its own unit of meaning.

54. The label "jargon" for a Jewish variety of a local language is not new. Nineteenth-century opponents of Yiddish and Judeo-Spanish, as well as writers who fondly wrote in Yiddish and Judeo-Spanish, used variants of the word "jargon" to refer to those languages.

55. Jerry Hellman, "Yeshivishe Reid: Is Frumspeak a Real Language?" *Ami Magazine*, March 2011, citing Benor, "American."

56. Significant difference: p <0.05 (Chi square test). As a control, I included a set of "dummy" questions: two identical sentences. In this case, both groups' responses were significantly different from the dummy questions (p = 0.001 for BTs and 0.032 for FFBs).

57. The number presented is the mean difference between respondents' judgment of the speakers' Orthodox identity for excerpt A and excerpt B, and the significance level is based on the difference between the responses for that feature and the responses for the dummy questions. See details in Benor, *Second*.

58. The matched guise results for "by" and the rise-fall intonation contour would likely be higher if the stimuli had been worded differently (Benor, *Second*).

5. *"TORAH* OR *TOYRAH"*

1. Researchers use diverse terminology for the groups at the poles. Liebman, "Orthodoxy," uses "modern or church" and "sectarian," applying a theory that understands "churches" as more open than "sects" to the society around them. Ferziger, "Church/Sect," prefers "traditionalist" over "sectarian," based on Black Hat Jews' growing openness to non-Orthodox Jews, especially in the context of Orthodox outreach. Heilman and Cohen, *Cosmopolitans*, refer to the "two extremes" as "modernists" and "traditionalists," as well as "acculturative and contra-acculturative orientations." Helmreich, *World*, discusses three groups along a continuum: "Modern Orthodox," "Strictly Orthodox," and "Ultra-Orthodox."

2. Ayala Fader, "Gender, Morality, and Language: Socialization Practices in a Hasidic Community" (Ph.D. diss., New York University, 2000), 32. The pronunciation of *frum* as *frim* is common among Hasidic Jews who originated in Central and Southern Yiddish-speaking areas, especially Poland and Hungary.

3. Fader, *Mitzvah Girls*, 131.

4. Heilman, *Synagogue*.

5. http://northofbrooklyn.blogspot.com/2009/06/and-heres-another-one.html.

6. Liebman, "Orthodoxy"; Heilman, *Synagogue;* Heilman, *Defenders;* Heilman, *Sliding;* Heilman and Cohen, *Cosmopolitans;* Soloveitchik, "Rupture"; Gurock, *Orthodox;* Ferziger, "Holocaust."

7. As Heilman, *Sliding,* and Ferziger, "Holocaust," have shown, the continuum has shifted in recent decades, as Modern Orthodox Jews have taken on stringencies in halacha and gender separation.

8. Heilman, *Synagogue,* 218–219.

9. Ibid., 219.

10. E.g., Poll, "Hasidic"; Kaufman, *Rachel's Daughters;* Heilman, *Defenders;* Fader, *Mitzvah Girls.*

11. Frumster figures are from Sarah Bunin Benor, "Frumster.com and the Modern Orthodox to Yeshivish Continuum," presented at the annual meeting of the Association for Jewish Studies, San Diego, 2006.

12. Rebecca Press Schwartz, "Privilege, Perspective, and Modern Orthodox Youth," in *The Next Generation of Modern Orthodoxy,* ed. Shmuel Hain (New York: Yeshiva University Press, 2012), 23–35, 24.

13. Liebman, "Orthodoxy"; Heilman and Cohen, *Cosmopolitans;* Waxman, "Haredization"; Heilman, *Sliding.*

14. Blumen, "Criss-Crossing."

15. Heilman, *Sliding.*

16. Liebman, "Orthodoxy."

17. Bogoch, "Gender"; Isaacs, "Haredi"; Fader, "Reclaiming," *Mitzvah Girls.*

18. Hellman, "Yeshivishe Reid."

19. Heilman, *People.*

20. As Aviva Ben-Ur explains, some American schools and camps had switched from Ashkenazi to Israeli Hebrew pronunciation in the 1920s or even earlier, based on their "increasing attunement to Palestine for cultural and political cues." Aviva Ben-Ur, *Sephardic Jews in America: A Diasporic History* (New York: New York University Press, 2009). 62.

21. Sacknowitz, *Linguistic,* 253.

22. Benor, "Yavnish."

23. Silber, "Emergence"; Friedman, "Lost"; Soloveitchik, "Rupture"; Heilman, *Sliding;* Stolow, *Orthodox.*

24. In addition, Andrew's later e-mails to me include many Hebrew and Yiddish loanwords and constructions, as in this excerpt (italics are mine): "*Pesach* here was very nice. I was *by* two of the *rebbeim* and their *sedarim* were very nice, very long, but very interesting. *Be well* and talk to you soon." In Andrew's early interviews he used the word "Passover" rather than "Pesach" and "class" rather than "shiur."

25. I have observed Rabbi Fischer use a higher rate of [oy] with other audiences. His rate in this recording is lower likely because he is teaching a small group of BTs.

6. "JUST KEEPIN' IT REAL, *MAMISH*"

1. The scoring system is as follows:

Loanwords (types): 0 = none; 1 = one to seven; 2 = eight to fifteen; 3 = sixteen or more

Each Yiddish feature (tokens): 0 = none; 0.5 = one; 1 = two or more

Click hesitation marker (tokens): 0 = none; 1 = one to two; 2 = three or more

High-falling pitch boundary or rise-fall intonation (tokens): 0 = none; 1 = one or more

Word-final devoicing (tokens): 0 = none; 1 = one to two; 2 = three or more

Non-raised pre-coda-nasal short [a] (tokens): 0 = none; 1 = one or more

This is intended to be only a very rough measure of individuals' linguistic distinctiveness. Point values are necessarily arbitrary, but they are standard for all speakers. Some speakers undoubtedly used additional linguistic features when I was not recording or observing them.

2. During my year of research, some of the BTs started in one category and moved to another. For purposes of analysis, I considered them to be in the category they were in for the majority of my observations.

3. John R. Rickford, "Implicational Scales," in *Handbook of Language Variation and Change*, ed. J. K. Chambers, Peter Trudgill, and Natalie Schilling-Estes (Malden, Mass.: Blackwell, 2002), 142–167, 143.

4. On "standard language ideology" see Rosina Lippi-Green, *English with an Accent: Language, Ideology and Discrimination in the United States* (London: Routledge, 1997).

5. Shaffir, "Becoming," 338.

6. Davidman, *Tradition*, 187.

7. Greil and Rudy, "Social," 16.

8. Harding, *Book.*

9. See Levine, *Mystics*, for an example of an FFB girl who wishes she were a boy so she could study texts more intensively.

10. Rosenthal, "Désirez-vous."

11. Benor, "Talmid Chachams."

12. As Sands, "Social," demonstrates, many BTs identify strongly with other BTs and seek social networks with them. See also Danzger, *Returning.*

13. LePage and Tabouret-Keller, *Acts;* Irvine, "Style"; Bucholtz and Hall, "Language."

14. Rabbi Yisroel Reisman, "A Rebbe for Our Generation," *Jewish Observer*, December 2001, 14–21.

15. Levine, *Mystics*, 80.

7. "I FINALLY GOT THE LINGO"

1. Benor, "Sounding"; Benor, "Talmid Chachams."

2. While much work in sociolinguistics has focused on aggregated frequencies of linguistic variables among dozens or hundreds of speakers, that method often masks individual variation (see critiques in Johnstone, *Individual*, and Coupland, *Style*).

3. Lave and Wenger, *Situated;* Wenger, *Communities.*

4. Penelope Eckert and Sally McConnell-Ginet, "Think Practically and Look Locally: Language and Gender as Community-Based Practice," *Annual Review of Anthropology* 21 (1992): 461–490, 464.

5. E.g., Jitendra Thakerar, Howard Giles, and Jenny Cheshire, "Psychological and Linguistic Parameters of Speech Accommodation Theory," in *Advances in the Social Psychology of Language*, ed. Howard Giles and Robert St. Clair (Cambridge: Cambridge University Press, 1982), 205–255; John R. Rickford and Faye McNair-Knox, "Addressee- and Topic-Influenced Style Shift: A Quantitative Sociolinguistic Study," in *Sociolinguistic Perspectives on Register*, ed. Douglas Biber and Edward Finegan (Oxford: Oxford University Press, 1994), 235–276; Samy H. Alim, *You Know My Steez: An Ethnographic and Sociolinguistic Study of Styleshifting in a Black American Speech Community* (Durham, N.C.: Duke University Press, 2005).

6. Merrill Swain, "Integrating Language and Content Teaching through Collaborative Tasks," *Canadian Modern Language Review* 58/1 (2001): 44–63. Amy Snyder Ohta, *Second Language Acquisition Processes in the Classroom: Learning Japanese* (Mahwah, N.J.:

Lawrence Erlbaum Associates, 2001); Pauline Foster and Amy Snyder Ohta, "Negotiation for Meaning and Peer Assistance in Second Language Classrooms," *Applied Linguistics* 26/3 (2005): 402–430.

7. Schieffelin and Ochs, "Language Socialization," 166. The notion of "scaffolding" (David Wood, Jerome S. Bruner, and Gail Ross, "The Role of Tutoring in Problem Solving," *Journal of Child Psychology and Psychiatry* 17 [1976]: 89–100) builds on Vygotsky's work on the "zone of proximal development." Lev Vygotsky, *Mind and Society: The Development of Higher Psychological Processes* (Cambridge, Mass.: Harvard University Press, 1978). This notion has been applied in various ways in research on language socialization, e.g., Schieffelin and Ochs, eds., *Language Socialization*; Shoshana Blum-Kulka, *Dinner Talk: Cultural Patterns of Sociability and Socialization in Family Discourse* (Mahwah, N.J.: Lawrence Erlbaum, 1997); Amy Snyder Ohta, "Interactional Routines and the Socialization of Interactional Style in Adult Learners of Japanese," *Journal of Pragmatics* 31 (1999): 1493–1512; Ohta, *Second*; Caroline Vickers, "Second Language Socialization through Team Interaction among Electrical and Computer Engineering Students," *Modern Language Journal* 91/4 (2007), 621–640; Duff, "Higher Education"; Duff, "Academic." Poole's study of ESL classroom interactions characterizes the teachers' use of "known information questions" and expansions as scaffolding, explained as "the expert's interactional efforts to render a novice capable of completing a task beyond his or her level of competence" (Poole, "Language," 201–202).

8. Tatz, *Anatomy.*

9. Greenberg, *Pathways.*

10. Babylonian Talmud, Bava Metzia 58b.

11. Gail Jefferson, "On Exposed and Embedded Correction in Conversation," in *Talk and Social Organisation*, ed. Graham Button and J.R.E. Lee (Clevedon, UK: Multilingual Matters, 1987), 86–100; John Neil Bohannon and Laura Stanowicz, "The Issue of Negative Evidence: Adult Responses to Children's Language Errors," *Developmental Psychology* 24/5 (1988): 684–689; Alison Mackey and Jaemyung Goo, "Interaction Research in SLA: A Meta-Analysis and Research Synthesis," in *Conversational Interaction in Second Language Acquisition: A Collection of Empirical Studies*, ed. Alison Mackey (Oxford: Oxford University Press, 2007), 407–452; Olga V. Griswold, "Becoming a United States Citizen: Second Language Socialization in Adult Citizenship Classrooms" (Ph.D. diss., University of California, Los Angeles, 2007); Kira Gor and Michael Long, "Input and Second Language Processing," in *Handbook of Second Language Acquisition*, ed. William Ritchie and Tej Bhatia (New York: Academic Press, 2009), 445–472.

12. Katherine Demuth, "Prompting Routines in the Language Socialization of Basotho Children," in *Language Socialization across Cultures*, ed. Bambi Schieffelin and Elinor Ochs (Cambridge: Cambridge University Press, 1986), 51–79; Debra Friedman, "Speaking Correctly: Error Correction as a Language Socialization Practice in a Ukrainian Classroom," *Applied Linguistics* 31 (2010): 346–367.

13. Griswold, *Becoming*; Ohta, "Interactional"; Philips, "Language"; Mertz, *Language.*

14. Ochs and Schieffelin, "Acquisition"; Elinor Ochs, "Introduction," in *Language Socialization across Cultures*, ed. Bambi Schieffelin and Elinor Ochs (Cambridge: Cambridge University Press, 1986), 1–13; Barbara Johnstone, "An Introduction," "Perspectives on Repetition," special issue of *Text* 7 (1987): 205–214; Barbara Johnstone, ed., *Repetition in Discourse: Interdisciplinary Perspectives* (Norwood, N.J.: Ablex, 1994); Eve V. Clark, *First Language Acquisition* (Cambridge: Cambridge University Press, 2003); Cynthia Gordon, "Repetition and Identity Experimentation: One Child's Use of Repetition as a Resource for 'Trying On' Maternal Identities," in *Selves and Identities in Narrative and Discourse,*

ed. Michael Bamberg, Anna De Fina,and Deborah Schiffrin (Amsterdam: John Benjamins, 2007), 133–157; Eve V. Clark and J. Bernicot, "Repetition as Ratification: How Parents and Children Place Information in Common Ground," *Journal of Child Language* 35 (2008): 349–371; Leslie Moore, "Learning by Heart in Qur'anic and Public Schools in Northern Cameroon," *Social Analysis* 50 (2006): 109–126; Leslie Moore, "Language Socialization and Repetition," in *The Handbook of Language Socialization*, ed. Alessandro Duranti, Elinor Ochs, and Bambi Schieffelin (Oxford: Blackwell, 2011), 209–226.

15. Clark, *First*, 321.
16. See also Moore, "Learning."
17. This grammatical construction is common in nonstandard American English in general. Its frequency among Orthodox Jews is partly due to the influence of Yiddish, which has a parallel construction, "*Oyb ikh volt gehat gemeynt . . .*"
18. Karen Ann Watson-Gegeo and David W. Gegeo, "Calling-Out and Repeating Routines in Kwara'ae Children's Language Socialization," in *Language Socialization across Cultures*, ed. Bambi Schieffelin and Elinor Ochs (Cambridge: Cambridge University Press, 1986), 17–50, 25.
19. Ann M. Peters and Stephen T. Boggs, "Interactional Routines as Cultural Influences upon Language Acquisition," in *Language Socialization across Cultures*, ed. Bambi Schieffelin and Elinor Ochs (Cambridge: Cambridge University Press, 1986), 80–96; Ochs, *Culture*.
20. Poole, "Language," discusses the demeaning nature of repetition in an adult second-language classroom.
21. Mertz, "Linguistic," 155–156.
22. Weiser, *Frumspeak.*
23. Lave and Wenger, *Situated*, 57. See also William Evan, "Peer Group Interaction and Organizational Socialization: A Study of Employee Turnover," *American Sociological Review* 28 (1963): 436–440; Edgar H. Schein, "Organizational Socialization and the Profession of Management," *Industrial Management Review* 9 (1968): 1–15; Mortimer and Simmons, "Adult"; Ohta, *Second*; Foster and Ohta, "Negotiation"; Naoko Morita, "Discourse Socialization through Oral Classroom Activities in a TESL Graduate Program," *TESOL Quarterly* 34 (2000): 279–310; Masaki Kobayashi, "The Role of Peer Support in Students' Accomplishment of Oral Academic Tasks," *Canadian Modern Language Review* 59 (2003): 337–368.
24. I found many instances of this use of "daven" online, as well as in a Yiddish and Orthodox Jewish English coloring book geared toward (FFB) Hasidic boys (*"Ikh Bin Alt 3 Yohr—I Am Three Years Old" Coloring Book*, 3rd ed. [Monsey, N.Y.: R. M. Brandvayn, 10), which I purchased in 2002. The following sentences appear together (the first sentence appears in Hebrew letters; translations and italics are mine):
    a. *Di eltern* beten *az er zol oysvaksen an erlikher [y]id* [literally, "The parents pray that he should [will] grow up [to be] a serious/honest Jew"].
    b. The parents *daven* [pray] that their children should be Talmidei Chachomim [wise scholars] and Yirei Hashem [God-fearers].
    Yiddish *beten* is rendered as *daven* in the English sentence.

8. "A *BA'AL TESHUVA* FREAK"

1. Similarly, Sands, "Social," 97, found that despite "*baalei teshuvah*'s desire to blend in," "their status becomes visible when they try to pronounce Hebrew yeshiva-style or when they wear sneakers."

2. Note that these two strategies are instances of stages 4 and 5 in the acquisition of loanwords discussed in the previous chapter.

3. Trudgill, *Dialects*, 58; Siegel, *Second*.

4. E.g., Labov, *Sociolinguistic*.

5. Trudgill, *Dialects*, 66.

6. Yaeger-Dror, "Introduction," 184. See also Howard Giles, Richard Y. Bourhis, and Donald M. Taylor, "Toward a Theory of Language in Ethnic Group Relations," in *Language, Ethnicity, and Intergroup Relations*, ed. Howard Giles (London: Academic Press, 1977), 307–349; Malcah Yaeger-Dror, ed., "Communicative Accommodation: A New Perspective on 'Hypercorrect' Speech," special issue of *Language and Communication* 12/3–4 (1992); John Baugh, "Hypocorrection: Mistakes in Production of Vernacular African American English as a Second Dialect," *Language and Communication* 12/3–4 (1992): 317–326.

7. Labov, *Stratification*.

8. Richard D. Janda and Julie Auger, "Quantitative Evidence, Qualitative Hypercorrection, Sociolinguistic Variables—and French Speakers' Eadhaches with English h/0," *Language and Communication* 12/3–4 (1992): 195–236.

9. John Baugh, *Black Street Speech: Its History, Structure, and Survival* (Austin: University of Texas Press, 1983).

10. See variant and discussion here: http://ohr.edu/yhiy/article.php/3639, accessed November 2010.

11. Dina Kraft, "Rapper Finds Order in Orthodox Judaism in Israel," *New York Times*, November 10, 2010. http://www.nytimes.com/2010/11/11/arts/music/11shyne.html?_r=1.

12. http://www.frumsatire.net/2007/03/20/when-baal-teshuvas-shed-their-bt-status-how-to-stereotype/, accessed November 2010.

13. E.g., Aviad, *Return*, 115; Topel, *Jerusalem*, 119.

14. Aiken, *Survival*. See also discussion here: http://www.frumsatire.net/2009/08/11/the-baal-teshuva-survival-guide/.

15. Friedman, "Lost"; Silber, "Emergence"; Soloveitchik, "Rupture"; Heilman, *Sliding*; Stolow, *Orthodox*.

16. Heilman, *Sliding*; Ferziger, "Holocaust."

17. Heilman, *Sliding*, 96–122. See Goffman, *Asylums*, on the "total institution."

18. Phrase is from Heilman, *Sliding*.

19. Ben Rampton, *Crossing: Language and Ethnicity among Adolescents* (London: Longman, 1995).

20. Lave and Wenger, *Situated*, 95.

21. I thank an audience member at a talk I gave at Emory University for suggesting this term for what I was calling "the yo-yo effect."

22. Friedman the Tutor, "How to Get Deeper into Torah Without Going off the Deep End" (pamphlet circulated at some BT institutions in Israel, 1994).

23. http://www.frumsatire.net/2007/03/20/when-baal-teshuvas-shed-their-bt-status-how-to-stereotype/, accessed November 2010. Hebrew transliteration maintained.

24. Mock-Degen, *Dynamics*, 178.

25. Substituting a hyphen for a letter in "L-rd" is similar to the practice of writing "G-d": it allows Jews to throw away the paper on which the word appears without desecrating God's name.

26. Rabbi Moshe Shur, "B.T. Blues," from the album *King David Sang* (Forest Hills, N.Y.: M&M Enterprises). This song is reprinted verbatim from the liner notes (including inconsistencies in transliteration). Translations are mine. I am grateful to "Yakov

Tzvi" for introducing me to this song and to Rabbi Shur for writing it and giving me permission to reprint it.

27. Babylonian Talmud, Rosh Hashana 16b. Thank you to Aryeh Cohen and Dvora Weisberg for their help on this issue.

28. Tanya (a work of Hasidic philosophy by Chabad founder Rabbi Schneur Zalman of Liadi), chapter 12, cited at http://www.chabad.org/search/keyword_cdo/kid/9421/jewish/Beinoni.htm, accessed August 2010.

9. MATISYAHU AND *MY FAIR LADY*

1. Ohta, *Second*; Vickers, "Second."

2. Lave and Wenger, *Situated*; Wenger, *Communities*.

3. Howard S. Becker, "Becoming a Marihuana User," *American Journal of Sociology* 59/3 (1953): 235–242.

4. Greil and Rudy, "Conversion."

5. These studies shed light on the social processes surrounding professional training and other adult transitions. But by not analyzing language, they miss an important element of the socialization. For example, in Becker's classic study, his interview excerpts include distinctive phrases, such as "take a poke" and "turn on" (both meaning "smoke marijuana"), as well as more general 1950s slang. A language socialization approach might analyze how these phrases connect marijuana use to broader social structures and cultural phenomena, and it might investigate how novices learn them through interactions with more expert marijuana users. This type of analysis adds nuance to our understanding of adult socialization.

6. See Benor, "Adult."

7. Caplan, "Israeli."

8. Ibid. See also Tallen, "Jewish"; Sands, "Social."

9. Sands, "Social."

10. Greil and Rudy, "Conversion"; Lave and Wenger, *Situated*.

11. See Levine, *Mystics*.

12. Debra Kaufman, personal communication, December 23, 2003.

13. http://www.beyondbt.com/2008/07/22/are-bts-treated-as-second-class-citizens/, accessed June 2011.

14. Sands, "Social," 97.

15. Poole, "Language," using data on white middle-class American parents from Ochs, *Culture*, among other works.

16. Golden, "Teaching," 57.

17. Ibid., 63.

18. Fader, *Mitzvah Girls*.

19. Philips, "Language"; Mertz, *Language*.

BIBLIOGRAPHY

Agha, Asif. "The Social Life of a Cultural Value." *Language and Communication* 23 (2003): 231–273.

Aiken, Lisa. *The Baal Teshuva Survival Guide*. Beverly Hills, Calif.: Rossi Publications, 2009.

———. *To Be a Jewish Woman*. Northvale, N.J.: Jason Aronson, 1994.

Alim, H. Samy. *You Know My Steez: An Ethnographic and Sociolinguistic Study of Styleshifting in a Black American Speech Community*. Durham, N.C.: Duke University Press, 2005.

Amann, Paula. *Journeys to a Jewish Life*. Woodstock, Vt.: Jewish Lights Publishing, 2007.

Anzaldúa, Gloria. *Borderlands/La Frontera: The New Mestiza*. San Francisco: Aunt Lute Books, 1987.

Aron, Isa, Michael Zeldin, and Sara Lee. "Jewish Education." In *The Cambridge Companion to American Judaism*, ed. Dana Evan Kaplan, 145–168. Cambridge: Cambridge University Press, 2005.

Assouline, Dalit Berman. "Linguistic Maintenance and Change in Israeli Haredi Yiddish." Ph.D. diss., Hebrew University of Jerusalem, 2007.

Aviad, Janet. *Return to Judaism: Religious Renewal in Israel*. Chicago: University of Chicago Press, 1983.

Barrière, Isa. "The Vitality of Yiddish among Hasidic Infants and Toddlers in a Low SES Preschool in Brooklyn." In *Proceedings of Czernowitz Yiddish Language 2008 International Centenary Conference (Jews and Slavs 22)*, ed. Wolf Moskovich, 170–196. Jerusalem: Hebrew University, 2010.

Baugh, John. *Black Street Speech: Its History, Structure, and Survival*. Austin: University of Texas Press, 1983.

———. "Hypocorrection: Mistakes in Production of Vernacular African American English as a Second Dialect." *Language and Communication* 12/3–4 (1992): 317–326.

Baumel, Simeon. *Sacred Speakers: Language and Culture among the Haredim in Israel*. New York: Berghahn Books, 2005.

Becher, Mordechai, Moshe Newman, and M. Nyuman. *After the Return: Maintaining Good Family Relations and Adjusting to Your New Lifestyle—A Practical Halachic Guide for the Newly Observant*. New York: Feldheim, 1995.

Bechhofer, Shani. "Day Schools in the Orthodox Sector—A Shifting Landscape." In *International Handbook of Jewish Education*, ed. Helena Miller, Lisa Grant, and Alex Pomson, 729–747. Dordrecht: Springer, 2011.

Becker, Howard S. "Becoming a Marihuana User." *American Journal of Sociology* 59/3 (1953): 235–242.

Belcove-Shalin, Janet S., ed. *New World Hasidim: Ethnographic Studies of Hasidic Jews in America*. Albany: State University of New York Press, 1995.

Bell, Allan. "Language Style as Audience Design." *Language in Society* 13 (1984): 145–204.

Benor, Sarah. "Loan Words in the English of Modern Orthodox Jews: Hebrew or Yiddish?" In *Proceedings of the Berkeley Linguistic Society's 25th Annual Meeting, 1999*, ed. Steve Chang et al., 287–298. Berkeley: Berkeley Linguistic Society, 2000.

———. "Yavnish: A Linguistic Study of the Orthodox Jewish Community at Columbia University." *'Iggrot ha'Ari: Columbia University Student Journal of Jewish Scholarship* 1/2 (1998): 8–50. New York: Columbia University Jewish Student Union.

Benor, Sarah Bunin. "Adult Language Socialization: How Newcomers Learn to Speak Like Orthodox Jews." Unpublished manuscript.

———. "Do American Jews Speak a 'Jewish Language'? A Model of Jewish Linguistic Distinctiveness." *Jewish Quarterly Review* 99/2 (2009): 230–269.

———. "Ethnolinguistic Repertoire: Shifting the Analytic Focus in Language and Ethnicity." *Journal of Sociolinguistics* 14/2 (2010): 159–183.

———. "Frumster.com and the Modern Orthodox to Yeshivish Continuum." Paper presented at the annual meeting of the Association for Jewish Studies, San Diego, 2006.

———. "Lexical Othering in Judezmo: How Ottoman Sephardim Refer to Non-Jews." In *Languages and Literatures of Sephardic and Oriental Jews: Proceedings of the Sixth International Congress*, ed. David M. Bunis, 65–85. Jerusalem: Bialik Institute and Misgav Yerushalayim, 2009.

———. "*Mensch, Bentsh,* and *Balagan*: Variation in the American Jewish Linguistic Repertoire." *Language and Communication* 31/2 (2011): 141–154.

———. "Second Style Acquisition: The Linguistic Socialization of Newly Orthodox Jews." Ph.D. diss., Stanford University, 2004.

———. "Sounding Learned: The Gendered Use of [t] in Orthodox Jewish English." In *Penn Working Papers in Linguistics: Selected Papers from NWAV 29*, ed. Daniel Ezra Johnson and Tara Sanchez, 1–16. Philadelphia: University of Pennsylvania, 2001.

———. "*Talmid Chachams* and *Tsedeykeses*: Language, Learnedness, and Masculinity among Orthodox Jews." *Jewish Social Studies* 11/1 (2004): 147–170.

———. "Towards a New Understanding of Jewish Language in the 21st Century." *Religion Compass* 2/6 (2008): 1062–1080.

Benor, Sarah Bunin, and Steven M. Cohen. "Talking Jewish: The 'Ethnic English' of American Jews." In *Ethnicity and Beyond: Theories and Dilemmas of Jewish Group Demarcation* (*Studies in Contemporary Jewry* 25), ed. Eli Lederhendler, 62–78. Oxford: Oxford University Press, 2011.

Ben-Ur, Aviva. *Sephardic Jews in America: A Diasporic History.* New York: New York University Press, 2009.

Berger, Shalom, Daniel Jacobson, and Chaim Waxman. *Flipping Out? Myth or Fact: The Impact of the "Year in Israel."* New York: Yashar Books, 2007.

Bhabha, Homi. *The Location of Culture.* New York: Routledge, 1994.

Blum-Kulka, Shoshana. *Dinner Talk: Cultural Patterns of Sociability and Socialization in Family Discourse.* Mahwah, N.J.: Lawrence Erlbaum, 1997.

Blumen, Orna. "Criss-Crossing Boundaries: Ultraorthodox Jewish Women Go to Work." *Gender, Place and Culture* 9/2 (2002): 133–151.

Blutinger, Jeffrey C. "So-Called Orthodoxy: The History of an Unwanted Label." *Modern Judaism* 27/3 (2007): 310–328.

Bogoch, Bryna. "Gender, Literacy, and Religiosity: Dimensions of Yiddish Education in Israeli Government-Supported Schools." *International Journal of the Sociology of Language* 138 (1999): 123–160.

Bohannon, John Neil, and Laura Stanowicz. "The Issue of Negative Evidence: Adult Responses to Children's Language Errors." *Developmental Psychology* 24/5 (1988): 684–689.

Bongaerts, Theo, Brigitte Planken, and Erik Schils. "Can Late Starters Attain a Native Accent in a Foreign Language? A Test of the Critical Period Hypothesis." In *The Age Factor in Second Language Acquisition: A Critical Look at the Critical Period Hypothesis*, ed. David Singleton and Zsolt Lengyel, 30–50. Clevedon, UK: Multilingual Matters, 1997.

Bortoni-Ricardo, Stella. *The Urbanization of Rural Dialect Speakers: A Sociolinguistic Study in Brazil.* Cambridge: Cambridge University Press, 1985.

Bourdieu, Pierre. *Distinction: A Social Critique of the Judgement of Taste* (1979). Cambridge, Mass.: Harvard University Press, 1984.

———. "The Forms of Capital" (1983). In *Handbook for Theory and Research for the Sociology of Education*, ed. John G. Richardson, 241–258. New York: Greenwood, 1986.

———. *Language and Symbolic Power.* Cambridge: Polity Press, 1991.

———. *Outline of a Theory of Practice.* Cambridge: Cambridge University Press, 1977.

Boyarin, Jonathan. "Marginal Redemption at the Eighth Street Shul." In *Between Two Worlds: Ethnographic Essays on American Jewry*, ed. Jack Kugelmass, 52–76. Ithaca, N.Y.: Cornell University Press, 1988.

Brim, Orville, and Stanton Wheeler. *Socialization after Childhood: Two Essays.* New York: John Wiley, 1966.

Bucholtz, Mary. "Geek the Girl: Language, Femininity, and Female Nerds." In *Gender and Belief Systems*, ed. Natasha Warner et al., 119–131. Berkeley: Berkeley Women and Language Group, 1996.

Bucholtz, Mary, and Kira Hall. "Language and Identity." In *Companion to Linguistic Anthropology*, ed. Alessandro Duranti, 369–394. Oxford: Blackwell, 2003.

Buckser, Andrew. "Social Conversion and Group Definition in Jewish Copenhagen." In *The Anthropology of Religious Conversion*, ed. Andrew Buckser and Stephen D. Glazier, 69–84. Lanham, Md.: Rowman and Littlefield, 2003.

Buckser, Andrew, and Stephen D. Glazier, eds. *The Anthropology of Religious Conversion.* Lanham, Md.: Rowman and Littlefield, 2003.

Campbell-Kibler, Kathryn, Robert Podesva, and Sarah Roberts. "Sharing Resources and Indexing Meaning in the Production of Gay Styles." In *Language and Sexuality: Contesting Meaning in Theory and Practice*, ed. Kathryn Campbell-Kibler et al., 175–190. Stanford: CSLI Publications, 2001.

Caplan, Kimmy. *Internal Popular Discourse in Israeli Haredi Society* [in Hebrew]. Jerusalem: Zalman Shazar Center, 2007.

———. "Israeli Haredi Society and the Repentance (*Hazarah Biteshuvah*) Phenomenon." *Jewish Studies Quarterly* 8/4 (2001): 369–398.

Carter, Phillip. "Phonetic Variation and Speaker Agency: Mexicana Identity in a North Carolina Middle School." *University of Pennsylvania Working Papers in Linguistics* 13/2 (2007), Article 1.

Chambers, J. K. "Dialect Acquisition." *Language* 68/4 (1992): 673–705.

Chambers, J. K., Peter Trudgill, and Natalie Schilling-Estes, eds. *The Handbook of Language Variation and Change.* Oxford: Blackwell, 2002.

Clark, Eve V. *First Language Acquisition.* Cambridge: Cambridge University Press, 2003.

Clark, Eve V., and J. Bernicot. "Repetition as Ratification: How Parents and Children Place Information in Common Ground. *Journal of Child Language* 35 (2008): 349–371.

Clifford, James. "Introduction: Partial Truths." In *Writing Culture: The Poetics and Politics of Ethnography.* Berkeley: University of California Press, 1986.

——. *The Predicament of Culture: Twentieth-Century Ethnography, Literature, and Art.* Cambridge, Mass.: Harvard University Press, 1988.

Cohen, Steven M. *American Assimilation or Jewish Revival?* Bloomington: Indiana University Press, 1988.

Cohen, Steven M., and Arnold M. Eisen. *The Jew Within: Self, Family, and Community in America.* Bloomington: Indiana University Press, 2000.

Cohen, Steven M., and Ari Y. Kelman. "The Continuity of Discontinuity: How Young Jews are Connecting, Creating, and Organizing their Jewish Lives." New York: Andrea and Charles Bronfman Philanthropies, 2007. http://www.bjpa.org/Publications/details .cfm?PublicationID=327.

Cohen, Steven M., J. Shawn Landres, Elie Kaunfer, and Michelle Shain. "Emergent Jewish Communities and their Participants: Preliminary Findings from the 2007 National Spiritual Communities Study." New York: S3K Synagogue Studies Institute and Mechon Hadar, 2007. http://www.synagogue3000.0rg/files/NatSpirComStudyReport _S3K_Hadar.pdf.

Coupland, Nikolas. *Style: Language Variation and Identity.* Cambridge: Cambridge University Press, 2007.

——. "Style-Shifting in a Cardiff Work-Setting." *Language in Society* 9/1 (1980): 1–12.

Cutler, Cecilia. "'Keepin' It Real': White Hip-Hoppers' Discourses of Language, Race, and Authenticity." *Journal of Linguistic Anthropology* 13/2 (2003): 211–233.

Danzger, M. Herbert. *Returning to Tradition: The Contemporary Revival of Orthodox Judaism.* New Haven, Conn.: Yale University Press, 1989.

Davidman, Lynn. *Tradition in a Rootless World: Women Turn to Orthodox Judaism.* Berkeley: University of California Press, 1991.

Davidman, Lynn, and Arthur Greil. "Characters in Search of a Script: The Exit Narratives of Formerly Ultra-Orthodox Jews." *Journal for the Scientific Study of Religion* 46/2 (2007): 201–216.

Demuth, Katherine. "Prompting Routines in the Language Socialization of Basotho Children." In *Language Socialization across Cultures,* ed. Bambi Schieffelin and Elinor Ochs, 51–79. Cambridge: Cambridge University Press, 1986.

Deutsch, Nathaniel. "The Forbidden Fork, the Cell Phone Holocaust, and Other Haredi Encounters with Technology." *Contemporary Jewry* 29 (2009): 3–19.

Duff, Patricia. "Language Socialization into Academic Discourse Communities." *Annual Review of Applied Linguistics* 30 (2010): 169–192.

——. "Language Socialization, Higher Education, and Work." In *Encyclopedia of Language and Education: Vol. 8. Language Socialization,* ed. Patricia Duff and Nancy Hornberger, 257–270. New York: Springer, 2008.

——. "Second Language Socialization as Sociocultural Theory: Insights and Issues." *Language Teaching* 40 (2007): 309–319.

Duff, Patricia, and Nancy Hornberger, eds. *Encyclopedia of Language and Education.* Volume 8: *Language Socialization.* New York: Springer, 2008.

Eagleton, Terry. *Ideology: An Introduction.* London: Verso, 1991.

Eckert, Penelope. *Jocks and Burnouts: Social Categories and Identity in the High School.* New York: Teachers College Press, 1989.

——. *Linguistic Variation as Social Practice.* Oxford: Blackwell, 2000.

——. "Variation and the Indexical Field." *Journal of Sociolinguistics* 12 (2008): 453–476.

Eckert, Penelope, and Sally McConnell-Ginet. "Think Practically and Look Locally: Language and Gender as Community-Based Practice. *Annual Review of Anthropology* 21 (1992): 461–490.

Eisenberg, Joyce, and Ellen Scolnic. *The JPS Dictionary of Jewish Words*. Philadelphia: Jewish Publication Society, 2001.

El-Or, Tamar. *Educated and Ignorant: Ultraorthodox Jewish Women and Their World*. Boulder, Colo.: Rienner, 1994.

Ervin-Tripp, Susan. "On Sociolinguistic Rules: Alternation and Co-occurrence." In *Directions in Sociolinguistics: The Ethnography of Communication*, ed. John Gumperz and Dell Hymes, 213–250. New York: Holt, Rinehart, and Winston, 1972.

———. "Variety, Style-Shifting, and Ideology." In *Style and Sociolinguistic Variation*, ed. Penelope Eckert and John Rickford, 44–56. Cambridge: Cambridge University Press, 2001.

Evan, William. "Peer Group Interaction and Organizational Socialization: A Study of Employee Turnover." *American Sociological Review* 28 (1963): 436–440.

Fader, Ayala. "Gender, Morality, and Language: Socialization Practices in a Hasidic Community." Ph.D. diss., New York University, 2000.

———. "Learning Faith: Language Socialization in a Hasidic Community." *Language in Society* 35/2 (2006): 207–229.

———. *Mitzvah Girls: Bringing Up the Next Generation of Hasidic Jews in Brooklyn*. Princeton, N.J.: Princeton University Press, 2009.

———. "Reclaiming Sacred Sparks: Linguistic Syncretism and Gendered Language Shift among Hasidic Jews in New York." *Journal of Linguistic Anthropology* 17/1 (2007): 1–22.

Ferguson, Charles. "Diglossia." *Word* 15 (1959): 325–340.

Ferziger, Adam. "Church/Sect Theory and American Orthodoxy Reconsidered." In *Ambivalent Jew: Charles Liebman in Memoriam*, ed. Stuart Cohen and Bernard Susser, 107–124. New York: Jewish Theological Seminary of America Press, 2007.

———. "Holocaust, Hurban, and Haredization: Pilgrimages to Eastern Europe and the Realignment of American Orthodoxy." *Contemporary Jewry* 31 (2011): 25–54.

Finkelman, Yoel. *Strictly Kosher Reading: Popular Literature and the Condition of Contemporary Orthodoxy*. Boston: Academic Studies Press, 2011.

Fishman, Joshua A. "The Holiness of Yiddish: Who Says Yiddish Is Holy and Why?" *Language Policy* 1/2 (2002): 123–141.

———. "The Sociology of Jewish Languages from a General Sociolinguistic Point of View." In *Readings in the Sociology of Jewish Languages*, ed. Joshua Fishman, 3–21. Leiden: Brill, 1985.

Foreman, Annik. "A Longitudinal Study of Americans in Australia." In *Proceedings of ALS2k, the 2000 Conference of the Australian Linguistics Society*, 2000. http://www.als.asn.au/proceedings/als2000/foreman.pdf.

Foster, Pauline, and Amy Snyder Ohta. "Negotiation for Meaning and Peer Assistance in Second Language Classrooms." *Applied Linguistics* 26/3 (2005): 402–430.

Friedman, Debby. "*Kiddush Hashem?* That's Easy!" *Jewish Observer*, December 2001, 44–46.

Friedman, Debra. "Speaking Correctly: Error Correction as a Language Socialization Practice in a Ukrainian Classroom." *Applied Linguistics* 31 (2010): 346–367.

Friedman, Menachem. "The Lost *Kiddush* Cup: Changes in Ashkenazi Haredi Culture—A Tradition in Crisis." In *The Uses of Tradition: Jewish Continuity in the Modern Era*, ed. Jack Wertheimer, 175–186. New York: Jewish Theological Seminary, 1992.

Garrett, Paul, and Patricia Baquedano-López. "Language Socialization: Reproduction and Continuity, Transformation and Change." *Annual Review of Anthropology* 31 (2002): 339–361.

Geertz, Clifford. "Religion as a Cultural System" (1966). In *The Interpretation of Cultures*, 87–125. New York: Basic Books, 1973.

Giddens, Anthony. *Central Problems in Social Theory: Action, Structure and Contradiction in Social Analysis*. Berkeley: University of California Press, 1979.

Giles, Howard, R. Y. Bourhis, and D. M. Taylor. "Toward a Theory of Language in Ethnic Group Relations." In *Language, Ethnicity, and Intergroup Relations*, ed. Howard Giles, 307–349. London: Academic Press, 1977.

Giles, Howard, and Nikolas Coupland. *Language: Contexts and Consequences*. Buckingham: Open University Press, 1991.

Glanz, David, and Michael I. Harrison. "Varieties of Identity Transformation: The Case of Newly Orthodox Jews." *Jewish Journal of Sociology* 20/2 (1978): 129–142.

Glinert, Lewis. *The Joys of Hebrew*. Oxford: Oxford University Press, 1992.

———. "Language Choice in Halakhic Speech Acts." In *Language, Society, and Thought: Essays in Honor of Joshua A. Fishman's 65th Birthday*, ed. Robert L. Cooper and Bernard Spolsky, 161–186. Berlin: Mouton de Gruyter, 1991.

———. "We Never Changed Our Language: Attitudes to Yiddish Acquisition among Hasidic Educators in Britain." *International Journal of the Sociology of Language* 138 (1999): 31–52.

Glinert, Lewis, Kate Miriam Loewenthal, and Vivienne Goldblatt. "Guarding the Tongue: A Thematic Analysis of Gossip Control Strategies among Orthodox Jewish Women in London." *Journal of Multilingual and Multicultural Development* 24/6 (2003): 513–524.

Glinert, Lewis, and Yoseph Shilhav. "Holy Land, Holy Language: Language and Territory in an Ultraorthodox Jewish Ideology." *Language in Society* 20 (1991): 59–86.

Goffman, Erving. *Asylums: Essays on the Social Situations of Mental Patients and Other Inmates*. New York: Anchor, 1961.

Gold, David. "Jewish English." In *Readings in the Sociology of Jewish Languages*, ed. J. Fishman, 280–298. Leiden: Brill, 1985.

———. "On Jewish English in the United States." *Jewish Language Review* 6 (1986): 121–135.

———. "The Pronunciation of ng as Taught in a New York City High School about 1962." *American Speech* 49/1–2 (1974): 159–160.

Golden, Deborah. "'Now, Like Real Israelis, Let's Stand Up and Sing': Teaching the National Language to Russian Newcomers in Israel." *Anthropology and Education Quarterly* 32 (2001): 52–79.

Gor, Kira, and Michael Long. "Input and Second Language Processing." In *Handbook of Second Language Acquisition*, ed. William Ritchie and Tej Bhatia, 445–472. New York: Academic Press, 2009.

Gordon, Cynthia. "Repetition and Identity Experimentation: One Child's Use of Repetition as a Resource for 'Trying On' Maternal Identities." In *Selves and Identities in Narrative and Discourse*, ed. Michael Bamberg, Anna De Fina, and Deborah Schiffrin, 133–157. Amsterdam: John Benjamins, 2007.

Greenberg, Richard H. *Pathways: Jews Who Return*. Northvale, N.J.: Jason Aronson, 1997.

Greil, Arthur, and David Rudy. "Conversion to the Worldview of Alcoholics Anonymous: A Refinement of Conversion Theory." *Qualitative Sociology* 6 (1983): 5–28.

———. "Social Cocoons: Encapsulation and Identity Transformation." *Sociological Inquiry* 54 (1984): 260–278.

Griswold, Olga. V. "Becoming a United States Citizen: Second Language Socialization in Adult Citizenship Classrooms." Ph.D. diss., University of California, Los Angeles, 2007.

Gurock, Jeffrey. *Orthodox Jews in America*. Bloomington: Indiana University Press, 2009.

Haas, Jack, and William Shaffir. *Becoming Doctors: The Adoption of a Cloak of Competence*. Greenwich, Conn.: JAI Press, 1987.

Harding, Susan. *The Book of Jerry Falwell: Fundamentalist Language and Politics*. Princeton, N.J.: Princeton University Press, 2000.

He, Agnes Weiyun. "Heritage Language Learning and Socialization." In *Encyclopedia of Language and Education. Volume 8: Language Socialization*, ed. Patricia Duff and Nancy Hornberger, 201–213. New York: Springer, 2008.

Heilman, Samuel. *Defenders of the Faith: Inside Ultra-Orthodox Jewry.* New York: Schocken, 1992.

———. *The People of the Book: Drama, Fellowship, and Religion.* Chicago: University of Chicago Press, 1983.

———. *Sliding to the Right: The Contest for the Future of American Jewish Orthodoxy.* Berkeley: University of California Press, 2006.

———. "Sounds of Modern Orthodoxy: The Language of Talmud Study." In *Never Say Die! A Thousand Years of Yiddish in Jewish Life and Letters*, ed. Joshua Fishman, 227–253. The Hague: Mouton, 1981.

———. *Synagogue Life: A Study in Symbolic Interaction.* Chicago: University of Chicago Press, 1973.

Heilman, Samuel, and Steven Cohen. *Cosmopolitans and Parochials: Modern Orthodox Jews in America.* Chicago: University of Chicago Press, 1989.

Heller, Tzipora. *More Precious Than Pearls: Selected Insights into the Qualities of the Ideal Woman.* New York: Feldheim, 2001.

Hellman, Jerry. "Yeshivishe Reid: Is Frumspeak a Real Language?" *Ami Magazine*, March 2011.

Helmreich, William. *The World of the Yeshiva: An Intimate Portrait of Orthodox Jewry.* Hoboken, N.J.: Ktav, 2000.

Herzog, Marvin, Uriel Weinreich, Vera Baviskar, et al. *The Language and Culture Atlas of Ashkenazi Jewry.* Vol. 1. Tübingen: M. Niemeyer, 1992.

Horowitz, Bethamie. "Connections and Journeys: Shifting Identities among American Jews." *Contemporary Jewry* 19 (1998): 63–94.

Irvine, Judith. "'Style' as Distinctiveness: The Culture and Ideology of Linguistic Differentiation." In *Style and Sociolinguistic Variation*, ed. Penelope Eckert and John Rickford, 21–43. Cambridge: Cambridge University Press, 2001.

Irvine, Judith, and Susan Gal. "Language Ideology and Linguistic Differentiation." In *Regimes of Language: Ideologies, Polities, and Identities*, ed. Paul Kroskrity, 35–83. Santa Fe: SAR Press, 2000.

Isaacs, Miriam. "Haredi, Haymish and Frim: Yiddish Vitality and Language Choice in a Transnational, Multilingual Community." *International Journal of the Sociology of Language* 138 (1999): 9–30.

Jacobs-Huey, Lanita. *From the Kitchen to the Parlor: Language and Becoming in African American Women's Hair Care.* Oxford: Oxford University Press, 2006.

Jacobson, Shari. "Modernity, Conservative Religious Movements, and the Female Subject: Newly Ultraorthodox Sephardi Women in Buenos Aires." *American Anthropologist* 108/2 (2006): 336–346.

Janda, Richard D., and Julie Auger. "Quantitative Evidence, Qualitative Hypercorrection, Sociolinguistic Variables—and French Speakers' Eadhaches with English h/0." *Language and Communication* 12/3–4 (1992): 195–236.

Jefferson, Gail. "On Exposed and Embedded Correction in Conversation." In *Talk and Social Organisation*, ed. Graham Button and J.R.E. Lee, 86–100. Clevedon, UK: Multilingual Matters, 1987.

Jochnowitz, George. "Bilingualism and Dialect Mixture among Lubavitcher Hasidic Children." *American Speech* 43/3 (1968): 188–200.

Johnstone, Barbara. "An Introduction." "Perspectives on Repetition," special issue of *Text 7* (1987): 205–214.

———. *The Linguistic Individual: Self-Expression in Language and Linguistics*. Oxford: Oxford University Press, 1996.

———, ed. *Repetition in Discourse: Interdisciplinary Perspectives*. Norwood, N.J.: Ablex, 1994.

Kurtz, Chani Aftergut. "We Wish You a Merry . . . Chanuka?" *Jewish Observer*, November 2001, 38.

Katz, Maya Balakirsky. *The Visual Culture of Chabad*. Cambridge: Cambridge University Press, 2011.

Kaufman, Debra Renee. *Rachel's Daughters: Newly Orthodox Jewish Women*. New Brunswick, N.J.: Rutgers University Press, 1991.

Kelner, Shaul. *Tours That Bind: Diaspora, Pilgrimage, and Israel Birthright Tourism*. New York: New York University Press, 2010.

Kerswill, Paul. *Dialects Converging: Rural Speech in Urban Norway*. Oxford: Clarendon Press, 1994.

Kligman, Mark. "Contemporary Jewish Music in America." *American Jewish Yearbook* 101 (2001): 88–141.

Kobayashi, Masaki. "The Role of Peer Support in Students' Accomplishment of Oral Academic Tasks." *Canadian Modern Language Review* 59 (2003): 337–368.

Koskoff, Ellen. "The Language of the Heart: Music in Lubavitcher Life." In *New World Hasidim: Ethnographic Studies of Hasidic Jews in America*, ed. Janet Belcove-Shalin, 87–106. Albany: State University of New York Press, 1995.

Kotler-Berkowitz, Laurence, Steven M. Cohen, Jonathon Ament, Vivian Klaff, Frank Mott, and Danyelle Peckerman-Neuman. *The National Jewish Population Survey 2000–01: Strength, Challenge and Diversity in the American Jewish Population*. New York: United Jewish Communities, 2003.

Kraft, Dina. "Rapper Finds Order in Orthodox Judaism in Israel." *New York Times*, November 10, 2010. http://www.nytimes.com/2010/11/11/arts/music/11shyne.html?_r=1.

Kulick, Don. *Language Shift and Cultural Reproduction: Socialization, Self, and Syncretism in a Papua New Guinea Village*. Cambridge: Cambridge University Press, 1992.

Kulick, Don, and Bambi Schieffelin. "Language Socialization." In *A Companion to Linguistic Anthropology*, ed. Alessandro Duranti, 349–368. Oxford: Blackwell, 2004.

Labov, William. "The Social Motivation of a Sound Change." *Word* 19 (1963): 273–309.

———. *The Social Stratification of English in New York City*. Washington, D.C.: Center for Applied Linguistics, 1966.

———. *Sociolinguistic Patterns*. Philadelphia: University of Pennsylvania Press, 1972.

Labov, William, Sharon Ash, and Charles Boberg. *The Atlas of North American English: Phonetics, Phonology, and Sound Change*. Berlin: Mouton de Gruyter, 2006.

Lambert, Wallace E. "A Social Psychology of Bilingualism." *Journal of Social Issues* 23 (1967): 91–109.

Lambert, Wallace E., Richard C. Hodgson, Robert C. Gardner, and Stanley Fillenbaum. "Evaluational Reactions to Spoken Language." *Journal of Abnormal Social Psychology* 60 (1960): 44–51.

Lapidus, Steven. "Creating Community through Isolation: Haredim Log Off the Internet." Paper presented at Association for Jewish Studies annual meeting, December, San Diego, 2006.

Lave, Jean, and Etienne Wenger. *Situated Learning: Legitimate Peripheral Participation*. Cambridge: Cambridge University Press, 1991.

Le Page, R. B., and Andrée Tabouret-Keller. *Acts of Identity: Creole-Based Approaches to Language and Ethnicity*. Cambridge: Cambridge University Press, 1985.

Levin, Michael Graubart. *Journey to Tradition: The Odyssey of a Born-Again Jew.* Hoboken, N.J.: Ktav, 1986.

Levine, Stephanie Wellen. *Mystics, Mavericks, and Merrymakers: An Intimate Journey among Hasidic Girls.* New York: New York University Press, 2003.

Levon, Erez. "Mosaic Identity and Style: Phonological Variation among Reform American Jews." *Journal of Sociolinguistics* 10 (2006): 185–205.

Liang, A. C. "The Creation of Coherence in Coming-Out Stories." In *Queerly Phrased: Language, Gender, and Sexuality*, ed. Anna Livia and Kira Hall, 287–309. Oxford: Oxford University Press, 1997.

Lieber, Andrea. "A Virtual 'Veibershul': Blogging and the Blurring of Public and Private among Orthodox Jewish Women." *College English* 72/6 (2009): 621–637.

Liebman, Charles S. "Orthodoxy in American Jewish Life." *American Jewish Year Book* 66 (1965): 21–97.

Lippi-Green, Rosina. *English with an Accent: Language, Ideology and Discrimination in the United States.* London: Routledge, 1997.

Lowenstein, Steven M. *The Jewish Cultural Tapestry: International Jewish Folk Traditions.* New York: Oxford University Press, 2000.

Mackey, Alison, and Jaemyung Goo. "Interaction Research in SLA: A Meta-Analysis and Research Synthesis." In *Conversational Interaction in Second Language Acquisition: A Collection of Empirical Studies*, ed. Alison Mackey, 407–452. Oxford: Oxford University Press, 2007.

Mahmood, Saba. *Politics of Piety: The Islamic Revival and the Feminist Subject.* Princeton, N.J.: Princeton University Press, 2005.

Malinowski, Bronislaw. *A Diary in the Strict Sense of the Term.* London: Routledge and Kegan Paul, 1967.

Malone, Dennis. *The In-Between People: Language and Culture Maintenance and Mother-Tongue Education in the Highlands of Papua New Guinea.* Dallas: SIL International, 2004.

Margolese, Faranak. *Off the Derech: Why Observant Jews Leave Judaism.* New York: Devora Publishing, 2005.

Matisoff, James A. *Blessings, Curses, Hopes, and Fears: Psycho-Ostensive Expressions in Yiddish.* 1979. 2nd ed., Stanford, Calif.: Stanford University Press, 2000.

Mendoza-Denton, Norma. *Homegirls: Language and Cultural Practice among Latina Youth Gangs.* Oxford: Blackwell, 2008.

——. "Style." *Journal of Linguistic Anthropology* 9/1–2 (2000): 238–240.

Mertz, Elizabeth. *The Language of Law School: Learning to "Think Like a Lawyer."* Oxford: Oxford University Press, 2007.

——. "Linguistic Ideology and Praxis in U.S. Law School Classrooms." In *Language Ideologies: Practice and Theory*, ed. Bambi Schieffelin, Kathryn Woolard, and Paul Kroskrity, 149–162. Oxford: Oxford University Press, 1998.

Milroy, Lesley. *Language and Social Networks.* Oxford: Blackwell, 1980.

Mitchell, Bruce. *Language Politics and Language Survival: Yiddish among the Haredim in Post-War Britain.* Paris: Peeters, 2006.

Mock-Degen, Minny E. *The Dynamics of Becoming Orthodox: Dutch Jewish Women Returning to Judaism and How Their Mothers Feel About It.* Amsterdam: Amphora Books, 2010.

Moore, Leslie. "Language Socialization and Repetition." In *The Handbook of Language Socialization*, ed. Alessandro Duranti, Elinor Ochs, and Bambi B. Schieffelin, 209–226. Oxford: Blackwell, 2011.

——. "Learning by Heart in Qur'anic and Public Schools in Northern Cameroon." *Social Analysis* 50 (2006): 109–126.

Morita, Naoko. "Discourse Socialization through Oral Classroom Activities in a TESL Graduate Program." *TESOL Quarterly* 34 (2000): 279–310.

Morita, Naoko, and Masaki Kobayashi. "Academic Discourse Socialization in a Second Language." In *Encyclopedia of Language and Education. Volume 8: Language Socialization*, ed. Patricia Duff and Nancy Hornberger, 243–255. New York: Springer, 2008.

Mortimer, Jeylan T., and Roberta G. Simmons. "Adult Socialization." *Annual Review of Sociology* 4 (1978): 421–454.

Newman, Zelda Kahan. "The Jewish Sound of Speech: Talmudic Chant, Yiddish Intonation and the Origins of Early Ashkenaz." *Jewish Quarterly Review* 90 (2000): 293–336.

Ochs, Elinor. *Culture and Language Development: Language Acquisition and Language Socialization in a Samoan Village*. Cambridge: Cambridge University Press, 1988.

——. "Indexing Gender." In *Rethinking Context: Language as an Interactive Phenomenon*, ed. Alessandro Duranti and Charles Goodwin, 335–358. Cambridge: Cambridge University Press, 1992.

——. "Introduction." In *Language Socialization across Cultures*, ed. Bambi Schieffelin and Elinor Ochs, 1–13. Cambridge: Cambridge University Press, 1986.

Ochs, Elinor, and Schieffelin, Bambi. "Language Acquisition and Socialization: Three Developmental Stories and Their Implications." In *Culture Theory: Essays on Mind, Self, and Emotion*, ed. Richard Shweder and Robert LeVine, 276–320. Cambridge: Cambridge University Press, 1984.

Ochs, Vanessa. *Inventing Jewish Ritual*. Philadelphia: Jewish Publication Society, 2007.

Ohta, Amy Snyder. "Interactional Routines and the Socialization of Interactional Style in Adult Learners of Japanese." *Journal of Pragmatics* 31 (1999): 1493–1512.

——. *Second Language Acquisition Processes in the Classroom: Learning Japanese*. Mahwah, N.J.: Lawrence Erlbaum Associates, 2001.

Oladipo, Salami. "Arabic and Sociocultural Change among the Yoruba." In *The Sociology of Language and Religion: Change, Conflict and Accommodation*, ed. Tope Omoniyi, 45–57. London: Palgrave MacMillan, 2010.

Patrick, Peter L., and Esther Figueroa. "Creole Paralinguistics across the African Diaspora: The Case of 'Kiss-Teeth.'" Paper presented at Sociolinguistics Symposium 15, Newcastle upon Tyne, 2004. Abstract at http://www.ncl.ac.uk/ss15/papers/paper_details .php?id=424.

Payne, Arvilla C. "Factors Controlling the Acquisition of the Philadelphia Dialect by Out-of-State Children." In *Locating Language in Time and Space*, ed. William Labov, 143–178. New York: Academic Press, 1980.

Penfield, Wilder. "A Consideration of the Neurophysiological Mechanisms of Speech and some Educational Consequences." *Proceedings of the American Academy of Arts and Sciences* 82/5 (1953): 201–214.

Peters, Ann M., and Stephen T. Boggs. "Interactional Routines as Cultural Influences upon Language Acquisition." In *Language Socialization across Cultures*, ed. Bambi Schieffelin and Elinor Ochs, 80–96. Cambridge: Cambridge University Press, 1986.

Philips, Susan Urmston. "The Language Socialization of Lawyers: Acquiring the 'Cant.'" In *Doing the Ethnography of Schooling*, ed. George Spindler, 176–209. New York: Holt, Rinehart, and Winston, 1982.

Podesva, Robert J. "Phonetic Detail in Sociolinguistic Variation: Its Linguistic Significance and Role in the Construction of Social Meaning." Ph.D. diss., Stanford University, 2006.

Poll, Solomon. *The Hasidic Community of Williamsburg: A Study in the Sociology of Religion*. New York: Schocken, 1962.

Poole, Deborah. "Language Socialization in the Second Language Classroom." *Language Learning* 42 (1992): 593–616.

Poplack, Shana, David Sankoff, and Christopher Miller. "The Social Correlates and Linguistic Processes of Lexical Borrowing and Assimilation." *Linguistics* 26 (1988): 47–104.

Prell, Riv-Ellen. "Developmental Judaism: Challenging the Study of American Jewish Identity in the Social Sciences." *Contemporary Jewry* 21 (2000): 33–54.

———. *Prayer and Community: The Havurah in American Judaism.* Detroit: Wayne State University Press, 1989.

Purnell, Thomas, Joseph C. Salmons, Dilara Tepeli, and Jennifer Mercer. "Structured Heterogeneity and Change in Laryngeal Phonetics: Upper Midwestern Final Obstruents." *Journal of English Linguistics* 33/4 (2005): 307–338.

Rambo, Lewis. *Understanding Religious Conversion.* New Haven, Conn.: Yale University Press, 1995.

Rampton, Ben. *Crossing: Language and Ethnicity among Adolescents.* London: Longman, 1995.

Reisman, Rabbi Yisroel. "A Rebbe for Our Generation." *Jewish Observer*, December 2001, 14–21.

Rickford, John R. "Implicational Scales." In *Handbook of Language Variation and Change*, ed. J. K. Chambers, Peter Trudgill, and Natalie Schilling-Estes, 142–167. Malden, Mass.: Blackwell, 2002.

Rickford, John R., and Faye McNair-Knox. "Addressee- and Topic-Influenced Style Shift: A Quantitative Sociolinguistic Study." In *Sociolinguistic Perspectives on Register*, ed. Douglas Biber and Edward Finegan, 235–276. Oxford: Oxford University Press, 1994.

Rickford, John R., and Angela E. Rickford. "Cut-Eye and Suck-Teeth: African Words and Gestures in New World Guise." *Journal of American Folklore* 89 (1976): 294–309. Reprinted in John R. Rickford, *African American Vernacular English: Features, Evolution, Educational Implications.* Oxford: Blackwell. 157–173, 1999.

Robbins, Joel. *Becoming Sinners: Christianity and Moral Torment in a Papua New Guinea Society.* Berkeley: University of California Press, 2004.

Roof, Wade Clark. *A Generation of Seekers: The Spiritual Journeys of the Baby Boom Generation.* San Francisco: Harper, 1993.

———. *Spiritual Marketplace: Baby Boomers and the Remaking of American Religion.* Princeton, N.J.: Princeton University Press, 1999.

Rose, Mary. "Language, Place and Identity in Later Life." Ph.D. diss., Stanford University, 2006.

Rosenthal, Michele. "'Désirez-vous vous couvrir la tête?' Les bénédictions de Rabbi Amnon Yitzhak." *Les Cahiers du Judaïsme* 31 (2011): 48–56.

Ruby, Jay, ed. *A Crack in the Mirror: Reflexive Perspectives in Anthropology.* Philadelphia: University of Pennsylvania Press, 1982.

Sacknowitz, Aliza. "Linguistic Means of Orthodox Jewish Identity Construction: Phonological Features, Lexical Features, and the Situated Discourse." Ph.D. diss., Georgetown University, 2007.

Sands, Roberta G. "The Social Integration of *Baalei Teshuvah.*" *Journal for the Scientific Study of Religion* 48/1 (2009): 86–102.

Sands, Roberta G., and Dorit Roer-Strier. "*Ba'alot Teshuvah* Daughters and Their Mothers: A View from South Africa." *Contemporary Jewry* 21 (2000): 55–77.

Schein, Edgar H. "Organizational Socialization and the Profession of Management." *Industrial Management Review* 9 (1968): 1–15.

Schieffelin, Bambi. *The Give and Take of Everyday Life: Language Socialization of Kaluli Children.* New York: Cambridge University Press, 1990.

———. "Introducing Kaluli Literacy: A Chronology of Influences." In *Regimes of Language: Ideologies, Polities, and Identities*, ed. Paul Kroskrity, 293–327. Santa Fe, N.M.: School of American Research Press, 2000.

Schieffelin, Bambi, and Rachelle Charlier Doucet. "The 'Real' Haitian Creole: Ideology, Metalinguistics, and Orthographic Choice." In *Language Ideologies: Practice and Theory*, ed. Bambi Schieffelin, Kathryn Woolard, and Paul Kroskrity, 285–316. Oxford: Oxford University Press, 1998.

Schieffelin, Bambi, and Elinor Ochs. "Language Socialization." *Annual Review of Anthrpology* 15 (1986): 163–191.

———, eds. *Language Socialization across Cultures*. Cambridge: Cambridge University Press, 1986.

Schieffelin, Bambi, Kathryn Woolard, and Paul Kroskrity, eds. *Language Ideologies: Practice and Theory*. Oxford: Oxford University Press, 1998.

Schiff, Alvin I. *The Mystique of Hebrew: An Ancient Language in the New World*. New York: Shengold, 1996.

Schilling-Estes, Natalie. "Investigating 'Self-Conscious' Speech: The Performance Register in Ocracoke English." *Language in Society* 27 (1998): 53–83.

Schreiber, Lynne, ed. *Hide and Seek: Jewish Women and Hair Covering*. Jerusalem: Urim Publications, 2003.

Schwartz, Rebecca Press. "Privilege, Perspective, and Modern Orthodox Youth." In *The Next Generation of Modern Orthodoxy*, ed. Shmuel Hain, 23–35. New York: Yeshiva University Press, 2012.

Sclafani, Jennifer. "Martha Stewart Behaving Badly: Parody and the Symbolic Meaning of Style." *Journal of Sociolinguistics* 13/5 (2009): 613–633.

Scovel, Thomas. *A Time to Speak: A Psycholinguistic Inquiry into the Critical Period for Human Speech*. Cambridge, Mass.: Newbury House, 1988.

Segalowitz, Norman. "Individual Differences in Second Language Acquisition." In *Tutorials in Bilingualism*, ed. A.M.B. de Groot and Judith Kroll, 85–112. Mahwah, N.J.: Erlbaum, 1997.

Shaffir, William. "Becoming Observant and Falling from the Faith: Variations of Jewish Conversion Experiences." In *Symbolic Interaction: An Introduction to Social Psychology*, ed. Nancy J. Herman and Larry T. Reynolds, 326–341. Lanham, Md.: Alta Mira, 1994.

———. "Conversion Experiences: Newcomers to and Defectors from Orthodox Judaism (*hozrim betshuvah* and *hozrim beshe'elah*)." In *Tradition, Innovation, Conflict: Jewishness and Judaism in Contemporary Israel*, ed. Zvi Sobel and Benjamin Beit-Hallahmi, 173–202. Albany: State University of New York Press, 1991.

———. "Movements In and Out of Orthodox Judaism: The Cases of Penitents and the Disaffected." In *Joining and Leaving Religion: Research Perspectives*, ed. Leslie J. Francis and Yaacov J. Katz, 269–285. Trowbridge, Waltshire: Gracewing, 2000.

———. "The Recruitment of *Baalei Tshuvah* in a Jerusalem Yeshiva." *Jewish Journal of Sociology* 25/1 (1983): 33–46.

Shandler, Jeffrey. *Adventures in Yiddishland: Postvernacular Language and Culture*. Berkeley: University of California Press, 2005.

Shtadler, Nurit. *Yeshiva Fundamentalism: Piety, Gender, and Resistance*. New York: New York University Press, 2009.

Shurkin, Michael Robert. "Decolonization and the Renewal of French Judaism: Reflections on the Contemporary French Jewish Scene." *Jewish Social Studies* 6/2 (2000): 156–177.

Siegel, Jeff. *Second Dialect Acquisition*. Cambridge: Cambridge University Press, 2010.

Silber, Michael K. "The Emergence of Ultra-Orthodoxy: The Invention of a Tradition." In *The Uses of Tradition: Jewish Continuity in the Modern Era*, ed. Jack Wertheimer, 23–84. New York: Jewish Theological Seminary of America Press, 1992.

Silberstein, Laurence J., ed. *Mapping Jewish Identities*. New York: New York University Press, 2000.

Silverstein, Michael. "Shifters, Linguistic Categories, and Cultural Description." In *Meaning in Anthropology*, ed. Keith Basso and Henry Selby, 11–55. Albuquerque: University of New Mexico Press, 1976.

Singleton, David, and Zsolt Lengyel, eds. *The Age Factor in Second Language Acquisition: A Critical Look at the Critical Period Hypothesis*. Clevedon, UK: Multilingual Matters, 1997.

Soloveitchik, Haym. "Rupture and Reconstruction: Transformation of Contemporary Orthodoxy." *Tradition* 28/4 (1994): 64–131.

Spolsky, Bernard, and Sarah Bunin Benor. "Jewish Languages." In *Encyclopedia of Language and Linguistics*, 2nd ed., ed. Keith Brown, 6:120–124. Oxford: Elsevier, 2006.

Steinmetz, Sol. *Dictionary of Jewish Usage: A Popular Guide to the Use of Jewish Terms*. Lanham, Md.: Rowman and Littlefield, 2005.

———. "Jewish English in the United States." *American Speech* 56/1 (1981): 3–16.

———. *Yiddish and English: A Century of Yiddish in America*. Tuscaloosa: University of Alabama Press, 1986.

Steinsaltz, Adin. *Teshuva: A Guide for the Newly Observant Jew*. New York: Free Press, 1987.

Stolow, Jeremy. *Orthodox by Design: Judaism, Print Politics, and the ArtScroll Revolution*. Berkeley: University of California Press, 2010.

Stromberg, Peter G. *Language and Self-Transformation: A Study of the Christian Conversion Narrative*. Cambridge: Cambridge University Press, 1993.

Swain, Merrill. "Integrating Language and Content Teaching through Collaborative Tasks." *Canadian Modern Language Review* 58/1 (2001): 44–63.

Swidler, Ann. "Culture in Action: Symbols and Strategies." *American Sociological Review* 51 (1986): 273–286.

Tagliamonte, Sali A., and Sonja Molfenter. "How'd You Get That Accent? Acquiring a Second Dialect of the Same Language." *Language in Society* 36 (2007): 649–675.

Tallen, Louise E. "Jewish Identity Writ Small: The Everyday Experience of *Baalot Teshuva*." In *Diasporas and Exiles: Varieties of Jewish Identity*, ed. Howard Wettstein, 234–252. Berkeley: University of California Press, 2002.

Tannenbaum, Michal, and Netta Abugov. "The Legacy of the Linguistic Fence: Linguistic Patterns among Ultra-Orthodox Jewish Girls." *Heritage Language Journal* 7/1 (2010): 74–90.

Tatz, Akiva. *Anatomy of a Search: Personal Drama in the Teshuva Revolution*. New York: Mesorah Publications, 1987.

Thakerar, Jitendra, Howard Giles, and Jenny Cheshire. "Psychological and Linguistic Parameters of Speech Accommodation Theory." In *Advances in the Social Psychology of Language*, ed. Howard Giles and Robert St. Clair, 205–255. Cambridge: Cambridge University Press, 1982.

Thomas, C. K. "Jewish Dialect and New York Dialect." *American Speech* 7/5 (1932): 321–326.

Thomason, Sarah. *Language Contact: An Introduction*. Washington, D.C.: Georgetown University Press, 2001.

Topel, Marta F. "Brazilian *Ba'alot Teshuvah* and the Paradoxes of Their Religious Conversion." *Judaism* 51/3 (2002): 329–345.

———. *Jerusalem and São Paulo: The New Jewish Orthodoxy in Focus*. Lanham, Md.: University Press of America, 2008.

Trudgill, Peter. *Dialects in Contact*. Oxford: Blackwell, 1986.

Turner, Victor. "Betwixt and Between: The Liminal Period in *Rites de Passage*." In *The Forest of Symbols: Aspects of Ndembu Ritual*, 93–111. Ithaca, N.Y.: Cornell University Press, 1967.

Vickers, Caroline. "Second Language Socialization through Team Interaction among Electrical and Computer Engineering Students." *Modern Language Journal* 91/4 (2007): 621–640.

Vygotsky, Lev. *Mind and Society: The Development of Higher Psychological Processes*. Cambridge, Mass.: Harvard University Press, 1978.

Wardhaugh, Ronald. *An Introduction to Sociolinguistics*. Fifth edition. Oxford: Blackwell, 2005.

Watson-Gegeo, Karen Ann, and David W. Gegeo. "Calling-Out and Repeating Routines in Kwara'ae Children's Language Socialization." In *Language Socialization across Cultures*, ed. Bambi Schieffelin and Elinor Ochs, 17–50. Cambridge: Cambridge University Press, 1986.

Waxman, Chaim I. "The Haredization of American Orthodox Jewry." *Jerusalem Letters* 376. Jerusalem: Jerusalem Center for Public Affairs, 1998. http://www.policyarchive.org/handle/10207/bitstreams/18274.pdf.

Weinreich, Max. *History of the Yiddish Language* (1973). Translated from Yiddish by S. Noble and J. Fishman. New Haven, Conn.: Yale University Press, 2008.

———. "The Reality of Jewishness Versus the Ghetto Myth: The Sociolinguistic Roots of Yiddish." In *To Honor Roman Jakobson: Essays on the Occasion of his Seventieth Birthday*, 3:2199–2211. The Hague: Mouton, 1966.

———. "Yiddishkayt and Yiddish: On the Impact of Religion on Language in Ashkenazi Jewry." In *Mordecai M. Kaplan: Jubilee Volume on the Occasion of his Seventieth Birthday*, ed. Moshe Davis, 481–514. New York: Jewish Theological Seminary of America Press, 1953.

Weinreich, Uriel. *English-Yiddish Yiddish-English Dictionary*. New York: YIVO Institute for Jewish Research, 1968.

———. *Languages in Contact: Findings and Problems* (1953). The Hague: Mouton, 1974.

———. "Notes on the Yiddish Rise-Fall Intonation Contour." In *For Roman Jakobson: Essays on the Occasion of his Sixtieth Birthday*, ed. Morris Halle, 633–643. The Hague: Mouton, 1956.

Weiser, Chaim. *Frumspeak: The First Dictionary of Yeshivish*. Northvale, N.J.: Jason Aronson, 1995.

Weissler, Chava. *Making Judaism Meaningful: Ambivalence and Tradition in a Havurah Community*. New York: AMS Press, 1989.

Wenger, Etienne. *Communities of Practice: Learning, Meaning, and Identity*. New York: Cambridge University Press, 1998.

Wertheimer, Jack. *A People Divided: Judaism in Contemporary America*. Waltham, Mass.: Brandeis University Press, 1997.

Wexler, Paul. "Jewish Inter-Linguistics: Facts and Conceptual Framework." *Language* 57/1 (1981): 99–149.

Winston, Hella. *Unchosen: The Hidden Lives of Hasidic Rebels*. Boston: Beacon, 2006.

Wolberger, Lionel A. "The Music of Holy Argument: The Ethnomusicology of Talmudic Debate." Ph.D. diss., Wesleyan University, 1991.

Wolfram, Walt. *A Sociolinguistic Description of Detroit Negro Speech*. Washington, D.C.: Center for Applied Linguistics, 1969.

Wood, David, Jerome S. Bruner, and Gail Ross. "The Role of Tutoring in Problem Solving." *Journal of Child Psychology and Psychiatry* 17 (1976): 89–100.

Wood, Kathleen M. "Narrative Iconicity in Electronic-Mail Lesbian Coming-Out Stories." In *Queerly Phrased: Language, Gender, and Sexuality*, ed. Anna Livia and Kira Hall, 257–273. Oxford: Oxford University Press, 1997.

Woolard, Kathryn A. "Language Ideology as a Field of Inquiry." In *Language Ideologies: Practice and Theory*, ed. Bambi Schieffelin, Kathryn Woolard, and Paul Kroskrity, 3–47. Oxford: Oxford University Press, 1998.

———. "Simultaneity and Bivalency as Strategies in Bilingualism." *Journal of Linguistic Anthropology* 8/1 (1998): 3–29.

Wuthnow, Robert. *After Heaven: Spirituality in America since the 1950s*. Cambridge, Mass.: Harvard University Press, 1998.

Yaeger-Dror, Malcah, ed. "Communicative Accommodation: A New Perspective on 'Hypercorrect' Speech." Special issue of *Language and Communication* 12/3–4 (1992).

———. "Introduction." "Hypercorrection," special issue of *Language and Communication* 12/3–4 (1992): 181–193.

Zuckermann, Ghil'ad. "Cultural Hybridity: Multisourced Neologization in 'Reinvented' Languages and in Languages with 'Phono-Logographic' Script." *Languages in Contrast* 4/2 (2004): 281–318.

———. "Hybridity versus Revivability: Multiple Causation, Forms and Patterns." *Journal of Language Contact* 2 (2009): 40–67.

INDEX

Page references to figures are in italics; references to tables are followed by T. Books and periodicals excepted, italicized subject entries refer to lexical items.

ABOUT THE AUTHOR

SARAH BUNIN BENOR is an associate professor of contemporary Jewish studies at Hebrew Union College–Jewish Institute of Religion. She received a Ph.D. in linguistics from Stanford University in 2004. She has published and lectured widely on sociolinguistics and American Jewish language and culture. She lives in Los Angeles with her husband and three daughters.

CPSIA information can be obtained at www.ICGtesting.com
Printed in the USA
BVOW07s0843261114

376748BV00001B/35/P